RED CARD
TO
RACISM

THE FIGHT
FOR EQUALITY
IN FOOTBALL

I am proud of the work of Kick It Out … but there is sadly more work to do stamping the blight of racism and discrimination out of football.

– HRH Prince William, President of the FA

There's not enough to be said to thank Kick It Out for what it is doing to stamp out racism and discrimination in football but also throughout the world.

– Martin Luther King III

For over 25 years, Kick It Out (KIO) has been the heart of the drive towards equality, inclusion and cohesion for everyone who plays, watches and works in football. Fights all forms of recrimination in the game we love.

– KICK IT OUT

When races come together, cultures are enriched.

– Eric Cantona

There was no conflict between religion and the fact that I wanted to play football. I was brought up correctly and in the right way and my parents are very proud of the fact that I am a professional footballer.

– Sadio Mané, Liverpool winger

RED CARD
TO
RACISM

THE FIGHT
FOR
EQUALITY IN
FOOTBALL

HARRY HARRIS

Foreword By
HERMAN OUSELEY

Dedicated to all who have fought discrimination in all its forms over more than 25 years and to those who will continue that fight to shape the next 25 years+.

First published in 2021 by Ad Lib Publishers Ltd
15 Church Road
London, SW13 9HE

www.adlibpublishers.com

Text © 2021 Harry Harris

Paperback ISBN 978-1-913543-68-6
eBook ISBN 978-1-913543-30-3

A CIP catalogue record for this book is available from the British Library.

Every reasonable effort has been made to trace copyright-holders of material reproduced in this book, but if any have been inadvertently overlooked the publishers would be glad to hear from them.

Printed in the UK
10 9 8 7 6 5 4 3 2 1

CONTENTS

ACKNOWLEDGEMENTS

My appreciation goes to the dedicated former Chairman of Kick It Out (KIO) Lord Herman Ouseley and to the outgoing long-serving PFA Chief Executive Gordon Taylor; both much maligned at times, but whose contribution to the game has been immense, notably in the campaign against racism.

The list of contributors who have personally given their time for interviews, providing statistics, content and information, is testimony to the importance of the fight against racism, now reaching a crescendo with Black Lives Matter:

Gordon Taylor, PFA CEO
Lord Herman Ouseley, KIO chair
Chris Hughton, Brighton manager
Hope Powell, Brighton Women's manager
Greg Dyke, ex-FA Chairman, ex-BBC Director General, ex-Manchester United board member
David Dein, ex-FA and Arsenal vice-chair
David Davies, ex-FA executive director
Garth Crooks, OBE, ex-Spurs/Manchester United/Stoke; BBC TV

Glenn Hoddle, ex-England/Tottenham/Chelsea manager; ITV/BT Sport

Harry Redknapp, one of the most experienced football managers

Viv Anderson, first black player for England

Les Ferdinand, QPR technical director, ex-QPR/Tottenham/Newcastle

Jermain Defoe, OBE, England/Spurs/Bournemouth

Ruud Gullit, first black manager to win a trophy in England and Europe, former World Footballer of the Year, AC Milan, Dutch captain who lifted European Championship

Andrew Cole, ex-Manchester United/Arsenal/Newcastle

Brendon Batson, OBE, ex-Arsenal/West Brom

Paul Elliott, CBE, MBE, FA chair, Inclusion Advisory Board, ex-Chelsea

Bill Kenwright, CBE, Everton chair

David Sullivan, West Ham co-owner. ex-Birmingham City co-owner

David Gold, West Ham co-owner, ex-Birmingham City co-owner

Pat Nevin, TV/radio pundit, ex-Chelsea/Everton

Paul Canoville, first black player for Chelsea

Marcus Gayle, KIO educator, ex-Wimbledon/Brentford

Ivor Baddiel, script writer

Mel Stein, Gazza's former agent

Clive Tyldesley, ITV World Cup commentator

Thanks to all the media departments, clubs and those who helped with interviews and content:

Tom Everett, Corporate Communications Officer, The FA Group

Karen Shotbolt, Football Media Relations Manager, Manchester United FC

Anthony Marshall, Head of Media and Communications, Bournemouth FC
Dan Francis, Communications Manager, West Ham United FC

Many thanks to the variety of online sources for retrospective quotes, information and content; especially to *Mail Online, Daily Mail, Daily Mirror, Guardian,* Sky, BBC Online and Football365.

Special thanks to John Blake, Jon Rippon and Robert Nichols at Ad Lib Publishers.

FOREWORD

25+ Years Campaigning

The issues of race, gender and class are at the heart of the struggle against inequality in society. That is something that has existed almost from day one of civilised societies. When it is mixed with ignorance, prejudice, fear and stereotypes, the result is discrimination, bias, exclusion and hatred of others because of their different characteristics, appearance and circumstances. On the one hand, there's hate-related abuse, harassment and violence delivered at a personal level. More insidious is the impenetrable institutionalised discrimination, where the people with power who make decisions and control resources can use that power to maintain the status quo and exclude others unlike themselves or can choose to use their power to end privilege and discrimination in favour of equal and fair treatment for all.

On many occasions during the 1970s, '80s and early '90s, I'd tried to get football to stop the race hate that infected the game. Very few people wanted to acknowledge that there was a problem that warranted action on their part and certainly those with the power to end it were not accessible.

Then, in 1993, I became the Chairman of the Commission for Racial Equality (CRE). At last, I could go to those people, with the authority of statutory duties behind me and either encourage them to change or, eventually, consider how to force them to change. The "Let's Kick Racism Out of Football" campaign was launched on 12 August 1993. It was needed then and still is today.

Kick It Out (KIO) was set up in 1993 at a time when extreme organisations such as the National Front (NF) and the British National Party (BNP) were active on the terraces and stands of many professional football clubs. That year, Stephen Lawrence was brutally murdered on the streets of South London, the BNP had a candidate elected to Tower Hamlets Council, the IRA bombed Warrington and Bishopsgate, the UK interest rate was 6% and unemployment stood at over three million.

Overt racist abuse, harassment and violence infected football. BAME (Black and Minority Ethnic) players faced discrimination, prejudice, bias and abuse not only from fans, but within dressing rooms, on training grounds and from coaching and management staff. They had no choice but to accept the situation, to try to overcome the odds, to stay quiet, if they wanted to remain in the game and further their careers. This was the reality at all levels of the game. Football authorities and most clubs buried their heads in the sand, hoping the problem would just disappear.

There *is* visible ethnic diversity reflected on the field, but we still await the breakthrough of British Asian players at the top level; more women are playing the game; disabled and older people have more opportunities to take part. There's an acknowledgement that the pursuit of equality, inclusion and cohesion is beneficial to both football and wider society, with equal emphasis applied to zero-tolerance principles when tackling issues associated with sexism, anti-Semitism, disability discrimination, homophobia and Islamophobia.

Today, BAME professional players experience less abuse than in previous years, *but* it's still more prevalent at grassroots level. Those affected appear more confident in reporting incidents and challenging unacceptable behaviour and the FA is much more resolute in applying disciplinary sanctions wherever appropriate. However, while the visibility of on-field progress is evident, there's less to applaud when it comes to equality of access to opportunities in other spheres of the game.

Kick It Out has been and continues to be pivotal to the processes of change, challenging all forms of discrimination and exclusion, encouraging progressive developments to open up opportunities for people from all backgrounds to those that have historically been closed to them, such as in the boardrooms, coaching, administration, management and other technical positions. Our education and mentoring programmes help to facilitate change in preparing the next generation to take up opportunities when available. These programmes help individuals to challenge bias and prejudice and are vital in supporting the change to positive and tolerant attitudes and conduct among players, officials and fans.

Kick It Out has been a catalyst for change, but the positive developments in football must be attributed to those people making it happen: the progressive fans, some of whom were campaigning courageously for change to tackle racism in football long before KIO appeared on the scene; the FA, the Premier and English Football Leagues, many others in the lower leagues and at grassroots; and, above all, the players, without whom there would be no game. Without Kick It Out, there might not have been the progress made. Without enterprising influential individuals, there would have been no Kick It Out. In particular, at the beginning, Gordon Taylor and the PFA were at the forefront of supporting the ideals of equality, inclusion, and cohesion – not only for members, who were the victims of relentless discrimination, but for the game as a whole. The PFA has been and remains a staunch KIO partner. Without the support of David Dein at the beginning of the Premier League, David Davies at the FA in 1993 and Richard (now Lord) Faulkner at the Football Trust, the campaign may have floundered into early oblivion, such was the reluctance of those with power to face up to the challenge of dealing with racism, sexism and homophobia in football. Other significant contributors from day one included key former players such as Paul Elliott and Garth Crooks.

When tackling institutional inertia, it is critical to challenge timid irresponsible leadership and it remains a truism that, if the powerful decision-makers in the game *want* to end exclusion, inequality and divisiveness, they can make it happen.

As well as highlighting the negative, one should also recognise the positive and progressive work being done to bring about greater community and social cohesion through the football foundations and charities. Bringing together and creating opportunities in the game for young people of all backgrounds so that they and we learn with and from each other provides a substantial contribution to building that cohesion for the next generation. Football can be proud that it is leading the way, but the importance and value of this contribution has to be put in the context of continuing bias, prejudice and hate-related activity across society. Examples include government promoting a "hostile environment" for migrants (including those who have lived here as British subjects since the 1950s), an upsurge in anti-Semitism, extreme racist fringe groups seeking to infiltrate football again and uncontrolled filth and abuse on social-media platforms.

Undoubtedly, the way forward is for football to lead on equality, inclusion and cohesion. It must reflect on what it has been doing for the past twenty-five years, what has been achieved, what is being done now and what is still to be done. Football must be more open, accessible, transparent, progressive and accountable. Those who run the game must take the pursuit of equality, inclusion and cohesion in a coherent and co-ordinated way across the entirety of the game. The FA must lead for the whole of football, and the Premier League, English Football League (EFL), Professional Footballers' Association (PFA), League Managers' Association (LMA) and Football Supporters' Federation (FSF) must all unite in collective action in pursuit of equality and inclusion. Above all, recognition must be given to the leadership, expertise, commitment and invaluable contribution to the game of the whole Kick It Out team, led magnificently by Roisin Wood.

– Lord Herman Ouseley, ex-Chair, KIO

INTRODUCTION

"Good ... as far as it goes"

"I've been very lucky to have a chairman and a managing director to whom colour doesn't matter. We've had a lot of support from the local council. It's a liberal-minded club. The fact that I'm black is immaterial. I must have been the best person to have applied for the job, or otherwise I wouldn't have got it."
– Keith Alexander, on becoming the first full-time black Football League manager

The Premier League, English Football League and Professional Footballers' Association instigated a new scheme to increase the number of BAME coaches as a direct consequence of the power of the Black Lives Matter campaign.

Good ... as far as it goes.

Premier League players' powerful statement of "taking the knee" in every game after Project Restart brought football back during the Covid-19 pandemic had an equally powerful consequence – bringing the anti-racism campaign to the forefront of the sport more significantly than the best part of three decades of campaigning by organisations including Kick It Out.

Football authorities are now united in a new initiative to help BAME players move into full-time coaching roles in the professional game, encouraged by the current powerful message of Black Lives Matters (BLM), which has gained in importance around the world during recent tragic events.

But there have been many initiatives that petered out once the headlines stopped and, more importantly, there have been numerous calls to see BAME representatives running the game.

Our national sport will not be seen as properly diverse, totally integrated, and given full respect until a BAME representative holds the role of FA chair or Premier League CEO.

No one is convinced that will happen in their lifetimes!

Kenny Dalglish once told me he wanted to see Liverpool FC team-sheets *not* balance sheets, so that supporters can see for themselves the lack of senior BAME figures. Nothing will truly change until a BAME member is at the pinnacle of the sport.

For years, there's been a glaring lack of proper representation on the touchline but at least there are now some measures to address this. The new scheme will give six coaches a twenty-three-month work placement at EFL clubs per campaign. PFA members at any age or stage in their careers can apply: "This is a critical time for black, Asian and minority ethnic coaches," said Doncaster Rovers manager Darren Moore, who is chair of the Premier League's Black Participants' Advisory Group. "We all know and agree that the diversity of coaches and managers must increase, and this placement scheme represents a positive step. There are lots of roles in the academy system, all the way through to first team, and young coaches can slot in at different points to begin that journey. We need to have the right structures and people in place to develop their careers. I know from my own experiences the value of strong support throughout the coaching journey."

At present, only six of the ninety-one Premier League and EFL managers or head coaches are BAME. The new scheme, supported by the FA, is jointly funded by the Premier League and the PFA, with bursaries to each participant from the placement club. Candidates must have a minimum of a UEFA B qualification and commit to the UEFA A coaching licence. They must also take the FA Advanced Youth Award and will be selected following panel and individual club interviews. "It is vital that there are no barriers to entry to the pipelines for employment in coaching," said Premier League CEO Richard Masters. "We need more BAME coaches entering the system to create greater opportunities throughout the professional game."

It was inevitable that football authorities had to act after the decision of players to "take a knee" at kick-off when football resumed after the coronavirus lockdown – backing a global campaign that mushroomed after the death by police in the US of George Floyd – with the names of players replaced by "Black Lives Matter" on their shirts for the opening twelve games. All top-flight shirts carried a BLM badge designed by Watford striker Troy Deeney and his partner Alisha Hosannah. They were Premier League policy and worn for the duration of the resumed season.

Black Lives Matter want to bring to an end racial injustice, something universally supported by all who believed it was time for change. The movement has galvanised many to protest in the streets, despite social-distancing rules brought about by the Covid-19 pandemic, to emphasise how important is the fight against racial inequality.

In the UK, Gordon Taylor and Baron Herman Ouseley are two among many who have dedicated much to the anti-racism movement. Both can be proud that, as they reach the conclusion of their formidable careers, they leave a proud legacy to the campaign for equality and diversity. "Experience has taught me that racism has to be dealt with as a group – a group of footballers or society as a whole," Taylor says. He and Ouseley created the anti-racism campaign Kick It Out. "Since its inception we had that group to build on and involve all the football family," Taylor adds. "We have agitated, educated and achieved. The football pitches of our professional game are full of players reflecting inclusion, diversity and equality and setting an example to society throughout the world.

"Our current challenge is on the touchline for BAME coaches and managers with many initiatives in place and in the boardroom so that the graduates of our courses can reveal the quality of their learning at the highest level for the good of the game.

"You only need to look at the make-up of teams on the pitch to see what has been achieved and look at our England teams and note that this country provided more players for the most countries in the World Cup.

"We have evolved from anti-racism to discriminatory issues of any kind, reinforced equality and respect and shown that football – as the world's most popular spectator and participant sport – can be a force for good in overcoming barriers of race, religion, culture, creed, politics and engaging with the younger generation. In the words of Nelson Mandela we can 'Bring hope where once there was only despair!' We have lobbied successfully for football's governing bodies, from FIFA and UEFA to our own FA to bring in new rules and new sanctions, and provided education and understanding of 'right from wrong', 'respect and disrespect' to 'appropriate and inappropriate'.

"With regard to many cases we have had to deal with, the most public was the Eniola Aluko case, which resulted in a successful conclusion for Eniola as a result of our support and the FA being called in front of the Parliamentary Committee for Media Culture and Sport. The next 25 years we need to see the same changes on the touchline and in boardrooms!

"In a world of conflict, where too many know only war and extremism, our message and work is even more necessary for the next 25 years than the last! Like football, the world has to work together as a team with the sum being greater than the individual parts! We cannot afford to fail! Together 'everybody achieves more'!"

Originally, the PFA joined with the CRE to form "Let's Kick Racism Out of Football". The campaign's objective was to halt the racist abuse from the terraces that black footballers were subjected to from fans on a weekly basis. Simone Pound, PFA Director of Equalities, commented: "As the players' union, the PFA considered it at the forefront of our responsibility to protect our members within their workplace, the football stadium and protect their human rights as people as well as professional footballers. A ten-point plan of measures that professional football clubs should follow to challenge racism was drawn up to ensure that there were targets to work towards (see 2: Pre-Kick It Out).

"Within a 12-month period, we had begun to make some visible differences and, in 1995, a film with Eric Cantona and Les Ferdinand was produced and shown at cinemas and matches around the country – 'Do you see a black man, a French man … or a footballer?"

In 1997, "Let's Kick Racism Out of Football" changed its name to Kick It Out and began its formal constitution, receiving funding from the PFA, Premier League, Football Foundation and FA and support from the LMA and EFL, as it does to this day.

In 2001, the game adopted the Kick It Out "Weeks of Action" with professional clubs and grassroots projects all working to make a united stand against discrimination and raise awareness of the campaign's work.

Pound again, in 2018: "Twenty-five years from where we began, and the game has seen many changes. Football has a more diverse workforce that is celebrated by fans across the world and the English game has provided a benchmark for what can be achieved to tackle racism and discrimination.

"There is still a long way to go; the under-representation of British-born Asian players in the professional game, BAME minority coaches and managers, [lack of] openly gay male players, coaches and managers in top-flight football and the commercialisation of the women's game are all key issues for us to challenge."

When Herman was plain old Mr Ouseley, as chair of the Commission for Racial Equality, he presented me with CRE Race in the Media award. With the *Daily Mirror* at the time, as Chief Football Writer, I led a campaign persuading some high-level black footballers to speak up about racial abuse, something which had never before been aired in public. Back then, it was one of the great taboos in football and journalists had little to no interest in championing the causes of ethnic minorities. Pride of place on my office wall is a letter from Neil Kinnock, then Leader of the Labour Party, on House of Commons-headed notepaper to the *Daily Mirror* editor, praising the groundbreaking campaign. Having collected 24 major industry awards in football journalism, the CRE award ranks as the least known of them all but is one of my proudest achievements.

When Ruud Gullit came to England to play for Chelsea, I felt compelled to write a biography of the former World Footballer of the Year. However, publishers at the time rejected the idea, telling me, "Books about black people don't sell"! That shocked me. Finally, Collins Willow, an imprint of HarperCollins, published the book and it proved a huge success. So much so, that it wasn't long before I was approached to write Gullit's *auto*biography, which went straight to number one in the *Sunday Times* best-sellers list. He became the first black manager in English football to lift a trophy – Chelsea's first trophy in twenty-six years!

It's been uplifting to listen to so many people's stories and insights. So many interviews freely given by such a wide range of people who have played their part. While 25 years have brought many positives, the negatives still exist and the big question is whether enough is being done, and how much more work there *needs* to be done?

– Harry Harris

1

BAME Representation

"Go any Saturday to the local parks in most cities in England and see how many BAME players are out there on the pitches. And then go and look at any FA meeting, from the FA Council right down to your local FA, and you find the vast majority are still dominated by old white men wearing ties and blazers. Take a look and you can see the scale of the problem football still faces. It's not that these organisations are blatantly prejudiced – in the overwhelming number of cases they are not – but what they haven't done is realise that the racial mix of people playing football in England has changed at almost every level and that they have a responsibility to reflect that in the structures of football at all levels."

– Greg Dyke, Former Director General of the BBC,
ex-FA Chairman,
former Manchester United FC board member

In January 2016, Greg Dyke announced that he would not seek re-election as FA Chairman when his term ended in June of that year. Dyke, appointed in 2013, had intended to stand for a further year, but said that opposition to proposed reforms from some FA councillors and a minority of board members had made him reconsider. He felt it would be a "fight" to convince the FA Council to see through other "much-needed, significant reform".

When he succeeded David Bernstein, Dyke famously said England should aim to reach the semi-finals of Euro 2020 and win the World Cup in 2022. "I had already decided that if no reform was possible I was going to leave anyway this summer, a position I had shared with a number of colleagues. What I now see is that even if we get the reform through, I am probably not the best person to pick up the pieces following the inevitable discord." Dyke had pursued policies aiming at modernising the FA and increasing the number of English players in the Premier League.

Bernstein was "not particularly surprised" by Dyke's decision, saying neither he nor Dyke had made "any substantial change" and that pushing reforms through is "extremely difficult". "I can understand his frustration, which matches my frustration," he told BBC Radio 5 Live Sport, adding that only "outside intervention" from government or a regulator would make a significant difference.

In an exclusive interview for this book, Dyke looks at the issues of diversity in English football today:

The change in English football since Kick It Out started 25+ years ago is quite remarkable. Back then, racism was widespread on the terraces and I suspect the boardrooms of some clubs. Organisations like the FA seemed incapable of doing anything about it. Today, blatant racism isn't tolerated in football. Officials, fans and players who make racist comments are dealt with pretty harshly by the FA and, largely due to pressure from organisations like Kick It Out, there has been a massive change in culture. However, that's not to say prejudice isn't still there in places.

Two examples spring to mind from my time as FA Chairman. First, was the FA council member who told me that this was a London issue, that prejudice and under-representation of people from BAME backgrounds wasn't a problem in his native Yorkshire. Second, was when a member of the FA board told me that "they" – by which, he meant people from ethnic minorities – "didn't want to run local football clubs and certainly didn't want to join committees run by their local FA". With people like him in authority, I'm not at all surprised.

I really didn't know what I was walking into that day early in my turbulent FA career when, unannounced, I attended a news conference at the Victoria offices of the Commission for Racial Equality (CRE). It was 1994.

To his great credit, Gordon Taylor of the Professional Footballers Association (PFA) was already working with the CRE and its charismatic boss, Herman Ouseley, to fight the scourge of racism that was scarring the national sport both at the top of the game and at the grassroots. And there they were together in front of the cameras and the assembled newspaper scribes.

I sat quietly in the audience ... and listened ... and learned. And felt quite at home.

After all, as a BBC TV hack for 23 years of my life before risking my sanity at the FA, this had been my world. Asking questions of others, of the great and the good, and yes, of the not so great, and not so good.

I thought I knew a little about racism, too. In South Africa, like so many of my college mates, I'd grown passionate about fighting apartheid. In the deep south of the US where several months travelling on a scholarship had taken me to Memphis and Alabama and changed my life.

But then to my extreme discomfort, from around me came questions about the FA and their apparent reluctance to be part of fighting racism. "Ask David Davies. He's here," said Herman. And now the cameras swung in my direction.

The honest answer, which I hope I gave, was that I hadn't got a clue why anybody anywhere would not want to be part of a campaign to use the significant power of football to combat racism. At that moment, I knew that I had to do something to persuade my new employers (some of whom I also knew were not my greatest supporters and didn't expect me to stay very long anyway) to get involved.

Back in the sanctuary of my new office of the time at Lancaster Gate, I would love to say I was swept along by the enthusiasm of everybody around me to get involved!

But by now, thankfully, the horror stories of racism on and off the pitch so eloquently expressed by the likes of John Barnes, Brendon Batson, Ian Wright and the late Laurie Cunningham, as well as lesser-known names in football were being listened to. Likewise, the activities of the National Front and others were being chronicled in TV documentaries. They were hard to ignore.

Which made it that little bit easier to build a new alliance within the game for a campaign that could make a difference. As always in such campaigns, dedicated individuals made the biggest contributions.

"Let's Kick Racism Out of Football" and its full-time successor Kick It Out were born thanks, of course, to Herman Ouseley and Gordon Taylor. But David Dein, then Vice Chairman of Arsenal and a founder and inspiration for the Premier League, brought the top clubs onside very quickly. Journalists like Harry Harris of the *Mirror* convinced their editors that football could be a power for good, no easy task after the nightmares of Heysel and Hillsborough and Bradford in the then still recent past. The new Football Foundation was an early supporter. However, the Football League, and at least some of its 72 club chairmen, continued to display some of the reluctance that I had experienced within the FA.

Their argument was the one we were to witness again and again in future years in Eastern Europe and closer to home in Italy. Football's job is football, not changing the world. If you highlight racism, you make it worse. In summary, shut your eyes, close your ears. Wrong, wrong, wrong.

The FA itself internally was hardy a trailblazer, though. The FA Council, its parliament, as is well documented, was jam packed with white, middle-aged and older, and largely middle-class men. Yes, a bit like me. Admittedly, there was one woman who coincidentally was married to one of those men. And they were, by the way, not by any means all "amateurs" as was the supposedly derogatory term with which they were branded. No, lots of professional types from insurance and the law and the rest. Mostly good people but not a black face in sight.

As for us staff members – "you downstairs" as a former bearded Chelsea Chairman used to describe us with his well-known charm – well, black or minority faces were mightily hard to find as well. Mind you, I owe my transition from new media Luddite to new CyberMan *par excellence* to a wonderful FA stalwart called Saty Gahir who brought me screaming into the new technological world. A miracle!

So, it was a proud day in 1997 when Kick It Out became a full-time organisation, not just a campaign, financed jointly by the FA, the Premier League, the Football Foundation and the PFA. And if the stories about the work of Piara Power and Ben Tegg in their tiny first office in Islington are even half true, they have even more to be proud of.

Yes, ridding top-level English football of its worst racist excesses meant that, in 2018, Lord Ouseley could be widely quoted saying, "We now have a situation where I think players are as comfortable playing here as in any country in the world. And black and minority fans are going to matches in increasing numbers to enjoy their football. Whereas, in days gone by, they were in fear of being abused or even attacked."

On top of this, the diversity of the England squad at the most recent World Cup in Russia was the best tribute possible, you hope, to those pioneers like John Barnes and Ian Wright who, in a previous generation, stood up so much to racism at its worst when they were in an England shirt. Likewise, the diversity apparent in the England Women's team – third in the world in Canada remember – is testament to what has changed.

And yet ... and yet, Kick It Out is busier than ever handling complaints. Yes, a third of male players in our top four divisions are now from ethnic minorities. But where are the black coaches and managers that, when Keith Alexander made history back in 1993 as the first full-time black coach in the Football League, some of us assumed would be flooding the game by now? The latest figure I saw was just 7% in such jobs in 2017. And then, of course, there are the administrators and blazers in the FA nationally and regionally, the Premier League, the

Football League and elsewhere in the National Game. Will I live to see a black chairman of the FA?

Even closer to home for me, is my embarrassment about a book I recommend, if you can find it, called *Asians Can't Play Football*. I remember discussing it with its excellent author Jas Bains. I told him that the near absence of Asian players at top-level would surely not be the case in the next generation. Not long afterwards, Michael Chopra became the first Asian male to play and score for an England team. But Jas was right and I was wrong. Football is still a closed world to too many people of Asian origin.

Meanwhile, in the parks on a Saturday and Sunday morning, is racism dead? Sadly, not. Time for some undercover filming on the touchline from my old TV profession to show it as it is even today.

Looking beyond England, Kick It Out was a founder of the Fare Network (Footballers Against Racism in Europe) across Europe. Chief Executive, Priara Powar, I hope, has a slightly bigger office than the one where it all started in Islington!

But we are still living in an age where the international football association, FIFA, imposes a fine of just £22,000 for an international match, during the Russia 2018 World Cup that produced a cacophony of racist chanting that shocked even seasoned observers. Hardly a punishment to fit the crime in an age of multi-million-pound sponsorship and transfers. And be certain that what really matters to such associations and, indeed, big football clubs are ground closures and expulsions from tournaments.

As for players walking off in response to racist chanting and abuse, I hope FIFA's orders to referees – which ultimately give them the power to abandon a match if racist chants will not stop – will make a difference. Watch this space.

Meanwhile, it's time for a new generation, and new initiatives, and new campaigns to confront the bigots at all levels of football. The most popular sport on the planet does have considerable power and influence.

This 70-year-old wishes he could have done more but Kick It Out and all it stands for is winning. It's been a privilege to play a small part.

Chris Hughton

Until his sacking by Brighton, Chris Hughton was the *only* black Premier League manager – that in itself should sound the alarm bells. I've known Chris since the first day he strode into White Hart Lane as a fresh-faced kid ready to embark on his move into big-time football. Few players of his era before or since have had a more engaging attitude towards life and the profession. Hughton was Norwich manager, the only black manager in the Premier League, when in 2013, he was hurt by the racist abuse directed at him by fans on Facebook. Like the majority of black players in the 1980s and '90s, he'd suffered regular abuse, but was shocked to have to deal with it again as a manager. Norwich vowed to ban for life any fan found responsible for posting the abuse.

Prior to becoming a football manager, Hughton enjoyed a successful playing career, winning two FA Cups and the UEFA Cup and becoming the first-ever BAME player to represent the Republic of Ireland at full international level. From 1977–1993, he featured in 297 league games for Tottenham Hotspur (398 in total), won 53 caps for Ireland, and also played for West Ham United and Brentford. As team coach, caretaker manager and then manager, Hughton made his mark at Newcastle

United, returning the club to the Premier League before Mike Ashley sacked him in December 2010 when the club dropped to 11th position. Norwich enticed him away from Birmingham, but he was again sacked in April 2014 and unemployed for eight months. Hughton became Brighton's manager on New Year's Eve 2014 while undertaking study in corporate governance. "I was delighted to do it – even if it impinged a little on my job while I was at Brighton. It's a ten-month course and I had three months to do it […] So it overlapped but I was really pleased. The course is about getting more diversity in the boardroom – and learning about boardroom structures and how they're run. It was very interesting but tough. I have a thirst for knowledge because you're always trying to have the best relationship with the directors. I also won't always be a manager. It might open up another future pathway.

"The Football Association decreed they will include a BAME coach with every one of their national football teams; not the main man, but at least one coach at each level right the way through all the different age groups. A very positive step, it represents in our stakeholders a welcome change of attitude and mentality and will help all of us work towards greater diversity in our workplace. That said, we need to be realistic and accept that there's still a lack of change at senior management level and until that change happens, it's very difficult to gauge real progression.

"I'm delighted that this book contains interviews with the likes of Greg Dyke, David Dein and David Davies – people who know what really goes on inside the FA, and it's fascinating to hear their perspective. The big question is a simple one: 'Who will pave the way?' The answer is an equally simple one: 'It has to be the game's main stakeholders – the FA, the Football League, the Premier League.'

"Looking back, it's clear to me that a change of attitude by the football authorities and our governing bodies rather than the supporters' groups themselves ended the days when crowds of fans on the terraces, were allowed to be as disruptive and racist as they wanted to be.

"Surely, having already witnessed the election of a black President of the United States and two women UK prime ministers, we can look forward to one day welcoming a black or ethnic leader of the FA? At the moment, there's an imbalance between the number of BAME players in the game and those that have gone into management and coaching. What has increased, though, is the number of BAME players coaching in academy football. Transferring that to elite football is a challenge and the reasons for that are a bigger conversation. But I'm happy with the role because there are a lot of BAME coaches striving to see it happen, and if I can help in any way I'm happy to do so."

Chris Hughton has urged UEFA to show they're serious about fighting racism by handing out tougher punishments to clubs. Too often, it seems, this has translated into fines, which are easily paid by the bigger clubs, so harsher penalties need to be considered.

Chris Hughton first joined the youth system at Tottenham Hotspur in 1971. "I went to Tottenham at 13, having grown up at Upton Park, ten minutes from West Ham. I would have been very average at school but, if you weren't a footballer, you got an apprenticeship. So, I stayed on as an amateur and did a four-year apprenticeship as a lift engineer. At 18, they offered me full-time as a pro, which I turned down, to finish my apprenticeship. I signed pro as a 20-year-old and made my debut against Manchester United in the League Cup in 1979. I signed full-time in the summer and – this is the lucky part – we'd brought in Gordon Smith to play left-back. After three games, he done his hamstring and I ended up making my debut and that was it: I stayed in!

"At the time, I would have been the only black player. I think I was the second black player to play for Tottenham. Then Garth [Crooks] would have come in 1980. These are the eras when there would be things I would be conscious of that others wouldn't, and there would have been particular places – I'll let you guess them – that were worse than others. As a player, I was always conscious of that. And things around you that weren't right or that you felt had racial overtones, but the only way to cope with that was to get on with it. It was the only way to cope. What happened over the years – stakeholders and clubs became more aware of it. No, sorry: they paid more attention to it. Some of the organisations in the game have worked tirelessly and they've been listened to. It's not something that has completely gone, but it's a far healthier environment now.

"I was brought up in a football environment where we saw a lot of racism – whether it was abuse from other players or huge groups of supporters in away matches. I remember going to stadiums and huge sections of the stand gave you racial abuse. It was never nice, but it wasn't a surprise – particularly when I was first at Spurs. You were used to it if somebody made a racial comment to you on the pitch. I wouldn't say you accepted it, but you had to get on with it. It was in society, too. Those were also the days where the perception of black players was that, 'They can play on the wing, and they're really quick, but they're not captaincy or organisation material.' Even now it's about getting away from that myth.

"You had to be thick-skinned. It was a different era then, '70s Britain, for a black family or a young black player trying to come through the system. I was the first black player for the Republic of Ireland, but I never experienced anything [racist] in Ireland, itself. Going abroad, yes, but people in Ireland were wonderfully welcoming.

"I don't think any black footballer in the late 1970s and '80s would not have experienced it. The only way to combat and work around it was to get on with the job, to work as hard as you could to prove as many people wrong as you could and to ignore it as much as you could.

"It's shocking and the more we speak about the lack of BAME managers, and reflect on it, the more it hits home that there's an incredible imbalance between those of ethnic backgrounds playing football, often at very good clubs, having good careers, being captains of their teams, and an absence in senior management. There have been some changes and it has been encouraging at academy and grassroots level – but still not at the top level. The game has a responsibility to redress the balance. The Football League [but not the Premier League] came out and said with any [coaching or management] position the club must interview at least one black or ethnic candidate. I certainly believe in a type of Rooney Rule [a rule introduced by the NFL] – in legislation that doesn't give BAME individuals a job but, at least, puts them in the frame. We're in an age of big business and I'm sure there will be future legislation about the workplace. All of the stakeholders in our game appear to have an enthusiasm for change. You see it with the big broadcasters. We're broadcasting English football all over the world – including many African countries. I feel people in the game want to see diverse players and multiracial cultures – which means [black] people in better positions at the stadium, doing the actual interviewing in the boardrooms, because the game on the field is multiracial.

"Am I hopeful of more representation in the boardroom? The stats over the last ten to twenty years don't suggest [much hope]. But the stakeholders seem to say we need a harder push. It's the same battle women have had. We don't see enough women in the boardroom. There was always a saying that 'a woman or a black person needed to work twice as hard to get a position someone else would reach far more comfortably'."

2

Pre-Kick It Out

"Albert was quite a brave man to actually go on the pitch in the first place, wasn't he? And he went out and did it. He had a lot of skill. A nice man as well – which is, I suppose, the more important thing, isn't it? More important than anything."

– George Best

It was quite a shock to discover, during the vast amount of research required for such an important football tome, that the FA, realising they had selected a black player for the England team, then had no hesitation about deselecting him. He was picked to play for England against Ireland in 1925, before being suddenly ditched. It would be 53 years later, in 1978, before a black player – Viv Anderson – would receive the honour of becoming the first-ever to represent England at senior level, making his debut against Czechoslovakia.

Jack Leslie was born in Canning Town in 1901, the son of an English mother and Jamaican father, and played for Barking Town until his move to Plymouth Argyle at the age of 20. He was the only black professional player in

England during his time at the club, where he remained for the rest of his professional career.

After the First World War, London-born Leslie became a prolific scorer with Argyle between 1920 and 1935, scoring 137 goals. His manager, Bob Jack, told him he had been selected to play for England, before receiving communication cancelling his call-up, stating that they didn't realise he was "a man of colour". Leslie told a journalist in 1982: "They must have forgot I was a coloured boy." When the papers published the team days later, he was named as a travelling reserve, but didn't even go to Belfast for the game.

Just when his story was long lost and forgotten and no one was interested, the *Daily Mirror* and *Mail Online* took it up again at the beginning of July 2020, reporting that a campaign had been launched to build a statue of the player. The Jack Leslie Campaign reads: "After his selection, his name mysteriously disappeared from the team-sheet, seemingly because FA officials had come to look at him in person and discovered that he was black."

Leslie's story was first told in 1978 by acclaimed sportswriter Brian James in the *Daily Mail*. In the interview, Leslie recalled the day his manager told him that the selection committee wanted him to play for England. "Well, can you imagine?" said Leslie. "Everybody in the club knew about it. The town was full of it. It was quite a thing for a little club like Plymouth. I was proud. All of a sudden everyone stopped talking about it. Sort of went dead quiet. Didn't look me in the eye. Then the papers came out a day or so later and Billy Walker of Aston Villa was in the team, not me. I didn't ask outright. I could see by their faces it was awkward. But I did hear that the FA had come to have another look at me. Not at my football but at my face. I suppose they thought that was like finding out I was foreign."

There is no physical evidence to support the story either at the FA or at Argyle's ground, Home Park, which was destroyed when Plymouth was blitzed in the war, and some club historians argue that Leslie's physical stature counted against him as well as his colour. However, his granddaughter Lesley Hiscott says, "Someone came to watch him. They weren't watching his football – they were looking at the colour of his skin."

His footballing exploits were highlighted by *Mail Online*: "As an inside-left, he forged a prolific partnership at Home Park with outside-left Sammy Black – although he sometimes appeared at centre-half – during a successful decade for the club. For six years in a row, they were runners-up in Division Three (South) – they even toured in Argentina – and finally won promotion as champions in 1930. By way of celebration, a giant pasty was carried onto the pitch before the final game of the season against Watford and presented to their captain, former England full-back Fred Titmuss. In Division Two, Argyle could attract crowds of more than 30,000. At the time, the *Plymouth Herald* described Leslie as "a versatile player" who was "known throughout England for his skill and complexion". Everton tried to sign both him and Black, but Leslie would spend his entire career at Argyle, where he made 401 appearances and is the fourth highest scorer of all time with 137 goals, the last of them against Fulham in 1934. "He is a hugely important figure at Home Park," said Plymouth's head of communications Rick Cowdery. "Ninth in the list of all-time appearance-makers and always a torch-bearer for diversity and inclusion. Since I joined Argyle more than 30 years ago, I've heard the story of his England call-up. We are 100% behind anything anyone can do to honour Jack. It's a tale of regret because he missed the chance to play for England but also of hope because society can change and *has* changed."

Campaigners hope to raise through crowdfunding over £100,000 for a statue to be erected at Home Park, saying, "Not only was Jack an incredible player [...] his is also a story of great historical significance [that] sadly still resonates."

Leslie's legend lives on at Home Park, though – the boardroom was named in his honour in 2019. Having first run a pub in Cornwall for a time after his playing career ended then returning to his roots as a boilermaker, he then worked as a boot-boy in the 1970s for West Ham United, where players including Clyde Best (himself one of only a very small number of black players in top-flight English football at the time) learned of his story. "Jack was already part of the furniture at Upton Park when I arrived," said Alvin Martin, who spent 22 years with the club from 1974. "He was reserved and quite shy, but he was a lovely man. John Lyall always found time for him and would treat him with a lot of respect. John knew he'd been one hell of a player and made sure all the boys knew that as well."

Leslie finally retired aged 80, with TV cameras filming his final day at work, and died in 1988, aged 87 – with, sadly, no formal recognition of him being a pioneering black footballer.

Today, FA chairman Greg Clarke says: "Stories like this are incredibly sad. Discrimination in the game, in any form or from any time period, is unacceptable. We must always remember pioneers like Jack Leslie and be thankful that football is in a very different place today. We are very pleased to support this [crowdfunding] campaign, which will hopefully ensure that Jack's career is appropriately recognised."

Fast-forward to 24 January 2004, when Vivek Chaudhary reported in the *Guardian* that a former England manager had "alleged that during his tenure he was told by senior FA officials not to pick too many black players". The manager, Chaudhary wrote, "claims that he was called into an office where two senior FA officials were present, and they told him that his England team should be made up of predominantly white footballers." Chaudhary's story said the manager, who "has a long history of closely working with some of England's leading black players over the past 25 years, privately spoke about the incident at the lunch" marking the tenth anniversary of KIO, but "refused to go public with his allegation". The manager in question is thought to be Graham Taylor. On several occasions during his three-year managerial reign, from 1990 to late 1993, Taylor fielded England teams featuring a large number of BAME players and was the one England manager most likely to have been the recipient of such a proposal for a racial quota on the England team. He worked closely with England's leading BAME players at Watford in the late 1970s.

In Clarke Carlisle's 2012 documentary *Is Football Racist?*, Carlisle, who had received a solitary England under-21 cap, revealed that a current England international refused to contribute to the programme, because he believed that his place in the squad could be at risk from the FA.

Having met and spoken with the current FA chairman Greg Clarke, I've no doubt that such obnoxious bigotry no longer exists at the highest level of the game's powerbrokers. That said, there's still no sign of a woman or black FA chair! Worse, there is still only one Premier League black manager, and so few in the Football League that – while much has been achieved, so much to be admired and applauded in the KIO's twenty-five years – there's still much to be done.

Pre-KIO there was no person, no organisation, representing the specific needs of ethnic minorities involved in football. There were, however, some notable landmarks and some immensely important trailblazers against all the odds.

The first black footballer in Britain was Andrew Watson, the son of a Scottish sugar planter Peter Miller and a local girl Rose Watson, born in Georgetown, British Guiana, in 1857.

Watson was sent to England to be educated at Halifax Grammar School and Rugby College before enrolling at Glasgow University in 1875 to study philosophy, mathematics and civil engineering. He joined Queen's Park, Britain's largest football team in 1880, became club secretary a year later, and led his team to several Scottish Cup wins. On 12 March 1881, Watson won his first cap playing right-back for Scotland against England, leading his country to a 6–1 victory as captain. Two days later, he played in the team that beat Wales 5–1. The following year he won his third cap when Scotland beat England 5–1. Watson sacrificed his international career by moving to England in 1882 – the Scottish FA refused to select men who played football outside Scotland – joining London Swifts and becoming the first black player in the FA Cup. In 1884, he joined the elite amateur club, Corinthians.

Arthur Wharton, the son of the Rev. Henry Wharton, a Wesleyan Methodist missionary from the West Indies, was born in Accra, Ghana on 28 October, 1865. Of mixed race, Wharton was educated at Dr. Cheyne's School, London, between 1875 and 1879. After spending time with his family in Grenada in the West Indies, Wharton returned to Britain in 1882 to train as a missionary teacher. He studied at Shoal Hill College before moving to Cleveland College in 1884. He was an outstanding athlete and eventually decided to concentrate on being a sportsman and began competing in sprint races in Darlington. Manny Harbon, a local coach, was impressed with Wharton and suggested he entered the AAA Championships at Stamford Bridge. In July, 1886, he set a new world record when he ran the 100 yards in ten seconds, making him the first black athlete to win an AAA. This brought him to the attention of Major William Sudall, manager of Preston North End, the club he joined later that year.

"Good judges say that if Wharton keeps goal for Preston North End in their English cup-tie, the odds will be considerably lengthened against them. I am of the same opinion [...] Is the darkie's pate too thick for it to dawn upon him that between the posts is no place for a skylark? By some it's called coolness – *bosh!*"

– *Athletic Journal*, 29 October 1887

Despite his tremendous speed, he played in goal, his trademark being his "prodigious punch" which had two targets: the ball and the opponent's head – always connecting with one. A number of match reports mention the run-ins he had with forwards. Goalkeepers could handle the ball anywhere in their own half and could be shoulder-charged with or without the ball. The physicality appealed to Wharton. In 1887, he played against West Brom in the FA Cup semi-final, losing 3–1. He played so well during this period that one football writer suggested he should play for England. In 1889, he signed for Rotherham United and also became licensee of the Albert Tavern in the town. Later, he ran the Plough Inn public house and, in September 1893, married a local girl, Emma Lister.

They had two daughters together, Minnie and Nora. In the late 1890s, Wharton coached Stalybridge Rovers.

After five years at Rotherham, he moved to Sheffield United, and also ran the Sportsman Cottage public house in the city. However, he had difficulty holding his place in the team, was replaced by Bill Foulke, and, in 1895, returned to Rotherham, where he played another 15 league games before joining Stockport County in 1901. During this period, Wharton developed a drink problem and, in 1902, was forced to retire from football, finding alternative employment as a colliery haulage worker at the Yorkshire Main Colliery, Edlington, joining the Miners' Federation of Great Britain and taking part in the 1926 General Strike.

Sadly, Wharton died a penniless alcoholic on 12 December 1930 at Doncaster's Springhill House Sanatorium – cause of death recorded as "epithelioma" and "syphilis" – and was buried in an unmarked grave for more than two thirds of a century before Football Unites, Racism Divides (FURD) raised the money to place a proper headstone on his resting place in 1997. The organisation also honoured him with the first of their *Pioneers* comic-book series.

According to Phil Vasili, in *Colouring Over the White Line: The History of Black Footballers in Britain* (2002), the next black player to play professional football in England was Fred Corbett, centre-forward for West Ham between 1900-02, before moving to Bristol Rovers, Bristol City and Brentford.

The first-ever black player for West Ham, he'd made his footballing debut as an 18-year-old right-winger for its predecessor Thames Ironworks during the 1899/1900 season, transferring to the inaugural West Ham United. Of mixed race, Corbett was a product of the East End and a prolific scorer at youth-team level, playing for St Luke's, the local side who produced many players for the club. His debut was the 1–0 away defeat to Reading on 16 September 1899. His first goal was the winner in his fifth game on 6 October 1900 in a 0–1 away win at Swindon. His finest moment came on 30 September 1901, when he scored a hat-trick in the 4–2 win against Wellingborough Town. In total, he played 35, scoring 15 before moving on to a long professional career with Bristol Rovers.

Cairo-born Hassan Hegazi played for Fulham in the club's 3–1 win over Stockport County. He scored one of the goals and the *Fulham Observer* commented that "with persistence, something might be made of him [...] Hegazi has the makings of a League player." Hegazi also played for Millwall, before completing his studies at Cambridge University.

In 1908, Tottenham Hotspur signed Walter Tull, a 20-year-old apprentice printer. Tull scored two goals in ten games in the 1909/10 season, before being transferred for a large fee to Northampton Town, where he played 110 first team games. Playing at wing-half, Tull became the club's most popular player. Some newspaper reports of his Spurs' matches refer to Tull as "West Indian" and "darkie". One in the *Northampton Echo*, however, dated 9 October 1909, had this to say about abuse levelled at him: "A section of the spectators made a cowardly attack upon him [Walter Tull] in language lower than Billingsgate [...] Let me tell these Bristol hooligans [there were but few of them in a crowd of nearly 20,000] that Tull is so clean in mind and method as to be a model for all white men who play football, whether they be amateur or professional. In point of ability, if not in actual achievement, Tull was the best forward on the field."

Other clubs wanted to sign him and, in 1914, Glasgow Rangers began negotiations with Northampton Town. Before he could play for them, however, there came the outbreak of the First World War.

Tull abandoned his career for the British Army, joining the 1st Football Battalion of the Middlesex Regiment. The army soon recognised his leadership qualities, promoting him to the rank of sergeant. In July 1916, he took part in the Somme offensive. Tull survived but, in December 1916, developed trench fever and was sent home to England. On recovery, he trained at Gailes Officer Training School, Scotland.

Lieutenant Tull was sent to the Italian Front as the British Army's first-ever black officer, leading his men at the Battle of Piave, and he is mentioned in dispatches for his "gallantry and coolness" under fire. He stayed in Italy until 1918 when he was transferred to France to take part in the attempt to break through the German lines on the Western Front. On 25 March 1918, 2nd Lieutenant Tull was ordered to lead his men on an attack on the Favreuil German trenches, and, soon after entering No Man's Land, was hit by a German bullet. Tull was such a popular officer that several of his men made valiant efforts under heavy fire to bring him back to the trenches, but Tull died soon after being hit, and his body was never recovered. He's to be honoured in an upcoming edition of FURD's *Pioneers* comic-book series.

Hong Ying "Frank" Soo was born in Buxton, Derbyshire, in 1914, and raised in Liverpool, to a Chinese father and an English mother. His football career began at the age of 18 at Prescot Cables FC and he was rated one of the best inside-forwards of the pre-war era, renowned for his perfectly placed passing and free-kicks. He was the first player of Chinese origin to play in the English Football

League and the first non-white player to represent England, on 9 May 1942, against Wales at Ninian Park – and *still* the only player of an Asian background to reach that level! In total, he played in nine unofficial English internationals during the Second World War, and also captained the RAF team during the conflict. Soo's life-story came back to life recently through a reader's question to the *Daily Mail*: "Did a Chinese footballer play for Stoke City in the '30s?"

Nicknamed "The Smiler", Soo was an admired and skilful footballer, charming and charismatic, a role model for any aspiring young player – now as much as he was during his lifetime – despite being somewhat the forgotten man of 20th-century football. Yet, in his time, he was a household name, his life chronicled by national newspapers in Britain and around the world. He had a successful club career, playing for many years alongside, and later captaining, Stanley Matthews for Stoke City. After the war, he played for Leicester City, Luton Town and Chelmsford City, and appeared as a guest player for Everton, Newcastle United, Chelsea, Brentford and Millwall.

Soo's later career as a football manager, mainly in Scandinavia, included a spell at the 1952 Helsinki Olympics, as the coach of the Norwegian national football team. He was appointed manager of Djurgårdens IF in the 1954/55 season, leading them to the Allsvenskan title, the highest football league in Sweden. Other clubs he managed included Italy's Padova, Sweden's AIK and England's Scunthorpe United, the latter of which he took to 15th in the League table after only one season in charge.

Soo passed away in Cheadle, England, on 25 January 1991, aged 76 years. His family believe a highly racist cartoon derailed his England career (though no evidence of this cartoon has been found), while others believe that managing and living in Scandinavia meant his name was not spoken of as often in British households and eventually disappeared. Today, the Frank Soo Foundation actively promotes and advances his legacy, and, on 9 May 2020, in partnership with Google, they released the Frank Soo Google Doodle.

Soo's great-niece, Jacqui, who didn't meet him until he was 66, says he was still an inspiration long after his playing days were over: "He never drank and he never smoked, he made a point of telling us that. Then he dropped to the floor and began to do a load of press-ups. He was clapping between them and then doing them with one hand. It was amazing. My friends still talk about it to this day."

Roy Brown had a Nigerian father, Eugene Brown, and an English mother. He, too, had a successful career with Stoke City. Two further BAME footballers made an impact between the two world wars: Salim Bachi Khan, an Indian international, played barefoot for Glasgow Rangers in the 1936/37 season, while Trinidad-born Alfred Charles was a centre-forward for Southampton in 1936.

The first BAME player to represent England at *any* level was West Ham United defender John Charles, who earned three Youth Caps for England, twice against Israel, once against USSR. It would be another decade, however, before the Schoolboy level saw their first representation – by two players, Ben Odeje and Cliff Marshall, who played against Northern Ireland Schoolboys at Wembley Stadium, on 6 March 1971, the first of five appearances for Odeje, the first of four for Marshall.

West Ham have been serial trailblazers, providing opportunities for black players when it was unheard of elsewhere.

In his autobiography, Clyde Best argues West Ham has never done enough to celebrate their positive trailblazing role. He points out how West Ham were the first team to field three black players in a team a decade before West Brom's more famous "Three Degrees" (Cyrille Regis, Laurie Cunningham and Brendon Batson). Best, Ade Coker and Clive Charles were the Hammers' own "Three Degrees" and, as Best points out, if West Ham had not paved the way the West Brom trio would have found it more difficult. Regis personally told Best that it was, as a teenager, watching him on TV, that he'd developed his belief that he also could make it as a black centre-forward. Best's book is littered with statements from other players, too, including Garth Crooks, who took inspiration from the West Ham player. Best describes support he received from players such as Bobby Moore, Harry Redknapp, Geoff Hurst, and manager Ron Greenwood, who was determined to allow black players to succeed at the top-level.

Although Viv Anderson holds the "First Black Player to Play for England" distinction, receiving his call-up in 1978, Paul Reaney, of mixed-race heritage, played for the national team a decade earlier in 1968 – as substitute in a match against Bulgaria. Born in Fulham on 22 October 1944, Reaney moved to West Yorkshire as a child, leaving school at 15. He worked briefly as a car mechanic before signing for Leeds United as an apprentice, making his debut shortly before his 18th birthday.

A long-serving full-back with the hugely successful 1960–70's team, Reaney was seen as "white" during his appearance for England but, today, his position has assumed greater importance because he's now viewed by many as black/mixed-race. Unfortunately, having suffered a broken leg in a game against West Ham, he missed the 1970 Mexico World Cup, though went on to receive two more England caps. During his peak, he was the only player who could mark George Best out of a game, a fact acknowledged by Best himself. Continuing at Elland Road until 1978, he was given a free transfer after 745 appearances, joining neighbours Bradford City before completing his playing career in Australia. On returning to England, Reaney became a soccer-school coach.

It is another Leeds United star, though, who holds the distinction of being the first "black icon": outside-left Albert Johanneson. A teacher recommended Johanneson to Leeds United after seeing him play for Germiston Coloured School and Germiston Colliers in his native South Africa. Playing with no boots, bare-footed, he set up one goal, scored another and left the pitch in the arms of his teammates. His youth in Germiston had been characterised by racism and violence – such as the time when, aged six, he and some friends were playing on a street corner when a car stopped and a white boy of the same age leaned out and spat in his face. Johanneson did not move. The boy giggled and did it again, then the driver of the car reached out and whipped Johanneson across his neck with a cane. His friends ran when the man got out of his car but Johanneson was on the ground in pain, whereupon the man kicked him and drove off. In comparison to South Africa, the player saw England as a place where he could live out a dream, earn enough to provide for his family and escape the racism of apartheid.

Although nervous and retiring, Johanneson signed a three-month trial in 1961, making his debut in the first-team against Swansea. Soon he was again the target of racist abuse, coming first from the opposite dressing room and then the stands – fans making monkey noises and jumping up and down. Johanneson didn't score but he did make a mockery of the full-backs, using his quick feet and deft touch to leave them stuck in the mud, and he set up several chances for Jack Charlton, one of which led to a goal as Leeds drew 2–2.

"When we walked out," he told Paul Harrison, for his book about the player, *The Black Flash*, "all I could hear was a cacophony of Zulu-like noises coming from the terraces. It was dreadful, I could barely hear myself think for those screams. I wanted to run back down the tunnel". In Don Revie's words, it was a "shit pitch for fancy football", and he advised his winger to use his pace, "run like the wind and don't let the jungle-bunny chanting get to you." However, fellow player Johnny Giles observed, that he "did not contribute" and "he had a very, very bad match." After the match, Johanneson wasn't sure whether he could bath with his white teammates, till they, jokingly and good naturedly, stripped him, picked him up and threw him in!

There was no escaping the abuse around the away grounds *but* the supporters at Elland Road worshipped him. "Albert was a hero to the Leeds fans," Giles says, "they loved him."

In 1965, the South African made history as the first black man to play in the FA Cup Final, Leeds losing 2–1 to Liverpool at Wembley. The constant racial abuse sometimes undermined his confidence, and, before this historic appearance, he spent much of the time in the toilet vomiting and suffering from diarrhoea. He asked Revie if he could be dropped, but the manager refused. Then, waiting to go out onto the pitch, he was approached by someone, who said, "You've got no chance, looking like you do. Our fans will murder you."

"I'd heard of him but never seen him play," said Giles, who'd joined Leeds two years after Johanneson. "He played on the left-wing, very quick, good control, good goal scorer. He was outstanding." Billy Bremner was similarly enthusiastic. "When he joined Leeds, the rest of the team stood open-mouthed, drooling over his trickery. He was a bloody excellent player and had so much pace and strength, he was a great athlete." Jock Stein, the great Celtic manager, believed the South African "had no balls" and that "he wasn't tough enough," but Giles had little doubt about his resilience. "If he got a kick, he [would get up and] would go again." George Best was impressed, too: "In those days, Albert was quite a brave man to go on the pitch in the first place, wasn't he?"

Tragically, Johanneson died a forgotten man in September 1995, his marriage having dissolved along with his career. He'd moved to the Fourth Division, then York City in 1970 but, two years later, overweight and over drinking, he'd moved back to South Africa for a season, only to be back in Leeds soon after, working odd jobs, including washing dishes in a Chinese restaurant. Broke by now, he'd resorted to begging for money, approaching people with a telegram informing him of his father's death, claiming he needed cash for a flight home. His father had, in fact, died years earlier. Friends tried to get him clean, but he ended his days in his squalid Leeds high-rise flat, drinking cider, eating sausages and watching *Hawaii Five-O* on a black-and-white TV.

Johanneson's gravestone is etched with words from a Maya Angelou poem: "I rise, I rise, I rise" – he rose from South Africa to help ignite football's long journey against racism. In 2015, FURD's Howard Holmes joined with the Cape Town-based illustrator Archie Birch to produce *Albert Johanneson: The First Black Superstar*, a comic-book based on his life.

Sport reflects society, none more so than football, our national sport, and the life story of Cyrille Regis is a chilling reminder of a time when the evil of racism was at its zenith. Football, at the time, attracted the National Front to its doors, recruiting the vulnerable and disillusioned, spewing its evil doctrines.

The toxic nature of that evil is no better illustrated than by what was written across an Aston Villa team photo – "Aston N*****" – which referred to the side put out by "Big Ron" Atkinson, when Mark Bosnich and Shaun Teale were the only white faces in the team.

In his autobiography, *Cyrille Regis: My Story*, Regis recalls the "monkey chants whenever we touched the ball. Newspapers were highlighting it by referring to our colour. Black pearls, black gold, black magic. It was a new phenomenon [...] Laurie Cunningham and I both scored in a 3–1 win. You could almost hear people thinking, 'Where have they come from?' It was a constant noise, booing and monkey chants rather than individual shouts of abuse, but it soon became the norm."

Regis, who remembered Garth Crooks scoring a hat-trick for England against Denmark in 1978 and still being abused by England fans, and Regis himself receiving a bullet through the post, accompanied by a letter that read: "If you put a foot on our Wembley turf, you'll get one of these through your knees."

He was a powerhouse of a centre-forward who played for his country with pride and endured the racism with dignity. Along with Laurie Cunningham and Brendon Batson at West Brom, he was part of the famous "Three Degrees", put together by Atkinson. They even featured in a crass photo-opportunity with the eponymous pop group the Three Degrees, allowing themselves to be dressed up in Santa outfits under the headline, LOOK WHO'S DREAMING OF A WHITE CHRISTMAS – unfortunately, stereotyping was the norm.

Regis scored 81 goals in 241 games for Albion, before moving across the Midlands to Coventry, then to Aston Villa, before switching to Wolves at the time of KIO's birth in 1993. His epitaph describes him as "one of the great symbols of the fight against racism" and "a pioneer for black footballers across the world." His nephew – former West Brom, Blackburn and Wigan striker, Jason Roberts – in a moving BBC online article, paid his own touching tribute:

Cyrille Regis might have been a hero or a pioneer to many, but to me he was just my uncle. Growing up as a young kid on the Stonebridge Estate in north London, I never realised what he did was so special. I just thought that all uncles played in the First Division and for England! He was one of my three football-playing uncles, and when we all went round to my grandparents' house for Sunday dinner, he'd be there at the end of the table. He was no one special, just one of us. But there were several moments in my life where it struck me how big a star he was and how much he inspired people. In time, he proved to offer me the same inspiration – and for that I owe him so much. [Turning down the] chance to join French club Saint-Etienne, [because] he felt English [...] he went onto be a West Brom and Coventry legend [and] I came to realise how much people were in awe of him when he lived with me and my mum while playing for Wycombe Wanderers a few years later [...] As I grew older and more aware, I just remember being very proud; proud that it was my uncle out on the pitch scoring those wonderful goals, proud that he was taking on the racists, and then just having time for his nephew. [...] He was always so calm, measured and respectful – in many ways the opposite of me – and to do that after the sort of abuse he suffered shows the kind of man he was. [He] understood his impact on the community and on social issues, but he never sought to gain benefit from it. It was just what he did and who he was – and that has left a lasting impact on me. [...] My family have been completely overwhelmed by the love and messages from everyone since his passing. As he was to many people, he was our hero. But to me he was just my uncle.

Howard Holmes of FURD highlights the anti-racist campaigning by fans that existed before KIO's inception in 1993 and the actions beginning to take place in youth services, community groups, trade unions and local authorities, all of which would lay the groundwork for a national anti-racist campaign in football. "In Sheffield, a group of youth workers and young people began experimenting with peer-led activities that challenged racist attitudes among young people," Holmes says. "We started with the Anne Frank in the World youth project in 1987 and followed this up with the launch of Sheffield SOS Racism a year later, inspired by the youth-led SOS Racism movement in France. Such activities helped create a bank of ideas for effective anti-racist work, including the setting up of Sheffield ARAG (Anti-Racist Action Group) in 1988. Later that year, Sheffield United's new manager, Dave Bassett, began to add a number of black players to his all-white squad; a novelty for the Blades, who, despite having had the world's first black footballer in 1894 (more of him later), had employed only a handful of black players in the near-century since. The Bramall Lane ground had endured the typical mundane abuse of opposition black players since the late '60s, when Albert Johanneson arrived with Leeds United. A growing number of Blades began challenging the racially abusive fans around them during the 1980s, but the arrival of Brian Deane and Tony Agana as their very own twin black strike force at the start of the 1988/89 season was the real catalyst for change. These 'Black Blades' pioneers – building on the courage and determination of the likes of Cyrille Regis, Laurie Cunningham, Brendon Batson, John Barnes and Garth Crooks – helped give confidence to the fans that were standing up to the racists among them. The birth of the *Flashing Blade* fanzine helped create the space for writers to extol the virtues of our own black pioneers and the culture began to change. However, there were still disturbing reports of young BAME people being attacked by football fans standing outside pubs close to the United stadium, as well as local residents suffering harassment on match days and the virtual absence of any black faces on the terraces or in the stands. The launch of the "Let's Kick Racism Out of Football" initiative in 1993 gave much-needed confidence to anti-racist supporters across the UK.

"Football Unites, Racism Divides (FURD) was formed in 1995 and two larger-than-life characters have been a key part of our story since the start: Arthur Wharton and Kyle Walker. Walker attended one of FURD's free coaching sessions in 1997 as a seven-year-old. He was a little young and, originally, his older mates on the Lansdowne Estate close to Sheffield United's Bramall Lane ground told him there was no room in their car driving out to the pitch … until fate intervened: one lad didn't turn up so there was now a spare seat. I remember that first session clearly: he literally ran, ran and ran *again* around for a good hour, keen to learn new little tricks from FURD coaches Luis Silva and Paul Archer. It was the latter who took him down to Sheffield United, where he stayed for 11 years before the club sold him for a song to Spurs. Nothing unusual there, as Harry Maguire's career post-Blades proves!

"Kyle, his dad Michael and mum Tracey always acknowledge the role that FURD played in his very early career and he remains an inspiration for thousands of young kids in Sheffield."

Times have certainly changed for sure: around a hundred BAME players have appeared for England since Viv Anderson was the first to do so. Anderson was the 936th player to appear for England since their first match in 1872 and Dominic Solanke was the 1,230th player to appear for England. Thus, since Anderson broke the "colour barrier" in 1978, roughly one in every three-and-a-half players making an England debut has been BAME. With the possible exception of France, it's unlikely any other European national side comes close to that achievement.

3

25+ Years of KIO

"I didn't realise how I had affected so many people, not just in the football world, but kids who were struggling in life and had said I was an inspiration because it'd changed their mindset on what they wanted to do in life and how they wanted to be successful."

– Paul Ince, first-ever BAME England football captain

Paul Ince became the first-ever black England captain in 1993, the same year "Let's Kick Racism Out of Football" was launched.

The campaign's objectives were to halt the racist abuse from the terraces that black footballers were subjected to on a weekly basis. The PFA considered their responsibility to protect their members within the workplace, the football stadium, and to protect their human rights as people as well as professional footballers. A ten-point plan to tackle racism was drawn up for football clubs to work towards, as follows:

1. Tannoy announcements condemning racism.
2. Pitch-side hoardings and match-day programme articles condemning racism.

3. Condition for season-ticket holders not to take part in racist behaviour.
4. Take action to prevent sale of racist literature inside and outside of the stadium.
5. Disciplinary action against players who engage in racist behaviour.
6. Work with clubs to reinforce the anti-racism message.
7. Work with the police to deal with racist abuse.
8. Remove all graffiti from the ground.
9. Adopt an equal opportunity plan for the club.
10. Work with other groups and agencies to develop programmes and campaigns in the community to eliminate abuse and discrimination.

Within a 12-month period, it had begun to make some visible differences and, in 1995, a film – *Do you see a black man, a French man … or a footballer?* starring Eric Cantona and Les Ferdinand – was produced and shown at cinemas and matches around the country.

Simone Pound, Director of Equalities, PFA, commented: "In 1997, "Let's Kick Racism Out of Football" changes its name to Kick It Out, begins its formal constitution, is funded by the PFA, the Premier League, Football Foundation and FA, and supported by the LMA and the EFL. In 2001, the game adopted the Kick It Out Week of Action, with professional clubs and grassroots projects all working to make a united stand against discrimination and raising awareness of the campaign's work. The game has seen many changes: football has a more diverse workforce that is celebrated by fans across the world, and the English game has provided a benchmark for what can be achieved to tackle racism and discrimination. There is still a long way to go; the under-representation of British-born Asian players in the professional game, BAME coaches and managers; openly gay male players, coaches and managers in top-flight football and the commercialisation of the women's game are all key issues for us to challenge."

As England manager, Glenn Hoddle says he experienced no pressure from the FA in picking players, black or white: "All I know, from my own perspective, I had zero interference from above in terms of team selection, and I wouldn't have expected anything else."

Hoddle selected Paul Ince as his captain, entrusting him with the armband in one of the manager's most important World Cup qualifying ties during his two-year reign as national coach. Ince lead the team to one of their most famous performances, and results – a goalless draw in Italy that earned England a place at the 1998 World Cup Final in France.

In an exclusive interview for this book, Hoddle told me: "Alan Shearer was my captain, but he was not available and, although I would normally go for club captains and had a few in my team, such as Tony Adams, I went for Paul Ince for a number of reasons [...] Incy had played in Italy and I felt that might just give him and the team an edge. It turned out to be the right choice. But the choice was based on leadership qualities, absolutely no other criteria, just 100% leadership qualities."

Hoddle is now a lead commentator on England games for ITV, and was on World Cup duty in Russia, while also a leading pundit for BT Sport.

Yet, according to *Pitch Black* author Emy Onuora, the FA tried to impose an unofficial quota system on the number of black players an England manager should be allowed to use. Onuora claims Graham Taylor admitted to him he'd been summoned by two members of the FA's hierarchy and told "in no uncertain terms" he should not go beyond a certain limit.

Taylor is said to have revealed this during a function at Watford's ground during the 1999/2000 season, when Richie Moran was the guest speaker. Moran, a Birmingham City player in the 1990s who eventually quit the game because of the racial abuse he suffered, recalls in the book: "Graham Taylor came up to me and said: 'Look, I'm going to tell you something ... I'm never going to admit it, I will be sued for libel.' He said, 'When I was manager of England, I was called in by two members of the FA, who I won't name ...' I volunteered two names. He said: 'I'm not prepared to say, but I was told in no uncertain terms not to pick too many black players for the national side'." There's absolutely no suggestion that Taylor agreed to this policy.

The episode came up at a Kick It Out function on its 10th anniversary, in 2004, attended by Taylor. The *Guardian* claimed that it had spoken to one of the event's organisers, another senior figure in football-related race issues, who said he could confirm Taylor was the manager quoted. Taylor told the *Guardian* he couldn't specifically remember the conversation with Moran. "That is not me trying to evade it – and it also doesn't mean I didn't say it – but if anyone looks at my record with club and country, it would be obvious to everyone anyway that I didn't follow what was apparently said. If anyone looks at my record, I could never be accused of blocking the way for any black player."

Later, on BBC Radio Five Live he said of Moran's claim, "Certainly never during my time at the Football Association, I had no FA people coming up to me and telling me which team to pick and to pick less black players. I would have remembered that. I have no memory of that conversation. There certainly *was* an event at Watford. I can remember that, but I certainly have no memory of a conversation about black players [...] I never had any problems regarding team selection concerning black players from the Football Association."

Moran, in the *Guardian*, refuted Taylor's denials. "I have a very vivid memory of the conversation. My then girlfriend said to me after he'd told me, 'Who was that?' I said, 'It's the former England manager!' She said: 'Well, why did he tell you that, then?' I've mentioned it on numerous occasions, and I've even had a cease-and-desist letter, I think seven years ago, from the FA. But I'm happy for them to sue me for two reasons: one, I don't have any personal assets for them to take; and, two, I'm telling the truth. I'm not saying for one moment that Graham Taylor had any intentions [...] all I'm saying, is that that is a conversation I had with him. I have no reason to make it up."

Whatever the truth, no other England manager has ever suggested they were pressured into limiting the number of black players chosen for the national team.

However, Sol Campbell believes the game's governing body is institutionally racist, claiming in his 2014 authorised biography that he'd have led England for a decade had he been white. The 73 times-capped defender claimed the FA and the majority of fans don't want a black England captain, labelling the appointment of "fantastic forward" Michael Owen as skipper ahead of him as "embarrassing". "I think the FA wished I was white. I had the credibility, performance-wise to be captain. I was consistently in the heart of the defence and I was a club captain early in my career [...] It's all right to have black captains and mixed-race in the under-18s and under-21s but not for the full national side."

Ince, however, disagrees, telling the *Daily Mail* in 2014, "There's been me, Adams, Pearce, Seaman,

Shearer, Terry, Ferdinand [...] that's a lot of big names with a lot of big egos. Sol's a clever, articulate man and he's a friend of mine, but he wouldn't have been England captain for ten years – nobody is. He has obviously had different experiences to me as a footballer and I can only really talk about my own. We can make too much of the captaincy and what it means. I was captain of pretty much every team I played for – Manchester United, Inter Milan, Liverpool, Middlesbrough, Wolves and England – so my colour didn't come into it. Sol was around for Euro '96 under Terry Venables and again at the World Cup in 1998. I didn't deal with the FA often enough, but there was never any issue over my skin colour with my teammates or people I came across within the organisation. I have no reason to believe they are racist [...] I loved people like (ex-FA director) David Davies and I just never encountered it. Sol has every right to his view, and we all have opinions but, in my experience, I just didn't see it."

Ince was captain in 1993 against the USA in Foxboro, Massachusetts, the first black England player to wear the armband. "For me, it was the pinnacle of my career when Graham Taylor made me captain, but I can remember feeling uncomfortable with the questions. I just wanted to be the England captain, I didn't want to be remembered as the first black England captain because I didn't look at it in that way. Then, after the game, I began to look at it in a different way because I had a lot of parents from the ghetto sending me letters, telling me it had inspired their children to get jobs or to start playing football. I don't know whether they were black, white or Asian, or whatever, but it didn't matter. That meant a lot, to think that somehow I had inspired people I had never even met."

In total, Ince captained England seven times, leading the country to the World Cup finals in 1998. "Adams, Gascoigne, Southgate, Wright and Sol all played in that game and I had a responsibility to wear the armband against a very good Italy team. I can remember the night before the Italy game. I was with Ian Wright and we were both so nervous that we couldn't sleep because we didn't want to let the country down the next night. I felt a responsibility to the country, but the captaincy would have meant nothing to me if I didn't have the respect of the other players. That was important to me. My England teammates didn't look at me and think, 'Paul Ince is a black England captain', and neither did the manager. Why is that an issue?

"Glenn Hoddle was the manager and he chose the person he felt could do the job the best at that particular time – he could pick who he wanted [...] as Graham Taylor and Terry Venables did before him and the FA never had any say in it."

Ince represented his country 53 times and retired from international football after England's Euro 2000 exit, going on to manage Blackburn, Macclesfield and Blackpool, but he fears that a number of top, former black England players are being lost to the game. "We have lost a lot of good black players [...] such as Sol, Wright, Bright. We have to give them inspiration to stay involved because this is the 21st century. I was 32 when I started thinking about what was next for me. I understand there are obstacles in the way because we have to be prepared to do our A Licence and our Pro Licence if we want to be managers. [...] People like Keith Alexander, RIP, did so much for the game and showed black players that they could go on to become managers. Last year there was a lot of talk about the Rooney Rule, giving an ethnic minority candidate the opportunity to make a case for a job. We jumped on that and then it's all gone away. Maybe Sol [Campbell] needs to decide what he wants to do with his career now that he has stopped playing and commit to whatever it is he wants to do."

John Barnes also disagrees with Campbell's view: "Whatever Sol's frustrations may have been, the England captains he played under were worthy choices and deserved to lead their country. He played under Tony Adams at Arsenal, Alan Shearer was at the peak of his powers when he was appointed England captain, and [...] David Beckham brought more to the armband than football. To promote the image of English football, there may have been political and marketing reasons for making Beckham captain, but colour had nothing to do with any of them in a way detrimental to Sol's career."

Barnes cites Hoddle's selection of Ince, referring to Campbell's own captaincy for the three friendly internationals: "Maybe he feels he should have been given the job in more games [...] but black players *have* been chosen on merit for big games – none bigger than Paul Ince when England went to Rome [...] Sol talks of the FA being 'institutionally racist' [but] remember that institutions are run by people and it's people who are racist, not the abstract institutions themselves. Where he has a point is the absence of black people who run football, but boardrooms and directors in any walk of life tend to mirror society as a whole. The absence of black faces is no different to most industries, whether they are milkmen, bankers or whatever. The problem we've had for hundreds of years is a perception that black people lack the intellectual capacity to perform top jobs [...] I don't see discrimination being detrimental to his career."

ENGLAND'S BLACK CAPTAINS	
Paul Ince	7 (inc. 6 friendlies)
Sol Campbell	3 (3)
Rio Ferdinand	7(4)
Ashley Cole	1 (1)
TOTAL	18 (14)

In *Black Lions*, the account of the emergence of black footballers in England, Rodney Hinds – sports editor of *The Voice* – writes that, in under 25 years, "the black footballer has turned from freak show into a respected member of the football fraternity." He tells the individual stories of key figures – *pioneers* – who broke barriers, set precedents, endured the hate and harassment of fans and fellow professionals alike, and became icons for the black community. He charts the rise and decline of racism in English football, a tale of partial progress that, he rightly points out, is far from complete. Among the many players he features in his book is Ian Wright, who he describes as "without question, the most influential player of his generation." *Black Lions* updates Brian Woolnough's book *Black Magic: England's Black Footballers*, originally published in 1983.

Reviewing the book in *When Saturday Comes*, Matthew Brown applauds Hinds for highlighting what black players went through to "win respect and overcome stereotypes, often wrestling with their own questions of personal identity and national loyalty. In doing so he shines a light on the role they've played in changing football and, to some degree, changing society, too."

Brown does reserve some criticism of Hinds, for not calling out John Fashanu, who "regurgitates all the old, tired stereotypes about black players being naturally faster, fitter and more skilful than whites", but acknowledges that Hinds *does* explicitly expose such "notions as nonsense" elsewhere and, overall, describes the book as "uplifting."

Founded by Val McCalla in 1982, *The Voice* celebrated its 35th anniversary in 2017, and outlined plans to develop a closer relationship with Kick It Out.

4

Kung-fu Kick

"I do not feel at all that the guilty verdict is a clear reflection of the incident."

– Kiko Casilla, Leeds United goalkeeper

Manchester United striker Eric Cantona, one of world football's greatest enigmas. Genius. Rebel. Poet ... *but* also a victim of discrimination at a high-profile match during the 1994/95 season against Crystal Palace at Selhurst Park, which later prompted him to become one of the high-profile players to lend his voice, alongside Les Ferdinand, to the battle against racism.

Cantona is clearly a volatile character, with a long history of on-field incidents to add to his reputation. In 1987, in France, he punched his own team's goalkeeper at Auxerre, leaving the man with a black eye, and was suspended by Marseille for kicking a ball into the crowd and throwing his shirt at the referee after being substituted. Cantona retaliated by moving to England.

The debate still rages, though, whether a fan shouting, "Your mother's a French whore" justifies Cantona's kung-fu-kick retaliation. It doesn't – two wrongs never make a right – but Cantona was painted the "Red Devil" villain, when he was also the victim of racial abuse.

The "kung-fu" incident took place on 25 January 1995, when defending champions Manchester United travelled to south-east London. They were, at the time, in second place in the Premier League, two points behind leaders Blackburn, who they had beaten 1–0 at Old Trafford three days earlier with Cantona scoring the winner. Victory at lowly Crystal Palace would return United to the top of the league. United boss Sir Alex Ferguson, writing in his autobiography *Managing My Life*, commented, "(Referee) Alan Wilkie's inability to stamp out the disgraceful tackles from Crystal Palace's two central defenders made subsequent trouble unavoidable." In the 48th minute, Shaw comes into contact with Cantona as he chases a punt from keeper Peter Schmeichel and the Frenchman retaliates with a petulant kick. He is red-carded and walks off down the side of the pitch, with United kitman Norman Davies escorting him towards the dressing rooms. A fan came straight down the gangway and started screaming abuse at Cantona – who seemed okay when the guy was simply swearing at him – but not when the abuser then called the player's mother a "French whore" – Cantona leapt over the barrier delivering a kung-fu kick to the man's chest, and throwing several punches, before police, stewards and other members of the crowd pulled him off.

In court, Cantona – who, in mitigation, claimed the fan, Matthew Simmons, shouted racial insults and threw a missile at him as he walked off – was sentenced to two weeks in prison, reduced to 120 hours community service. His club fined him £20,000 and imposed a four-month suspension, (extended to nine months, with a further £10,000 fine, by the FA). Cantona was also stripped of his captaincy of the French national team and lost his place in the side. Simmons, meanwhile, had his season-ticket withdrawn by Crystal Palace for breaking ground rules!

Former Manchester United director and solicitor Maurice Watkins referred to this being "the most famous common-assault case in the history of the English legal system." "I think the club acted properly in the way they handled it," Watkins says, "[though] there were all kinds of suggestions that the club should terminate his contract [but] the club felt they had to stand by their player [which] is why we were disappointed when, subsequently, the FA decided to heap on a greater punishment."

United teammate Gary Pallister recalls: "Eric was always the number-one target for supporters around the country. It wasn't just players who tried to wind him up, fans felt as though they could do it as well. Some of the abuse he got was terrible. Eventually, it took its toll on him, I think, and it all came to a head that night. He was such a hate figure because he was such a good player. I think I was one of the only players that didn't run over. I just stood there in disbelief. I was more in shock at what I'd just witnessed. He had his mind set that he wasn't going to return to English football because of the way he was treated – he thought it was unfair – but the manager was obviously very persuasive. He came back the same player, the same genius."

His manager, Sir Alex, himself observed of it all: "By 4 a.m., I was up and watching a video. It was pretty appalling. Over the years since, I have never been able to elicit an explanation from Eric but my own feeling is that anger at himself over the ordering off and resentment at the referee's earlier inaction combined to take him over the brink."

On Cantona's eventual return to the field, he scored a penalty for Manchester United in a 2–2 draw against Liverpool. He scored the winning goal in the 1996 FA Cup final against Liverpool, to give United the double for the second time in three seasons and was voted the Football Writers' Association "Footballer of the Year". After winning the Premiership with United in 1997, he announced his retirement, at the age of 30, and has since turned to acting, appearing in several films, including in Ken Loach's Palme D'or-nominated 2009 film *Looking for Eric*. He returned to United to coach children and is also an ambassador for beach football.

Kiko Casilla

Leeds United goalkeeper Kiko Casilla was banned for eight matches and fined £60,000 after being found guilty of racially abusing Charlton Athletic forward Jonathan Leko, during Charlton's win over Leeds on 28 September 2019. The charge was found proven by an independent regulatory commission, though it reduced the FA's request for a ten-game ban for the Spaniard to eight.

Under rules introduced for the 2019/20 season, the minimum suspension for a player found guilty of an aggravated breach of the FA's discrimination rules is six matches, which can be increased depending on any additional aggravating factors.

Casilla was charged with breaching the FA's Rule E3 – which he denied – and was also ordered to attend a face-to-face education session. "I do not feel at all that the guilty verdict is a clear reflection of the incident," he said in a statement.

It was alleged the Spaniard's words "made reference to race and/or colour and/or ethnic origin", constituting an aggravated breach – Casilla was accused by Leko of calling him a "f****** n*****" after the pair clashed prior to a corner being taken. Leko and teammate Macauley Bonne, who also heard the words, both gave evidence to the FA.

Casilla had tweeted that he felt "truly sad and devastated" about being accused of making a racist comment. "[The] last five months have been the most difficult ones in my professional career. I am sure my family, friends, colleagues and the different technical teams whom I have been working with for all these years know that I would *never* use my words with a racist meaning. I would like to deeply thank Leeds for its support during this time and I appreciate the support of our amazing fans, whose warmth has strengthened me."

Leeds responded to the suspension, saying that they "do not tolerate any form of discrimination", but added it is "important to recognise [Casilla] has always denied making any racist comment." The club added that the decision had been made "on the balance of probability rather than proving Kiko to be guilty beyond reasonable doubt, which we have always believed is the more appropriate burden of proof."

Charlton players were said to be furious that Casilla was banned for just eight games. The Addicks were also upset that trolls targeted Congo-born Leko on social media.

A key defence used by the Spaniard was that, given his limited English, he did not even know that the "N-word" existed. The FA did "not accept" this argument, instead maintaining that Casilla "was aware of the English word", as well as the "meaning and connotation of that word, and that it was a racial insult." The FA were at pains to stress that they used the civil standard of proof.

The FA felt Casilla tried "to deceive the tribunal" and his high-profile character witnesses, including former Liverpool, Real Madrid and Newcastle boss Rafa Benitez, were a "shameless ploy." Other witnesses summoned by Casilla's defence included Leeds players Ben White, Kalvin Phillips and Liam Cooper, former coach at Espanyol Thomas N'Kono and former teammate Mubarak Wakaso.

N'Kono stressed that he "simply cannot believe" that Casilla would use that sort of language, a sentiment that Wakaso agreed with.

Among those called for the FA's case included Charlton striker Macauley Bonne, as well as Casilla's then teammate Eddie Nketiah. The Arsenal striker, who was on loan at Leeds at the time, had come on at half-time for Marcelo Bielsa's side and was on the pitch when the incident took place.

The FA commission found Leko and Bonne to have been "impressive and straightforward witnesses." They also concluded that they "could not reliably place any significant weight on his [Casilla] denials that he had not uttered the words alleged," and that "having successfully defended the corner and punched the ball clear, he determined to direct one last utterance at JL [Leko]."

The FA accepted that Casilla is "not a racist", and that the use of language was "out of character." But they were also "satisfied on the balance of probabilities" that the remark had been said.

The three-man independent panel consisted of Graeme McPherson, QC, former footballer Marvin Robinson and ex-Blackburn, Southampton and England winger Stuart Ripley. The keeper denied the charge, but the commission rejected his evidence and that of Leeds team manager Matt Grice, who, they said, "was not seeking to assist us to ascertain the truth." The FA argued that Casilla's evidence along with a lack of any apology to Leko were aggravating factors requiring a longer ban.

The FA released a statement to accompany the 62-page document of their findings: "Following this thorough process, the independent Regulatory Commission came to the unanimous decision that Mr Casilla had racially abused a fellow player on the field of play. The FA would also like to reiterate its firm and unwavering commitment to tackling all forms of discrimination at every level of the game and encourages any participant or spectator who believes that they have been the subject of, or witness to, discriminatory abuse to report it through the respective appropriate channel: the match referee; CFA network; The FA or its partners at Kick It Out."

David James

Former England goalkeeper David James wants his first manager's job in English football, but accepts in all probability it will be tough to get it, certainly at any elite level – a damning indictment on the current on-going issues of racism, inequality and diversity.

James played for five different Premier League clubs, including Liverpool and Manchester City, over four decades, earning 53 caps for England. His 572 Premier League appearances places him fourth on the all-time list. James, given an MBE in 2012 for his services to football and charity, played his last game in England for Bournemouth in 2013.

After two spells in charge of Indian Super League side Kerala Blasters, he says: "I'm starting the process of applying now. If there's an opportunity to be a manager or, more importantly, an opportunity to bring people through and be successful, I will be looking and applying, yes. Any level. I'm not averse to any level. I've worked a lot with John Still in the Conference when we were at Luton. Or League Two, it's football."

James was player/coach at Icelandic club IBV Vestmannaeyjar under then manager Hermann Hreidarsson, a former teammate at Portsmouth, and he also had a spell as coach at Luton while qualifying for his UEFA A Licence. During his second stint as manager of

Kerala Blasters in 2018, he obtained the elite-level Pro Licence, completing the course alongside Nicky Butt and Nemanja Vidic.

"The Covid-19 lockdown has given me plenty of time for reflection," said James, who was sacked by the Blasters at the end of 2018. "I had been quite happy and content working in Asia. I've got a lot of friends out there and loved travelling. The situation in England was always difficult because it seemed it was more about who you knew rather than what you knew and I was happy in Asia anyway. I haven't applied before because I didn't want to, I didn't need to, but lockdown has made me think about it and I love football."

Hreidarsson had worked as assistant to Southend manager Sol Campbell. "I've been speaking with Hermann, who has been working with Sol over the last couple of seasons, and again it's given me a hunger to get involved in the English game. I've got a lot of family here, who I need to see more of. I think the last 18 months or two years of travelling around Asia have made me realise that I need to be home.

"I love doing punditry work, but the pundit doesn't change anything. And I love change. I love the opportunity of being able to be successful. I can't do that as a pundit. [...] managing or being involved at any level [...] there is an opportunity. So, yes, I am hungry again."

James said the lack of diversity of managers and coaches in English football "is a very difficult topic to understand." He elaborated: "First of all you have to have the qualifications and once you've got the qualifications, it's how many have actually applied for the jobs. So, to argue we haven't got representation, we need to know how many coaches there are available and how many want a position.

"On my Pro Licence, I did ask the question: 'How many BAME coaches had passed the A or Pro Licences?' And that information wasn't available. When you apply, you don't have to state your ethnic background, which is right. It's a qualification, not a race thing.

"If you had a group of people with high grades not getting positions, then you ask the question. At the moment, it's very loose in many different contexts. I navigate around statistics and without the proof of statistics, it's difficult. In the Premier League, I think we're actually in a very positive position at the moment with regards to English managers. I think there are eight, which I think is the highest for a long time. So, if you're using basic statistics on equality, there should be one to two managers from the BAME community to every eight white English managers. Well, if there aren't ten positions available, then equality is difficult to achieve.

"So as a Pro Licence holder, am I part of the problem? I struggle to find a scenario where my ethnicity has hampered my career. That may purely be because my physical attributes are enough and they satisfied whatever was needed. People might just say I am a bad manager, in which case I can't really argue, but at least I'm going to put myself in a position to find out. It will be down to me as a person rather than anything else."

5

Asian Footballers

"Because I wasn't called Jimmy Patel, nobody in football asked about my background."
— Jimmy Carter, Liverpool and Arsenal winger,
first British Asian footballer

Problems faced by British Asian footballers trying to break into the professional game were highlighted in 1996 in Jas Bains's book, *Asians Can't Play Football*. Another eight years passed before Zesh Rehman became the first British Asian to start a Premier League match, when making his full debut for Fulham against Tottenham Hotspur. Though Rehman went on to become the first to play in all four English divisions, just three others – Neil Taylor, Michael Chopra and Hamza Choudhury – have followed him into the Premier League since.

Prior to all four, however, Jimmy Carter was one of the first Asian footballers – if not *the* first Asian footballer – in the history of the English game, though few knew it at the time. It's surely a terrible indictment of the way people perceived non-whites in this country that Carter felt compelled to keep his true identity and heritage a secret until very recently.

Nonetheless, escaping poverty in Hackney, he went on to play for two of the world's biggest clubs, Arsenal and Liverpool.

Jimmy is someone I feel proud to call a friend and, having got to know him well over recent years, I think he'd have every right to feel aggrieved, but he doesn't seem the least bit concerned that he had to carry such a secret for such a long time.

"Dad was a disciplinarian, who'd pull the sheets off the bed at 6 a.m. during winter and tell me to run twice around the park. On the way back, if someone had four pints of milk outside, I was to grab one so we had something for our cornflakes."

It is only now Jimmy has been prepared to "come out" publicly, as a tribute to his late father and to inspire people in his community to play football. His Anglicised name meant he wasn't quizzed about his ethnic background. Orphaned at 14, his Indian father, Maurice, was born and raised in Lucknow, the state capital of Uttar Pradesh, and brought up a Christian. Two years later, he joined the Indian Navy and travelled, before settling in England, where he raised two children, Jimmy and Philip, in London, after splitting up with their mother, Theresa. "Dad came from a privileged family in India. He was privately educated and his father was one of the first over there to own a car. They even had a Carter crest on their turbans," explains Jimmy. "I've got my family tree back to the 1700s. Because I wasn't called Jimmy Patel, nobody in football asked about my background.

"Food-wise, we were Indian kids. We had curry and rice every day. Dad would get the spices. He would send us to buy boiling chickens, the cheapest ones at £1. If we couldn't afford meat, he'd make a sauce and drop in a boiled potato, or eggs. It was only when I met my wife

Ann-Marie that I had a roast dinner. At first, the roast potatoes would give me hiccups – I wasn't used to them going down my throat.

"Ironically, my nickname at Portsmouth was 'Bhuna', because I loved a curry after a game. But they didn't know I had Indian roots. I'd get some racial abuse on the terraces for being dark, but in the dressing room, people just thought I'd been on too many sunbeds."

Crystal Palace offered him pro terms at 18: "I went up to £70-a-week and thought I'd made it. I grew my hair, got an earring and went clubbing in the West End. I got married and took on a second job at night as a double-glazing canvasser for extra money. I'd get home at 1 a.m. and be late for training the next day. Palace's manager Alan Mullery said he wouldn't pick me as long as I had a hole in my *a****!" Palace terminated the teenager's contract. With a mortgage and no job, Carter wrote to all 92 league clubs for a trial. The PFA put him in touch with scout Paddy Sowden, who was mates with QPR boss Jim Smith. "Rangers played on astroturf, which was great for a winger because defenders didn't want to slide in – they got burnt to the bone. If you had a good first touch, you were laughing."

Millwall boss John Docherty signed Carter for £15,000 after watching him give Neil Ruddock a run around for the reserves and so began a special love affair with the club. "I identified with Millwall straight away and it helped that Teddy [Sheringham] was there. We'd been teammates for Beaumont Juniors at 13 and I knew his game. As a kid, he sometimes turned up on a Sunday with a black eye or bruised ribs. Teddy's dad was a policeman and if anyone said something bad about it, he'd stand up for himself."

In 1988, Millwall were promoted to the top flight for the first time. "I'd never seen grown men crying before.

That's how much it meant," said Carter. "We hired a room in a Hull hotel and partied there. Some lads ventured out afterwards. When they got back at 3 a.m., Doc was waiting, puffing on a cigar. He put them on a minibus to play for the reserves in London the next morning." Millwall had the fab four up front – Carter, Sheringham, Tony Cascarino and Kevin O'Callaghan – backed up by hard-men Terry Hurlock and Keith Stevens.

On 1 October 1988, a 3–2 win against QPR sent them top and they finished 10th above Alex Ferguson's Manchester United. "We were still on £250-a-week. We'd asked Doc for new contracts after promotion, but he said we still had to prove ourselves. After we went top, there was a queue outside his office on the Monday! In the end, we were only given a crowd bonus. We'd all be looking around in the warm up after that to see how many were in. Teams didn't like coming to play us. You could see them lining up, fearful, wanting to get out of the old Den as soon as possible. Brian Clough was clever. He made his players walk to the ground, so they were used to the abuse before kick-off."

Sheringham joined Brian Clough at Nottingham Forest, Cascarino was successful at Chelsea, Marseille and Celtic. Carter went to Anfield. After only four starts in ten months, he signed for Arsenal. It went better for him at Highbury: in 1993, Arsenal won the FA Cup and League Cup; Carter played in the semi-finals but was left out at Wembley.

Carter was in his prime as part of Millwall's greatest team when Kenny Dalglish made his move in 1991 to sign the then-25-year-old winger. "Kenny told us to get up to Lime Street station," recalled Carter in a *Daily Mail* interview. "The cab arrived to take me to Watford Junction. My missus came out to give me a hug and then the little fella [two-year-old son Luke] shut the door behind us to lock himself in the house. With the taxi still running, we spent the next half-hour trying to coax Luke through the cat-flap. He was small enough to fit but too scared. Eventually, he came out but I missed the train. I had to ring Kenny from the station to apologise and ended up catching a later one to Preston, where he picked us up. Looking back, it was a perfect forecast of how my time at Liverpool went!"

The £800,000 deal went through, but four weeks later, Dalglish resigned, "We turned up at Anfield on the Friday to catch our coach to Luton. Ronnie Moran came into the dressing room and said the boss had decided to walk away. There was total silence. We were in shock. Nobody had an inkling. For me, the consequences turned out severe. Graeme Souness came in and made it clear I wasn't part of his plans. It left a prolonged darkness over my career. Graeme even subbed me as a substitute against Chelsea. I was embarrassed, humiliated and locked myself in the hotel room. I wouldn't come down for dinner until Peter Beardsley was concerned enough to call my room and convince me I shouldn't hide away."

Following spells at Oxford and Portsmouth, Carter returned to Millwall before retiring in 1999. He's glad his own two sons, Luke and Jamie, know about their Indian roots. "As a player, I didn't have any urge to shout about it from the rooftops. Now, I think I could have said something, to encourage other young Asian players that football can be a good career if you give everything. I'm very proud of my background and I know my father was proud of me. As a kid, Dad would run around Lucknow barefoot. He created a son who was able to run around Anfield and Highbury."

Prior to learning about Jimmy Carter, Michael Chopra – who became the first Asian male footballer to play for

England in 1999 – was assumed to be the first British Asian to play in the Premier League. The gangling 19-year-old son of shopkeepers scored the winner in a 2–1 victory over Argentina at Wembley Stadium for the nation's Under-16's set-up.

Chopra, who was born in 1983, in Newcastle, to an English mother and Indian father, attended the same school as his idol, former England captain Alan Shearer.

When selected for the England Under-16s, his father was doubly proud: "I was proud enough that he had been picked to play for his country but the fact that he was the first South Asian to play for England made it doubly special." Chopra played alongside Shearer and came very near to scoring against the then-reigning champions Manchester United. "I am disappointed [at not scoring], but it's great to be involved. It was a good test for me against international defenders like Rio Ferdinand, Mikael Silverstre and John O'Shea," he said after the match.

British Asians featured prominently in English cricket but were conspicuous by their absence in football as players.

The same was the case for spectators. Asian youngsters had felt excluded from the football system, but Chopra's feats gave them a way into the game. "I don't feel under any extra pressure because of being an Asian player, but it's great that I can be a role model to Asian kids. Hopefully, I can inspire them to do well," he said.

At the time, football authorities were taking steps to redress the lack of Asian representation in football, with almost 100 teams registering for an Asia-Europe Football festival, backed by the FA and PFA. Event director Majid Lavji said, "We are still waiting for Asian footballers to make the impact that black footballers have made since the early seventies."

Manchester United manager Sir Alex Ferguson had branded it "a scandal" that there was only one Asian player in English football, adding, "They feel excluded. Ask clubs, such as Walsall or Bury, where the best teenage footballers are in their areas. They'll say it's the Asian kids who play on the street. Get them in, make them feel welcome."

Son Heung-min

In July 2020, Arsenal condemned a fan on supporters' channel AFTV for a racist slur made against South Korea's Son Heung-min during the North London derby. AFTV is one of the most popular fan-produced YouTube channels in the world with 1.18 million subscribers.

Claude Callegari was heard saying "DVD's going off" as Son was substituted during Tottenham's 2–1 win and attracted widespread criticism. The reference was to selling DVDs from a market stall and is a racist term that has been directed at Asian footballers, including Son, in the past. Callegari was removed from the channel "indefinitely" and apologised, but only after he and channel owner Robbie Lyle attempted to justify the remark. The Gunners distanced themselves from AFTV and condemned what happened in a statement: "We are aware of a video on social media in which an Arsenal supporter uses a racist slur towards Tottenham Hotspur's Son Heung-min during Sunday's match. We operate a zero-tolerance approach to any form of discrimination and we unreservedly condemn this unacceptable racist behaviour. Our records show that the individual involved is not an Arsenal season-ticket holder and does not hold any form of ticket membership. The platform in question has no official association with Arsenal."

Lyle and Callegari appeared in a video to address the issue, suggesting Callegari meant that Spurs would release a celebratory DVD of their derby win. Lyle later performed a U-turn and removed the outspoken Callegari from the channel. He tweeted: "I would like to sincerely apologise for the derogatory remark heard on the AFTV livestream on Sunday, and for the response video that we put out today where we failed to apologise and take onus for the comment. As a channel that has millions of viewers around the world, I fully recognise the power that comments made by myself or people on our platform have, and it is paramount that we do not allow comments of this nature to be made in any form. As such, it is only appropriate that Claude is removed from the channel indefinitely. In no way do I or AFTV condone racism of any kind and it is important we take appropriate action in line with the comment made."

Callegari, meanwhile, apologised in a video posted to Twitter. "Unfortunately, what's happened here is a few days ago, in the game against Spurs, I made a comment. My only thing was the timing was all wrong when I made the comment. It's caused a lot of offence to Son and all the Spurs fans, and I want to apologise to Spurs fans and Son for that because of the offence it has caused. What can I do? It's caused a lot of offence and I want to apologise because I admire Son as a player."

The FA's "Bringing Communities Together" was first published in 2015, its aim to increase the number of Asians at grassroots level. By the end of the 2018/19 season, however, there'd still only been four players of South Asian descent – Rehman, Taylor, Chopra, Choudhury – in the Premier League. Clearly, there's still a long way to go.

6

"Let's Kick Racism Out of Football"

"There was no occasion, no fanfare. Just the two of us in an office in the Business Design Centre, Islington. The first thing we did was write to all 92 professional clubs. We got five replies!"

– Ben Tegg, first KIO staff member

In 1997, the "Let's Kick Racism Out of Football" campaign became Kick It Out, and the FA, Premier League, Football Foundation and PFA joined together to fund the organisation. On becoming formally constituted, Ben Tegg and Piara Powar became its first two members of staff.

"There was no occasion, no fanfare. Just the two of us in an office in the Business Design Centre, Islington," Ben recalls. "The first thing we did was write to all 92 professional clubs, introducing who we were, and what we aimed to do, and that we were now being backed by the game's governing bodies. We got five replies!

"Within six months, however, we were swamped by the media [and] the clubs, slowly, but surely, began to come on board, with a geographical trend quickly emerging. If one club from, say, the north-west, was seen with the Kick

It Out T-shirts on, we'd get calls from other clubs in that area, so as not to fall behind to local rivals. The campaign began to take on a global significance, too. What we were doing was, after all, quite unique."

The following year, the government's Football Task Force submitted a report, entitled "Eliminating Racism from Football" to the Minister for Sport. One observation suggesting that "non-white" faces are few and far between in "shop-front" positions in football clubs.

Football's power to unite surpasses that of any other sport, but so does its power to divide. The game commands the hearts and minds of millions. There is no more powerful vehicle to take to young people a positive message of tolerance and respect. But football can also be a focal point for racism and xenophobia. Racism is not a problem of football's making. It is society's problem. Yet it is an issue the game cannot afford to sideline. It presents it with responsibilities, and new opportunities. The game's ruling bodies – and clubs and players as its ambassadors – have a responsibility to protect and promote its image as the game that unites the world. They must act wherever necessary to ensure people can watch and play free from prejudice and abuse. They also have an opportunity to make a positive contribution to creating a better society. The Football Association understands football's unique potential to communicate [...] working with teachers' representatives in taking an anti-racism message to tens of thousands of children in schools across England. For a game often accused of taking more than it gives, the value of work by football to "put something back into society" cannot be overstated. So racism must always be a mainstream concern for football. Yet commitment to tackling it – and by extension encouraging more people to watch and play – is not universal. Tackling racism is seen in some quarters of the English game as a fringe issue. A County Football Association has told the Task Force it has "far more pressing matters to attend to." It is to English football's detriment that such attitudes remain [...] there is still a problem to be addressed [...] and compelling reasons why we all should sign up to do something about it:

- Tackling racism in football is first and foremost a moral issue – it is a basic right to be able to play and watch the game free from the threat of abuse. **Fact:** Young black and Asian players in England still encounter unacceptable levels of racist abuse on and off the pitch.

- It is about the quality of English football – country and clubs need to draw on the talents of the whole community: the more players the national team manager can choose from, the stronger England's chances of success. **Fact:** An Asian player has still to break into top flight football even though the Asian community makes up 3.5% of the population (1.7m people).

- There will be a boost for the financial health of English clubs which draw support from all sections of the community and increase crowds and revenue. By tackling racism, clubs create a more welcoming, family atmosphere at matches. **Fact:** "Non-white" people make up 7.3% of England's population – 3.5 million people – but just 1% of Premier League crowds. As long as black and Asian fans do not have confidence that they can attend matches and be treated with respect, clubs will continue to miss out on a big market. Encouraging steps have been taken over recent years – notably the development of the Kick It Out campaign, the growth of club-based anti-racism initiatives and educational work in schools – but more can and should be done. Until now, efforts have concentrated on confronting racist abuse in the stands. Football deserves credit for this work, but now is the time to take it forward and show renewed resolve to root out racism from all levels of the game. The Football Task Force has undertaken a thorough study of the nature and extent of the problem of racism in English football. It has taken soundings from all corners of the football community and also from representatives of the black and Asian communities. This report is the outcome of that consultation. It acknowledges that racism is still a deep-seated problem in English football. Commitment to tackle it must extend from the game's grassroots to the boot-rooms and boardrooms of its professional clubs. It focuses on key questions that must be addressed:

- Why are there no top flight Asian professional footballers when there is huge enthusiasm for the game among Asian children?
- Why do so few Asian people go to matches in England – even in cities where there is a large Asian population?
- Why is the number of black spectators decreasing at a time when more black players are succeeding at the highest level of the game?
- Why are so few black and Asian people employed in non-playing positions at football clubs and in administrative positions within the game?
- Why are there so few black and Asian referees and coaches?

A summary of these measures follows below.

Playing the game: eliminating racism
The Football Association should:

- issue new guidance to referees to make clear that an immediate red card should be shown to players making any racist comments on the field of play [This is now in place.]
- amend FA disciplinary rules to recognise racist abuse on and off the pitch as a distinct offence punishable by separate and severe disciplinary measures [This is now in place.]
- instruct County FA disciplinary committees that incidents of racism on the field of play should be punishable by severe penalties [This is now in place.]
- require County FAs to sign up to an anti-racism charter and pledge positive action to encourage wider participation in all aspects the game [In May 2020, the FA became the first national governing body in English sport to introduce a regional code of governance, which sets a higher precedent than the current gold standard for sport and aims to provide support and guidance to those running the grassroots game up and down the country. Diversity and inclusion is covered within this guidance, which ensures those officiating and leading the game at a local level are reflective of the communities that they serve.]
- establish a unit to monitor the implementation of the charter and to which all FA-affiliated teams can report suspected breaches of its provisions.

Local authorities should:

- exclude local football clubs with a record of involvement in racist incidents from council-owned playing facilities.

The Professional Footballers Association and League Managers Association should:

- recommend inserting an anti-racism pledge in players' and managers' contracts with breaches incurring severe sanctions (fines or dismissal).

Playing the game: encouraging wider participation
Local authorities should:

- promote special community coaching schemes with the specific aim of encouraging wider participation in football from all sections of the community.

The Government should:

- make efforts to ensure all schoolchildren – particularly those in inner city schools – have access to playing fields (preferably grass) on a regular basis.

Professional football clubs and Conference clubs should:

- review scouting activities to ensure teams from all sections of the local community are regularly watched.

The Football Association should:

- set targets for increasing the number of black and Asian qualified FA coaches and referees; and take positive action to meet those targets.

Watching the game: eliminating racism
The Government should:

- amend the Football Offences Act to make racist abuse by individual spectators at football matches a criminal offence.

The Football Trust (and bodies awarding grant-aid to football clubs) should:

- require recipients of grant-aid to implement the 9-point plan of the Kick It Out campaign on a regular and on-going basis.

The FA Premier League and Football League should:

- prepare written guidance for member clubs on action to counter racism.

All professional clubs and Conference clubs should:

- amend ground regulations to recognise racist abuse as a separate offence – distinct from the use of foul language – and set out the penalties involved.
- set up a confidential freephone hotline through which supporters can report incidents of racist abuse to club officials.
- implement measures in the Kick It Out campaign on a regular basis, including the broadcasting of a clear anti-racism message prior to kick-off of all home games.

The Football Association, Football Licensing Authority and Football Safety Officers Association should:

- ensure football stewards are trained to deal with incidents of racism at football matches as part of a mandatory NVQ or equivalent qualification.
- agree a simple procedure to deal with incidents of racism at football matches to be made standard at all grounds in England.

Watching the game: encouraging wider participation
All administrative organisations in football should:

- adopt a comprehensive written equal opportunities policy to cover the recruitment and treatment of all staff.

The Football Association should:

- ensure that the FA Council – and county FA councils – are more representative of the game and of the communities they serve.
- require all work to tackle racism in football to be co-ordinated under the banner of the Kick It Out campaign.
- create a Charter Mark to be awarded to clubs and football organisations making substantial efforts to tackle racism and encourage wider participation.

The Government should:

- set a clear timetable for any future work which arises out of this report and carry out a follow-up report to determine progress.

7

Unguarded Moments

*"He's what is known in some schools as a f***ing lazy thick n*****."*

– "Big Ron" Atkinson discussing Marcel Desailly

Former manager, Ron Atkinson had reinvented himself as a charismatic TV pundit, only to fall from grace with an unguarded moment in 2004 for which he was sacked by ITV. Following a post-match analysis – believing the mic to be switched off – he'd directed a racist comment at Chelsea player Marcel Desailly, who'd put in a lacklustre match performance. Atkinson's argument at the time – that he couldn't be racist because he picked the "Three Degrees" – fell on deaf ears, and still has little resonance today.

One of those "Three Degrees", Cyrille Regis, said the "words were racist, the speaker was not. People should be talking about what a fantastic football manager he was and the immense contribution he made to English football. I'd known him for 26 years, played for him, drank with him, had laughs and great times with him. He slips up once. Am I supposed to lock away the memories of all those good times because of that? With the many mistakes I've made in my life, I'm the last person to judge him."

Atkinson also provided a weekly column and tactical chalkboard for the *Guardian*, who took the incident "extremely seriously." Admitting he "*had* made a stupid mistake", he was left with no option but to resign his column too.

Piara Powar, director of Kick It Out at the time, said, "It's always disappointing to hear someone of [that] stature make the type of comment that he has. Regardless of his record, that sort of terminology is just simply out of bounds." The CRE added that he'd "done the right thing" by resigning.

Out of the limelight for almost a decade, in 2013, Atkinson joined *Celebrity Big Brother*. Big mistake! Four days after he strode into the *BB* house, Vanessa Feltz summed things up in the *Sunday Express*: "*Big Brother* won't expose your follies and foibles, or your darker side. You will. The TV programme will simply have given you an adequate quantity of rope with which to hang yourself." Wondering why he was doing the show, Feltz said "experts" had proffered that it was "partly for the cash but largely [...] to show his detractors he's a decent fellow without a racist bone in his body" and that his previous outburst "a mere aberration." However, "Just 48 hours after becoming a housemate, Ron saw Danielle Marr pull her cardie round her head to protect her blonde ponytail from the rain, thought it resembled a hijab, and said: 'You're not carrying a bomb with you, are you?' His thought processes were transparent. Head covering means Muslim. Muslim must mean terrorist. Terrorist must mean bomb. Therefore, all Muslims are terrorists. One thing was suddenly glaringly clear. Nine years of humiliation had taught Ron Atkinson absolutely nothing. The man is still not only racist but so profoundly racist he has no idea that what he says or thinks might be construed as deeply offensive."

Formally warned by Big Brother, Atkinson, looking downright flummoxed, issued the time-honoured *non*-apology apology: "If I have said anything offensive, I'm sorry."

Later, Atkinson was interviewed by Michael Eboda, editor of *New Nation*, Britain's biggest-selling black-community newspaper. Referring to *Big Brother*, Atkinson said, "I think I'd have been better off shooting somebody."

Referring back to the incident in 2004, he conceded that what he'd said was racist, but insisted he wasn't a racist. "Don't forget, I was brought up... look, I've had pairs of shoes that have been n*****-brown, that's what they used to say [...] all I can say is, sorry, I genuinely did not mean to offend anybody. What else can I say? I'm an idiot, but I'm not a racist. A racist is someone who won't give a black man a chance. My actions over the years prove that I have no problem with that [...] if somebody had said what I said about Desailly to one of my players, I would have got 'em by the throat and chinned 'em."

Atkinson then asked Eboda: "So, tell me, do *you* think I'm a racist?" To which the editor said, no, but that he had "a racist element" in him and, "I don't think you're aware of what racism is. You don't see colour when you are giving a person a job [...] but you come from an era when certain things were acceptable and I think you're not quite aware of what those things are [...] I don't think that had Desailly been white you would have mentioned his colour. You might have called him a lazy bastard, but you certainly wouldn't have called him a lazy, white nigger."

In 2019, he tried again to apologise, in another reality-TV appearance, *Celebrity Wife Swap*, in which Olympic javelin-thrower Tessa Sanderson went to live with him at his Birmingham home. Although he refused point-blank to discuss his 2004 gaffe with the athlete, his wife, Maggie, raised the subject with Sanderson's boyfriend, former judo champion Densign White. White explained that people were so offended not just because he'd used the N-word but because a stereotype black people often face is that they're "lazy and work-shy."

When she returned to the family home, Maggie explained to her husband what White had told her. "It made me realise quite how offensive my comments had been to people," he said. "I'm genuinely sorry about that." However, he continued to try to justify himself: "I've always said actions speak louder than words. I was very instrumental in bringing black players into the English game and I'd hope I'd be remembered more for that than a muttered comment."

In 2016, he wrote that he would "always regret" the comment. But the truth is that he'll now always be remembered for his racist outburst.

8

Weeks of Action

"Tell that black s*** [Thierry Henry] that you are much better than him. Don't hold back, tell him. Tell him from me. You have to believe in yourself, you're better than that black s***."

– Luis Aragonés, Spanish coach

Kick It Out developed its first "Week of Action" in 2001, for clubs and grassroots projects to take a unified stand against discrimination. It quickly became a prime feature in the footballing calendar, the initiative was supported by all clubs and had started to generate a lot of awareness about the campaign's work. But much was going on to undermine all this good work: discrimination, prejudice and racism still purveying the dressing room.

In 2007, "Week of Action" relaunched as "One Game, One Community Week of Action". The initiative continued to act as a focal point for players, managers, fans, grassroots teams, community groups and schools to join together and celebrate football's ability to unite people from all walks of life.

But Everton defender Joleon Lescott expressed his dismay after Newcastle United midfielder Emre Belözoğlu was cleared, by an independent commission, of racially abusing Joseph Yobo. In protest, Lescott hinted he may not wear a Kick It Out T-shirt in the future.

In 2009, Manchester City took part in the campaign, its players and mascots wearing "Unite Against Racism" T-shirts for a home match against Polish club Lech Poznan. In 2011, Lionel Messi was pictured with a mascot wearing an anti-racism shirt ahead of Barcelona's UEFA Champions League match against Czech team Viktoria Plzen.

So many initiatives, but was it really having much effect?

Proof that racism in football wasn't consigned to the English game, came when Spain's coach Luis Aragonés caused a global storm after making racist comments in 2014 about Thierry Henry to the player's Arsenal teammate Jose Antonio Reyes: "Tell that black s*** [Henry] that you are much better than him. Don't hold back, tell him. Tell him from me. You have to believe in yourself, you're better than that black s***."

Jozy Altidore, a former teammate of Henry's when they were both at New York Red Bulls, has documented the sheer abuse he himself suffered during his time with Villarreal in Spain, including being told to "go hang" himself.

As a pundit for Sky Sports, Henry had refused to criticise Chelsea following the Paris Metro race row when a group of supporters were filmed refusing to allow a black man on to a train following the Blues clash with Paris Saint-German. He didn't feel the club should be blamed for the behaviour of a small minority of their fans.

And speaking on *The Jonathan Ross Show*, the player talked about his experiences: "I've played games away from home in Europe, in countries that are not very clever. A lack of education can be the thing. You play a game and you try to concentrate and keep your composure and what you hear sometimes is 'black this' and 'monkey' and monkey chants, and people spitting at you when you take a corner kick. It is not easy [...] not easy to deal with."

In 2005, Henry teamed up with fellow professionals, including Rio Ferdinand and Ronaldinho, to front the Nike "Stand Up, Speak Up" campaign, which saw players all over Europe wear two interlocked wristbands, one black, one white.

Interviewed by Bryant Gumbel for HBO Sports, Henry wasn't surprised that, in the ten years since, there'd been no real change in racism in football, because "[It's] still a problem in society, so it will always be in the game."

9

Causing Mayhem

"We don't want any more Africans."
— Tony Henry, ex-Director of Player Recruitment,
West Ham United

In 2018, West Ham co-chairs David Sullivan and David Gold acted swiftly, first suspending then sacking Tony Henry, Director of Player Recruitment, following a claim made in the *Daily Mail* that he said African players "cause mayhem." Henry, it was reported, had sent an e-mail, dated 27 January of that year, explaining that the club didn't want any more players from the Continent. The paper claimed to have a leaked copy of the e-mail, in which the head of recruitment wrote of a Cameroonian player: "We don't want any more Africans and he's not good enough." Contacted by the *Mail*, Henry claimed, "It's nothing racist at all. It's just sometimes they can have a bad attitude. We find that when they are not in the team they cause mayhem. It's nothing against the African race at all. It's just sometimes they cause a lot of problems when they are not playing, as we had with Diafra (Sakho). He's left, so great. It's nothing personal at all." The paper also quoted him criticising other nationalities: "I just find with Russian players that they don't settle in England. How many Italians come and settle in England? As a club we are not discriminatory at all."

At the time, West Ham had employed seven African players: André Ayew (Ghana), who left for Swansea; Cheikhou Kouyaté (Senegal); João Mário (Angola); Arthur Masuaku (DR Congo); Pedro Obiang (Equatorial Guinea), Angelo Ogbonna (Nigeria), and Diafra Sakho (Senegal).

Suspending Henry while an investigation was carried out, West Ham confirmed its commitment to being inclusive "regardless of gender, age, ability, race, religion or sexual orientation."

Henry apologised for his actions on Sky Sports News but denied that he was racist, claiming the reason for limiting the number of African players was because the club "could struggle" with losing them to the looming African Nations Cup. "I was wrong for what I said [...] I'm sorry. I want to apologise most to the African players, the players of African descent, but also everybody, because I feel I've let them down." Of the forthcoming African Nations Cup, he said, the club would "lose them in January and February, and we could struggle with that."

Tony Henry's contract as West Ham chief scout – a position he'd held for four years – was terminated on 2 February.

Peter Beardsley

Former Newcastle United Under-23s coach Peter Beardsley was charged by the FA with three counts of using racist language to players.

Beardsley, who left United after a 14-month club investigation, "categorically denied" the claims. Kick It

Out was "concerned" that Newcastle had not revealed the reasons for his departure. Beardsley faced multiple complaints, including one of bullying by 22-year-old midfielder Yasin Ben El-Mhanni.

Newcastle declined to comment. The FA said, "It is alleged Mr Beardsley used abusive and/or insulting words towards Newcastle United FC Under-23 players, which were contrary to FA Rule E3(1), while employed as their coach. It is further alleged these words also constituted an 'aggravated breach', which is defined in FA Rule E3(2), as they included reference to ethnic origin and/or colour and/ or race and/or nationality."

KIO noted the FA charge and repeated its "call for the club to be transparent about the findings of their own investigation into this case."

Beardsley, who had been the U23s coach at Newcastle since 2009, had been on leave since a club investigation into racism and bullying allegations began. After he left the club, Beardsley, who made 326 appearances for Newcastle, said the "time was right to seek a new challenge." He added, "I have always honoured my contractual obligations of confidentiality to the club and maintained my silence, which has in itself been very difficult." Newcastle said they were "grateful for the contribution Peter has given over the years as a player, coach and ambassador and we wish him well for the future".

In 2003, Beardsley and Academy director Kenny Wharton had faced a Premier League investigation over allegations of bullying made by youth players, James Beaumont and Ross Gardner, but the case was dismissed.

An independent regulatory commission suspended Beardsley from all football and football-related activity for a period of 32 weeks until 29 April 2020. Beardsley was ordered to complete a face-to-face education course.

Beardsley was found guilty of questioning the legitimacy of the age of an African player, which the commission concluded was "a negative stereotype that players of black African origin commit fraud as to their true age."

John Barnes dismissed Peter Beardsley's use of racially abusive language as "banter", claiming his former England teammate had a fair point when he questioned the age of African players after Beardsley was found guilty by an independent Football Association commission on three counts of racially abusing Newcastle's young black players and was banned from football for seven months.

Beardsley had been sacked as the club's Under-23s boss for gross misconduct after an internal investigation also found it proven that he had used racist language to several players, including calling one of them a "monkey."

Barnes said, "Peter Beardsley is from a particularl era where what was called banter back then was completely accepted but isn't acceptable now. It's unfortunate for Peter, because Peter is one of the old school who are still involved in football. There are a lot of people who would use language or banter that Peter uses, but they're not involved in football, so therefore they don't do it. It's difficult for people who are over a certain age who are still involved in football and involved with young kids, because the intent is the most important thing. I never felt the intent was ever to be racist. But things that Peter said are clearly unacceptable now. I understand why he has to go through what he's going through. I understand why Peter has been banned."

However, Kick It Out branded Beardsley's language "appalling [and a] horrific use of racial stereotypes."

Barnes says Beardsley was right, *though*: "One of the things Peter is meant to have said is talking about the age of African players," he told beIN SPORTS. "I have spent time in South Africa and, if you ask African players their age, they will say, 'Football age or real age?' So this is not a problem. It's not right, it's not wrong, it's a cultural thing whereby they have separate ages. If Peter makes that point then that's not racist, because Africans says that themselves. Another thing he said was about the state of the pitches in Africa. The pitches in Africa are bad. By saying that, it's not being racist. Now other things he said are completely unacceptable, but we have to look at the nuances around that situation. Anybody who gets caught saying the wrong thing, you have to be seen to be coming down on them like a ton of bricks to prove to yourself that everything else is okay, the problem is Peter Beardsley. But when you're in that environment and you're coaching a team, and you're trying to inspire, make fun, have a laugh, and this is what we did 20 years ago, and you then do it, you then get caught out, unfortunately."

Emile Heskey

Emile Heskey spoke out about racism and how it was brushed off as banter during his playing days. Heskey suffered vile abuse. The former England, Liverpool and Leicester striker spoke on *The Gary Newbon Sports Show*, in association with MailOnline Sport.

"The racism, that we would class as racism, we get in the UK was brushed off as banter," Heskey said in the interview. Like I said, my parents didn't smoke, but if I was to make a bad pass, the shout would be 'Have you been on that wacky baccy?' I was like, I don't smoke, my mum or dad don't smoke, so what do you mean? I kind of just brushed it off. You wouldn't see them saying that to a white player if they did a bad pass or something. It would be something different."

The footballer endured horrific racism playing abroad for England. "Obviously, with England Under-21s I got it when we were playing Yugoslavia. Yugoslavia were going through what they were going through and then split up. We played them and had to play in a neutral stadium which was in Barcelona. It was at their reserve stadium, nice stadium but small, and you got a guy in the crowd shouting, 'Kunta Kinte. Hey, Kunta Kinte' every time I touched the ball. Kunta Kinte is just an African slave. And then you get the monkey chants from when I was playing for England against Slovakia and Croatia."

Heskey spoke out about the lack of support and action from UEFA and FIFA when players complain about the abuse. Heskey said, "It's not nice at the end of the day but what can I do? I can complain to the FA, what are they going to do? Complain to FIFA, what are they going to do?

"You know what it is? I don't think they are terrible. But the thing is, it's about understanding. They don't come and ask you, sit down with me or sit down with Rhian Brewster or sit down with Sol or sit down with someone who is going through that and understand, and try to understand, and try to get us to explain what we are going through and why it is wrong. Again, the only thing they think about is 'Oh, it's not that bad.' And I have heard commentators say that as well. I've heard people I would class as friends saying things like, 'It's not that bad here, it's worse abroad.' Well how do you know? How do you know it's not that bad here but it's worse abroad? You just see what you see. You haven't felt what I feel. So how do you know it's bad? And this is the thing, you don't take the time to sit down and listen and talk to the people who are actually going through this. It is getting to the point where people are actually starting to stop talking and start listening to what people are actually saying."

10

Anti-Semitism

"The Y-word is a racist word for Jews. It doesn't matter that it has other meanings; for many, many Jewish people, its prime connotation is racist."
  – Ivor Baddiel, children's author and comedy scriptwriter

In 2011, looking to stimulate debate around the topic of anti-Semitism in football, Kick It Out released *The Y-Word*, a film written and produced by David and Ivor Baddiel, featuring Frank Lampard, Ledley King, Kieran Gibbs, Rachel Yankey, Gary Lineker and Zesh Rahman that aimed to tackle anti-Jewish abuse.

In the film, Tottenham fans are seen chanting "Yiddo!" and "Spurs are on their way to Auschwitz, Hitler's going to gas them again." Lampard then says: "For some reason, some fans still shout the Y-word. Some might think it's just a bit of a laugh, but racist chanting is against the law. It's against the law to call someone the Y-word on the street."

Regrettably, in reality, the issue of anti-Semitism was not high on the agenda of the football authorities. Violent attacks, the chanting of Adolf Hitler's name and anti-Semitic abuse are all too common.

Mark Bosnich, one of just two white players at Aston Villa at the time of the infamous "Aston N*****" episode, was himself charged with misconduct by the FA following his Basil Fawlty Nazi-salute impersonation at Tottenham, not realising, he claimed, that it would be offensive to Spurs' large contingent of Jewish fans.

A charity event video surfaced in 2013, which shows the Manchester United and Chelsea keeper telling his version of what happened. The Tottenham crowd had been baiting him with taunts of "Klinsmann! Klinsmann!", referring to an incident that happened several seasons previous when Bosnich poleaxed the German player, who was then with Spurs. The Aussie's response was the ill-fated Nazi salute. Having spoken with police after the game, Bosnich attempted to rectify the situation, calling into a BBC radio programme to apologise. "To be honest, I'm a bit distraught [...] it was something done out of ignorance."

During a game against West Ham at White Hart Lane, some fans made Nazi salutes, and accusations of anti-Semitic abuse included hissing to mimic the sound of gas chambers, a reminder of the millions of Jews killed during the Holocaust. Before a Europa tie with Lazio, in Rome, Italian fans were seen chanting "Juden Tottenham". All this helps create a dangerous undercurrent of anti-Semitism.

"There's a hardcore of racist and anti-Semitic fans in British football who really don't seem to have any regard for common sense or decency," Association of Black Players chair Peter Herbert said. "There has to be zero tolerance – if these people can be identified, they should be prosecuted and banned from football."

Five fans were arrested after the match, with one from West Ham receiving a banning order from the club after being identified as a season-ticket holder. "Any other individuals identified can expect a similar swift and robust response," the club added.

Despite what happened in Rome, Scunthorpe United manager Brian Laws subsequently described his team's performance as being "as bad as the Holocaust"; his comments received a robust response from the Board of Deputies of British Jews. "Anti-Semitism has no place in football or society in general," their statement read. "Holocaust imagery and chants glorifying Adolf Hitler are grossly offensive to the Jewish community and is a stain upon the character of British football."

Herbert said, "What you have to understand is that if only one person is offended it's one too many. All these chants, intentional or unintentional, have to stop. If this happened in athletics or rugby it wouldn't be tolerated, why should it be tolerated in football?" However, fans retort was to chant, "We'll sing what we want."

Clifford Stott, an adviser to governments and police forces internationally on crowd-management policy and practice called on the FA to deliver a reasoned response, to empower "the majority of those fans who aren't abusing other supporters. If the lessons of the past are anything to go by, solutions reside in working with fans' grassroots organisations to respond constructively to any criminal action that occurred. The key message is that an indiscriminate response is counterproductive. Don't forget there is already sufficient legislation to deal with anti-Semitic or racist chanting at football grounds. Where this has happened then, clearly, it must be condemned and, if the evidence exists, for criminal sanctions to follow."

Herbert also talked about empowerment, asking UEFA to empower referees. "We'd like to see a proactive stance on this, a vigorous approach, prosecute where possible, ban people from grounds and, if incidents like that do happen, call a halt to the game. There is a UEFA rule which is never used where a referee can call off the game. That's the sort of initiative which has to happen. Do you want to watch a football game or do you want to listen to this abuse?"

David Baddiel said of their film that it wasn't intended to censor football fans. "It's simply to raise awareness that the Y-word is, and has been for many, many years, a race-hate word. It's our belief that some football fans may not even realise this, and the film is designed therefore to inform and raise debate."

Ivor described David Cameron's defence of Tottenham fans use of the Y-word "utterly ridiculous", after the Prime Minister said they should be able to use the word in chants without fear of prosecution. "This is a British, non-Jewish prime minister effectively telling non-Jews that it's okay to use a race hate word for Jews." The FA, meanwhile, warned them they could face banning orders or even criminal charges if they continued to do so.

In an exclusive interview for this book, Ivor describes how he and his brother David came to make the KIO film, *The Y-Word*. "When I first started going to Chelsea in the mid-seventies, I remember standing in The Shed and joining in with some weird chant that I couldn't quite make out. It sounded like 'Ee-yo, ee-yo'. Sometime later, a friend told me that it was, in fact, 'Yiddo, Yiddo', and, immediately, I felt weird and uncomfortable about it. That weird and uncomfortable feeling whenever I heard the chant persisted for about the next 35 years until one day at Chelsea I confronted someone who had gone from shouting, at the top of his voice, 'F*** the Yids!' to

'F*** the Jews!'. A nasty altercation ensued which left me feeling that, after all this time, something needed to be done. Discussing it with my brother, we decided that we wanted to make a short film to highlight the issue, similar to films that Kick It Out had made over the years to tackle other forms of racism and discrimination.

"We approached Kick It Out, who were very receptive to the idea, and the wheels were put in motion. However, those wheels rumbled on for some time. It wasn't easy getting the film made. The issue is not as clear-cut as, for instance, racism against black players. Indeed, chanting the Y-word is a very divisive issue for both Jews and non-Jews alike, with many, at the time, believing it to be acceptable and, in fact a positive thing.

"For me, the issue is simple. The Y-word is a racist word for Jews. It doesn't matter that it has other meanings – for many, many Jewish people, its prime connotation is racist. Imagine if there was a football team in Brixton and because of its location it became known as the N-words? People may even have objected to that back in the 60s and 70s, but it most certainly wouldn't have persisted through to 2018.

"What's more, despite being known as a Jewish club, the vast, vast majority of Tottenham fans are not Jewish, so we have a situation in which non-Jews are apparently reclaiming a racist word for Jews and saying it is acceptable, positive even."

David made a similar point back in 2012 that the idea that fans were "reclaiming" the Y-word "is simply not true", comparing the scenario of a largely non-Jewish crowd calling themselves a "Yid Army" to a largely white crowd reclaiming the N-word if they were based in a predominantly black area of London such as Brixton.

"That means well over 90% of those chanting 'Yid Army' are not actually Jewish and that is just one of several reasons why it cannot be right," he said.

Ivor continues: "Even if I was to go along with [the 'reclaiming'] argument, it simply hasn't worked. When black people reclaimed the N-word, for the most part it worked, and people understood that it was a terrible, racist word and stopped using it. In the case of Tottenham fans, that hasn't worked and the exact opposite has happened with fans of other clubs chanting the Y-word back at them with venom, and going onto use far, far more offensive chants such as the horrific one about Auschwitz used in the film.

"I don't believe for one minute that Tottenham fans are being knowingly anti-Semitic when they chant the Y-word, but it *does* cause offence and, crucially, confusion – if a Jewish Spurs fan is called the Y-word, his response would have to be, 'Are you calling me that because I'm Jewish or because I'm a Spurs fan? I need to know first before I can tell you whether I'm offended or not.' It's ridiculous."

Ivor believes the film achieved what it set out to achieve: "To raise the issue and make people think about it. And, although it's impossible to gauge precisely, I do think that since it came out there has been less chanting of the Y-word and less anti-Semitism in football. Of course, there is a still a way to go, but we made a start and the issue is now on the map as it were. Throughout it all, the support and backing from Kick It Out has been phenomenal, and I would like to take this opportunity to thank everyone."

Mel Stein – Paul Gascogine's former agent – also gave this book an exclusive interview. "When I first joined one organisation, a member of its board thought it was fine to tell me what he perceived as a 'Jewish Joke'. He was horrified when I pointed out to him that it was blatantly anti-Semitic and then puzzled when I added that it would have been fine for me to tell it. That's the fine line we walk. We can mock ourselves, but we can't allow others to mock us. It's at that point, I shrug and say, 'Go figure', and, again, that shrug as described by anybody non-Jewish could be considered anti-Semitic. That's the line getting even finer.

"I did an interview for a Sunday paper magazine, in my days of high-profile Gazza representation when most people thought that my friend Len Lazarus (also Jewish) and I were making fortunes and taking advantage of the 'naïve Geordie lad'. It wasn't like that but the more we protested, the less we were believed and when this particular journalist ended a double-page spread with the word 'Oy vey', our flesh crept. I don't believe he intended it to be an anti-Semitic observation, but that was how we took it. Oversensitive? Perhaps, but goodness knows, over the years the Jewish people have earned the right to be sensitive, so why should they be any different in the world of football.

"Football is big money now and many agents are Jewish. The Nazis understood all too well the effect of putting the words 'money' and 'Jew' together. Nobody would have the temerity to do that in print nowadays but all too often I read or hear that so-and-so's 'Jewish agent' has delivered a great deal for him. Would they say his 'Christian agent'? I don't think so, and use of the J-word as a descriptive-adjective is a very easy way to get your message across if you really feel that it's only Jews who are into making money for their player-clients.

"The dog's abuse that the Glazers received at Manchester United was just a heartbeat away from anti-Semitism at times. Spurs, of course, have had Jewish ownership for many years. Irving Scholar, Alan Sugar and now Daniel Levy. You might expect nothing else from a team whose supporters (Jewish and non-Jewish) describe themselves as 'Yiddos', but just listen to the chilling gas chamber-replication hissing from the terraces at Stamford Bridge to convince yourself that anti-Semitism *does* exist in football in the vilest of ways.

"Jews love their football. Read, *Does Your Rabbi Know You're Here?*, a book all about Jews in football, if you need to be persuaded. But does football love the Jews? I don't think so. My own rabbi at the time said, at my son's bar mitzvah, when Gazza was in the congregation, that there was an awful rumour in our community that he [Gazza] saw more of them than did the rabbi. That merely reflected the easy conscience of members of the community for whom the sabbath is more a day of going to White Hart Lane or the Emirates or Old Trafford than going to their local synagogue. It was a light-hearted comment and harmless. Yet, all too often, those light-hearted comments in the mouths of those who are racially or religiously prejudiced can have a dark side. It would appear that there is nothing wrong in making money from football as a player or an agent or a club owner ... *unless* you're Jewish. Then it becomes a heinous sin, a blood libel of the 21st century.

"Anti-Semitism has existed since time immemorial. It will take far more than any Kick it Out campaign to remove it from football, let alone society. As has ever been the case, in football, as in everything else, Jews must tread carefully, walk on eggshells at all times to avoid engrained racial prejudice. It all begins with an ill-considered joke, a shrug, a Yiddish phrase used derogatively. We all know where it ends."

David Dein – the former FA and Arsenal vice-chair – is arguably the world's greatest networker and influencer in world football today. Few, if any, in the industry do not have his business card in their possession. An active campaigner for KIO, and an Ambassador for the Premier League, Dein spends much of his free time touring schools and prisons as a motivational speaker on a voluntary basis. Instrumental at the formation of the Champions League in 1994, he was the President of the G-14 group of European football clubs – the most powerful clubs in Europe – and has sat on various committees within FIFA and UEFA. He was International President of England's 2018 World Cup bid, boarding an estimated 116 flights, travelling 191,369 miles and visiting 27 countries to lobby on England's behalf.

Back in 1983, I was the first journalist to interview him. He's given few interviews since, so I'm very pleased at his agreeing to do so for this book!

Dein has supported KIO from its formation and his position within football is a massive asset for the campaign. "I was there in a dingy room at a small hotel in Lancaster Gate when a small group of us decided to form KIO," he told me. "From very humble beginnings, we've made tremendous strides to control and eradicate racism in football and indeed society.

"I've personally been a victim of anti-Semitic remarks. The spoken word can be so hurtful when delivered inappropriately. We've made huge strides. Every Premier League club now places an advert in their match-day programme and stewards are educated on how to deal with offenders. The organisation always responds immediately whenever there are any anti-social problems involving racism.

"Lord Herman Ouseley has been an inspirational figure with his strong leadership and clarity of thought. He assembled a very able group around him, including Gordon Taylor, the chief executive of the PFA. I have always been very proud to be associated with the organisation. Onwards and upwards!"

Perhaps appropriately for this book, few people will know that David's family business roots started when his mother had a shop in Shepherds Bush market catering for the Afro-Caribbean population back in the 1960s.

As for the future, Dein says simply that we need to "keep up the pressure to ensure that racism and all forms of discrimination have no place in our society."

In January 2020, Scott Shulton of Hemel Hempstead Town was the victim of anti-Semitic abuse from Billy Crook of Braintree Town at a National League South match. Crook was suspended for five domestic first team games, fined and ordered to complete an education course. "I'm really pleased with the outcome," Shulton said. "It's unacceptable in this day and age for anyone to be abused because of their race, religion or ethnicity. I'm grateful for all the support I've received from players, the management and everyone at Hemel since the incident took place, and also from Kick It Out, who backed me throughout the case."

Following the outcome, the Community Security Trust issued a statement: "This verdict sends an important message that anti-Semitism will not be tolerated at any level of football. We applaud Scott for persevering with this case for several months and Kick It Out for giving him invaluable support." KIO welcomed the verdict but raised concern over the length of time it took to reach a conclusion, and warned that without greater resources, cases like this may not get the attention and treatment they deserve.

Elsewhere, Sky Sport Italia ended its relationship with former West Ham and Lazio striker Paolo Di Canio after he revealed his "dux" tattoo – which represents Italy's ex-Fascist leader Benito Mussolini – while presenting a show on the network.

The former Italian international's club career included stints at Juventus, Napoli, AC Milan, Glasgow Celtic, Charlton Athletic, West Ham and Sheffield Wednesday. Di Canio scored one of the Premier League's greatest-ever goals. Having infamously pushed a referee to the ground during a 1998 Sheffield Wednesday game against Arsenal for which he was sent off, he redeemed himself three years later, in 2001, being awarded FIFA's Fair Play Award in recognition of his "special act of good sportsmanship" for picking up the ball during a West Ham match against Everton whilst the opposition goalkeeper lay injured on the ground.

However, Di Canio again attracted controversy in 2005, for giving straight-arm salutes to Lazio fans. Speaking to the Italian news agency, Ansa, he said, "I'm fascist, not a racist. I saluted my people with what for me is a sign of belonging to a group that holds true values, values of civility against the standardisation that this society imposes upon us. I'm proud to be able to count on such people and I will continue to salute them in this way."

Italian Jewish groups were outraged, the Italian Maccabi Federation president, Vittorio Pavoncello, calling on Lazio and the authorities to take action. Di Canio brushed their protests aside, however, saying, "If we're in the hand of the Jewish community, it's the end.

If action is taken because one community is up in arms, it could be dangerous."

The player expected "a robust defence" from his club. "I'm not going to settle for anything less. I expect my president to defend me, just like presidents do in other clubs, otherwise I'm going to be really pissed off." However, it wasn't to be. A statement released on their website read: "Lazio repudiates any kind of racism or politicisation of football, both on the pitch and off it, and invites its shareholders and its fans to react against any attempt to pollute the language of sport." Di Canio was later fined €10,000 for making the same gesture at the end of Lazio's win over arch-rivals Roma.

Despite the controversies surrounding Di Canio, in 2013, the Italian succeeded Martin O'Neill as Sunderland manager, an appointment that led former UK Foreign Secretary David Miliband to resign from its board. In a statement posted on his website, Miliband said, "I wish Sunderland AFC all success in the future. It is a great institution that does a huge amount for the north-east, and I wish the team very well over the next vital seven games. However, in the light of the new manager's past political statements, I think it right [for me] to step down." The former South Shields MP served as Sunderland vice-chair and a non-executive director, having joined the board in 2011 after losing out on the Labour leadership to his brother, Ed. He relocated to New York to become CEO of the International Rescue Committee.

Miliband's announcement was praised by fellow Labour MP Stella Creasy, in a tweet describing his actions "all the more powerful" given how much the role meant to him. However, commentator and former footballer Stan

Collymore tweeted, "Faux outrage as always on twitter. No Italian ex-footballer ever called me N*****. Just plenty from the wonderful UK shires."

Explaining his stance in his autobiography, Di Canio wrote of Mussolini that, "his actions were often vile. But all this was motivated by a higher purpose. He was basically a very principled individual."

11

T-shirt Tick box

"My mum had her windows smashed and bullets put
through her door and ended up in hospital because of
the stress."

– Rio Ferdinand

Individual players decided to show their discontent at what
they believed to be a lack of progress in tackling racism by
refusing to wear KIO T-shirts during its 2011 "One Game,
One Community Week of Action" campaign.

Each season, anti-discrimination organisation Kick It
Out holds a week of action to promote awareness about
its anti-racism work. But, in 2011, Reading's Grenadian
striker Jason Roberts, who had played in England for the
previous 15 years, refused to wear the campaign T-shirt
in protest at what he perceived to be the group's lack of
action in combating racism in football.

Manchester United's Rio Ferdinand also protested,
becoming one of the most vocal critics of the way the
T-shirt campaign had become a symbol of a once-a-year
protest that had little ongoing effect, causing a rift with his

manager, Sir Alex Ferguson, who described the player's stance as "out of order".

Ex-United defender Viv Anderson, the first black player to play for England, stood with his former boss – who had also criticised Jason Roberts for urging black players to boycott the KIO campaign – saying he disagreed with Ferdinand and that the manager had a right to expect his players to "set an example", adding, "If he says we're all doing it together, it should be the end of the story."

However, the PFA chair Clarke Carlisle defended Rio's right to make a personal protest, saying that Sir Alex should have listened to his player's reasoning and he vowed to help the player fight any punishment, financial or otherwise. "We will make sure Rio's rights as a human being – never mind as a footballer – are not undermined," he said. "Everyone has a right to free speech – just like you can't coerce anyone into shaking hands, you can't make somebody wear a T-shirt."

Elsewhere, Ferguson backed his vice-captain Patrice Evra, in Evra's own race-related dispute with Liverpool striker Luis Suárez, the manager calling on the FA to show "responsibility" in dealing with players found guilty of making racist comments. Sir Alex said, "I can't believe this is an issue in 2011, given the number of black players who have played in our game over the last 25 years. At our club, we have had fantastic (black) players with great personalities and I have been very lucky to have them." However, ex-Arsenal footballer and players' union coach Paul Davis complained of double standards, saying that United and QPR were not giving as much support to Evra and Ferdinand as Liverpool and Chelsea were giving to Suárez and Terry, which "might prevent other black players from speaking out."

Anton Ferdinand

Ferdinand's brother Anton also refused to wear the T-shirt, himself the subject of racist abuse from Chelsea captain John Terry, during Chelsea's 1–0 defeat at QPR. Terry was alleged to have used the words "f****** black c***." While Terry didn't deny using the words, he claimed the context in which he said them meant they couldn't be taken as racist abuse, the Chelsea and England centre-back insisting that he was simply asking Ferdinand *if* he was accusing him of using the highly offensive phrase. Ferdinand refused to back down. "I didn't know racism still existed in football until last weekend," he said. "I thought we were past all that here. I had no idea it had happened until I left the ground. It was pretty shocking. It's crazy, I can't believe it [but] it's all on YouTube, everyone can see what [Terry] said."

Despite being found "not guilty" of racial abuse "beyond all reasonable doubt" in an ensuing court case, the FA concluded "on the balance of probabilities" that Terry's defence against claims he racially abused Ferdinand was "improbable, implausible [and] contrived", and awarded the centre back a four-match ban for racial abuse.

John Barnes felt the FA verdict wouldn't change anyone's opinion of Terry. "I have an opinion. We all do. It won't be changed by this. There's racism in football and in society […] I'd change things through education. But it will take 20 years. In the meantime, there will be these issues."

Anton's brother, Rio Ferdinand, revealed in 2014 his deep animosity towards Terry, saying, "he will always be the biggest idiot." Nonetheless, in 2015, he said that, despite their differences, he still admired the Chelsea captain. Though it was "impossible to forgive or forget" what had happened between Terry and his brother, "His performances for Chelsea this season have been nothing short of outstanding and I'm not afraid to say it. John took the decision to retire from playing for England and had his reasons, but Chelsea are reaping the benefits."

Ferdinand revealed that their mother ended up in hospital after the family was targeted: "My mum had her windows smashed and bullets put through her door and ended up in hospital because of the stress." He was also disillusioned with Ashley Cole, a childhood friend and former England teammate, for supporting Terry. "We've known each other since we were kids, but for me it ended the day he decided to go to court in support of John Terry. Anton rang me and my head nearly blew off. He was betraying Anton, who he'd also known for years." Claiming that Cole had felt pressurised into doing so by his club, writing in his autobiography, *#2Sides*: "I told him he had a choice, 'You're my mate and you're John Terry's mate. You know both our families. So, go into court and tell the exact truth about what happened, or don't go at all.' He told me, 'I've got no choice, I've been told I've got to go.'" Ferdinand responded that, if Cole did support Terry in court, "We will never talk again." Nevertheless, he admitted it was a mistake calling Cole a "choc ice" – black on the outside, white on the inside – for which the FA fined him £45,000. "I shouldn't have done it, but it's what I felt at the time."

For his part, Cole released a statement through his representative, stating that he and Ferdinand were still "good friends", appreciating that tweeting is "so quick, it often results in offhand and stray comments" and that he had "no intention of making any sort of complaint."

Back in 2007, Ferdinand had revealed in the *Daily Mirror* how racism brutally affected his childhood. One day, he went to school to find a fifth form boy had been stabbed to death in a racist murder. That boy was Stephen Lawrence, the black teenager murdered in 1993. Seven years later, Damilola Taylor was killed on an estate close to where Rio and his brother Anton grew up. He experienced racism on the terraces both as a player and as a supporter and remembers the England under-21s game where Emile Heskey was racially abused by Yugoslavia fans. "I was at school with Stephen Lawrence. I was a first-year and he was a fifth-year, but we knew each other. The day he was killed, it was mad. The whole day got frozen. People were coming in saying: 'Stephen Lawrence got stabbed.' He was a quiet, nice boy, into art and music; he had a purpose and wanted to do something in life. For him, to be taken away that way seemed so unreal; people didn't know what was going on, or why. I grew up on an estate in Peckham, near where Damilola Taylor was killed. When I was older I got a BMW convertible and used to drive around Peckham and areas like New Cross, Deptford and Hackney, and I'd get stopped on a regular basis. I wasn't really known as a footballer at the time and they'd ask me, 'Where d'you get the money for this? Are you dealing? Are you nicking stuff?' I would say, 'I earned this car, I wouldn't drive it if I didn't earn it.' I don't get stopped now.

"I was at a game when I was about 16 [...] and a man started shouting 'black this, black that' at the players. He turned to me and said: 'Not you mate, you're all right.' I looked at a nearby policeman, as if to say, 'What are you going to do?", but he looked through me, he wasn't going to do anything. I just got up and left.

"That's why I support Kick It Out – because it challenges racism at all levels in the game and uses football to bring communities together. As a player, you get a certain amount of racism from crowds here and there, but it's not as apparent as it was before. When players like John Barnes, Ian Wright and Viv Anderson were playing, it was a lot worse. I think there should just be football leagues so scouts can see everybody playing, rather than segregating them."

Luis Suárez and Patrice Evra

On 15 October 2011, Liverpool's Louis Suárez was accused of using insulting words in an altercation with Manchester United's Patrice Evra, including reference to his skin colour, during a 1–1 draw at Anfield. Referee Andre Marriner, who'd been made aware of the allegation *after* the game, reported it to the FA, who launched a lengthy investigation. Suárez categorically denied any wrongdoing, but Evra told France's Canal+ TV, "There are cameras, you can see him say a certain word to me at least ten times."

Liverpool backed their player and were "very surprised" when he was fined £40,000 and given an eight-game ban by the FA. Manager Kenny Dalglish tweeted that he was "very disappointed [...] Suárez needs our full support," and a statement issued by the club read: "We find it extraordinary that Luis can be found guilty on the word of Patrice Evra alone. No one else [...] including Evra's own Manchester United teammates and all the match officials, heard the alleged conversation." The club claimed that the FA were determined to bring charges against Suárez, even before interviewing him, and promised continued support to their player in his bid to clear his name.

However, others agreed with the outcome. Piara Powar, declaring the governing body's decision a landmark judgement, told BBC Radio 5 Live, "This is the first time we've seen an insight into what is said between players on the pitch, and what may have been commonplace between players in the past [...] Suárez could be suspended for 20% of the season - it's devastating for Liverpool [but] I'd say the FA have dealt with this in the right way. They've taken their time and taken independent advice."

Lord Ouseley agreed. "The FA has shown leadership and intent through what has clearly been a difficult and complex complaint to deal with and invested time and expertise to ensure this outcome. It has demonstrated that it will not stand for discrimination, something organisations such as FIFA and UEFA should take heed of. This charge is not saying Luis Suárez is a racist. It's saying, on this occasion, he used racist language. It doesn't make him a bad guy – he needs to learn what is acceptable."

The PFA were in agreement, too, its chair, Clarke Carlisle, calling the decision "100% correct." "There are definitely cultural differences for a lot of players coming from South America and from the Continent into England [but] we still expect people who come and work here to adhere to the standards and the laws of this land. It's wholly acceptable in parts of the Middle East to chop off the hands of thieves but we wouldn't tolerate it here and it's just the same when it comes to racism."

Its CEO, Gordon Taylor, "was surprised at the severity of the punishment," suggesting there was some doubt about the claims. "But it shows the FA must have some compelling evidence." He suggested that clubs tend to adopt a "them and us" stance, giving automatic support to their players, "but some things are bigger than clubs, players and even the game itself. Racism is one of them."

Rodney Hinds, sports editor of *The Voice*, wrote an article for the *Guardian* about the affair. In it, he said, "The FA has now provided a deterrent to those within the game who feel it's all right to abuse another professional simply because of his colour.

"When the independent regulatory commission announced that Evra's allegations against Suárez were proven, football was the winner. If Suárez had escaped punishment, all the good work of campaigns such as Kick It Out, Show Racism the Red Card and the FA itself would have been consigned to the dustbin [but] what's the point of cleaning up the terraces if racism then finds its way to the field of play itself?

"Maybe the anti-racism T-shirts and badges should be worn all year round," he added, warning, "It's easy to tick a box, and complacency is the greatest threat to the outstanding work put in by so many."

When Suárez returned after his ban, his first game was, ironically, against United, before which, thousands of copies of *Red Issue*, featuring a "potentially offensive image", were seized by Greater Manchester Police. The United fanzine included a Ku Klux Klan hood accompanied with the words "LFC" and "Suárez is innocent".

An arrest was made outside Old Trafford in connection with the sale of T-shirts also deemed offensive, and police promised swift action against anyone involved in the distribution of offensive material. "In consultation with the Crown Prosecution Service, we will take appropriate action against anyone either found selling this particular fanzine or provocatively displaying the image in public," match commander Chief Superintendent Mark Roberts said.

In the build-up to the match, expectations had been high that Suárez and Evra would shake hands, to try to defuse the situation. In the event, Suárez snubbed Evra, ignoring the latter's proffered hand, going straight to goalkeeper David de Gea. Of that, Evra's teammate Darren Fletcher praised the Frenchman for being "the bigger man." "Credit to Patrice Evra," he said, "he's gone to shake his hand and obviously Suárez has rejected it." Former United full-back Gary Neville added, "Obviously it's quite clear that Luis Suárez has completely blanked Patrice Evra. I'm not sure it's the wisest thing for him to do, I'm not sure he's helped his football club."

Dalglish was heavily criticised for his post-match reaction. Quizzed by Sky Sport 2's Geoff Shreeves about Suárez's snub, the Liverpool manager claimed he didn't know Suárez had refused the handshake. "I don't know, I wasn't there, I never saw it. We haven't looked at the handshakes, but that's contrary to what I was told. We'll ask him and we'll take it from there [but] I think you're very severe […] bang out of order to blame Luis Suárez for anything that happened here today."

However, United manager Sir Alex Ferguson was having none of it: "I couldn't believe it. He's a disgrace to Liverpool Football Club. That certain player should not be allowed to play for Liverpool again. The history that club's got and he does that and in a situation like today could have caused a riot. I was really disappointed in that guy, it was terrible what he did."

Gordon Taylor, too, branded the player's conduct "disrespectful, inappropriate and embarrassing," adding, that the FA would have to step in. "Suárez had a chance to put everything [right] yesterday, in front of a worldwide audience. The fact that he chose not to is, quite frankly, depressing."

Alan Hansen's observation was withering: "Liverpool FC made a statement that there would be a handshake. Luis Suárez was party to the statement. He knew about it and obviously agreed with it. To snub Patrice Evra was, in my view, totally unacceptable. The football club and the manager have given him total and unequivocal support through thick and thin. He has let Kenny Dalglish down, the club down and himself down."

Subsequently, Suárez and Dalglish both apologised for their respective conduct. "I have spoken with [Dalglish] and I realise I got things wrong," Suárez said in a statement on Liverpool's official website. "I should have shaken Patrice Evra's hand before the game, and I want to apologise for my actions. I would like to put this whole issue behind me and concentrate on playing football." Dalglish said, "I was shocked to hear that the player had not shaken hands having been told earlier in the week that he would do [so]. [...] When I went on TV after yesterday's game I hadn't seen what had happened, but I did not conduct myself in a way befitting of a Liverpool manager during that interview and I'd like to apologise for that."

In a separate statement, Liverpool MD Ian Ayre said "We are extremely disappointed Luis Suárez did not shake hands with Patrice Evra before yesterday's game. The player had told us beforehand that he would, but then chose not to do so. He was wrong to mislead us and wrong not to offer his hand to Patrice Evra. He has not only let himself down, but also Kenny Dalglish, his teammates and the club. It has been made absolutely clear to Luis Suárez that his behaviour was not acceptable. [He] has now apologised for his actions, which was the right thing to do."

United accepted their apologies. "Manchester United thanks Liverpool for the apologies issued following Saturday's game," a statement read. "Everyone at Old Trafford wants to move on from this. The history of our two great clubs is one of success and rivalry unparalleled in British football. That should be the focus in the future of all those who love the clubs."

Sports Minister at the time, Hugh Robertson accepted the season's race controversies "tarnished" the reputation of the game but did not think the damage was irreparable. Speaking to Sky Sports News, he said, "This has been a bad season for this sort of thing, but it shouldn't for a moment obscure the enormous amount of good work and progress over the past 20 years [...] Show Racism the Red Card and Kick It Out, [and] the FA have done enormous good work."

Mark Clattenburg and John Obi Mikel

In 2012, Chelsea alleged that referee Mark Clattenburg used inappropriate language towards John Obi Mikel, calling their midfielder a "monkey", during a 3–2 defeat against Manchester United at Stamford Bridge on 28 October. In a separate incident, Clattenburg was also accused of calling United's Juan Mata a "Spanish t***" during the match. Chelsea manager Roberto Di Matteo and CEO Ron Gourlay spoke to Clattenburg, Gourlay later making a complaint to Premier League match delegate Nick Cusack. However, following a three-week investigation, the FA completely exonerated the referee, charging Mikel instead over the angry confrontation in Clattenburg's dressing room following the match. While believing Mikel's team-mate Ramires – from whom the allegation originated – "acted in good faith," the FA pointed out that English was not his first language, concluding, "his instinctive reaction was to seek confirmation from John Mikel Obi as to what the referee had said. [Obi], who was being spoken to by the referee, was much closer to the referee than Ramires and did not hear what it is suggested was said to him. Three other witnesses – the other match officials – who heard everything said by referee via their communication equipment, are adamant the alleged words were not uttered. There is nothing in the video footage to support the allegation. For completeness, but of lesser weight, two other players, whose first language is English and were in the vicinity, did not hear anything untoward."

Professional Game Match Officials Limited general manager Mark Riley then confirmed Clattenburg would soon return to duty, "without any stain on his character or reputation."

Following his exoneration, Clattenburg issued his own statement: "I'm looking forward to putting this behind me and concentrating on refereeing in the Premier League and other competitions. The messages of encouragement from those inside and outside of the game have helped me through the most stressful time of my professional life. To know you were innocent of something but that there was the opportunity for it to wreck your career was frightening. Racism has no place in football and this experience should not discourage those to speak out if they genuinely believe they are a victim of abuse. However, there are processes that should be adhered in order that any investigation can be carried out in a manner that is fair for all parties involved. I know first-hand the ramifications of allegations of this nature being placed into the public domain ahead of a formal process and investigation. I hope no referee has to go through this in the future. We are fortunate to be working in the world's most watched and scrutinised football league. With that comes a responsibility in regard to how the different parts of the game work together."

12

Racism Rife Throughout Europe

"The Premier League and FA have to start taking more effective action against home-grown racism at matches in this country. [T]here have been too many new incidences taking place in recent games."
– John McDonnell, former Labour Party shadow chancellor

Porto were fined a mere $27,000 after their fans were found guilty of subjecting Manchester City's Mario Balotelli and Yaya Toure to monkey chants during a Europa League game in February 2012. Incredibly, the sum was lower than the $40,000 fine City received for being late on the field at another match, and paled compared to the $126,000 fine Denmark's Nicklas Bendtner received for lifting his shirt to reveal a betting company's logo on his underwear while celebrating a goal against Portugal in a Euro 2012 group game – an indication of where exactly UEFA placed its priorities ... *not* with racism issues.

The sort of slap-wrist approach to racist offences made UEFA's "Unite Against Racism" campaign look like mere window dressing. As a consequence, racism on the Continent was to get worse, far worse.

In November 2011, on CNN, FIFA president Sepp Blatter denied football had a problem with racism on the field, suggesting that any incidents that did occur should be settled by a handshake. Little wonder that so many fans thought they could get away with all manner of racial abuse of players, as well as each other.

Brazil's Roberto Carlos had been racially abused in Russia while playing for Anzhi Makhachkala, asking to be substituted in a match after abuse was thrown at him from the stands.

A group of fans – going by the name of Landscrona – at one Russian club, Zenit St Petersburg, unveiled their "Selection 12" manifesto, urging the club *not* to sign any black or gay players. The Landscrona group posted the manifesto on its website. They claimed they weren't racists but saw the absence of black players as "an important tradition." "We're against representatives of sexual minorities playing for Zenit. For us, it is crucial [Zenit] has retained its own identity, and not turned into an average European team, with a standard set of foreign players. We only want players from other brotherly Slav nations, such as Ukraine and Belarus as well as from the Baltic states and Scandinavia. We have the same mentality and historical and cultural background as these nations. Any other continents except Europe, should not be a priority."

FC Zenit had spent almost £100 million on black players Hulk (Brazil) and Axel Witsel (Belgium) and, following the fan group's demands, were prompted to issue its own statement emphasising its policy of diversity and tolerance, telling CNN World Sport that the club did not "support archaic values" and pointing out that St Petersburg was an open city.

Russia, having had its fair share of racist incidents in football over the years was preparing to host the 2018 World

Cup when media attention highlighted the manifesto. Fines included $39,000 and $38,000, respectively, during Euro 2012 and $155,000 after clashes between supporters and police during and after their game against the Czech Republic.

Antonio Rudiger

Antonio Rudiger reported being the subject of monkey chants during the second half of his Chelsea side's 2–0 victory over Tottenham Hotspur. The Professional Footballers' Association called for a government inquiry into racism within football after the allegations of abuse at the game. The chants, which caused widespread outrage, were heard shortly after Tottenham's Son Heung-min had been sent off for kicking out at Rudiger. The referee halted play and announcements were made at the Tottenham Hotspur Stadium to say, "racist behaviour among spectators is interfering with the game."

Rudiger, who is German, tweeted: "It is really sad to see racism again at a football match, but I think it's very important to talk about it in public. If not, it will be forgotten again in a couple of days (as always). I don't want to involve Tottenham as an entire club into this situation as I know that just a couple of idiots were the offenders.

"I got a lot of supportive messages on social media from Spurs fans as well in the last hours – thank you a lot for this. I really hope that the offenders will be found and punished soon, and in such a modern football ground like the Tottenham Hotspur Stadium with dozens of TV and security cameras, it must be possible to find and subsequently punish them. If not, then there must have been witnesses in the stadium who saw and heard the incident. It's just such a shame that racism still exists in 2019. When will this nonsense stop?"

The PFA posted: "Now more than ever we must unite and stand strong and together to confront, challenge and eradicate racist abuse in our stadiums and in our country. We believe that the time has come for all governing bodies to unite collectively to end this abuse. The PFA calls for a government enquiry into racism and the rise in hate crime within football and immediate and urgent action from an all-party group at the Department of Culture, Media and Sport to address this urgent issue."

In a statement, Tottenham Hotspur said any fan found guilty of racist abuse will receive a lifetime ban, and said that they were currently investigating the incident.

Kick It Out said in their statement: "We are aware of the alleged racist incidents at today's game between Tottenham Hotspur and Chelsea. We applaud the action of referee Anthony Taylor in following step one of the protocols and the ensuing steps taken by Tottenham Hotspur in repeating the stadium announcements. We have offered our support to both of the clubs and also to Chelsea's Antonio Rudiger."

Speaking on Sky Sports News, KIO's head of development Troy Townsend said, "It has always been there, but now incidents are getting reported more so it was good to see what happened today highlighted in the commentary so everyone knew what was going on. But unfortunately, this minority, which continues to find its way into our grounds, are continuing to act in this disgraceful matter. It is something the game has to look at now as to what the next steps are. The Premier League, the FA and all the governing bodies have to take a long, hard look and say 'what do we do? because what we are doing is not enough."

An FA spokesman said, "Following the incident in the match between Tottenham Hotspur and Chelsea on

Sunday, 22 December, we are working with the match officials, the clubs and the relevant authorities to fully establish the facts and take the appropriate steps."

Rudiger said he was first made to feel like a "monkey" and then a "liar" after Tottenham and the police dropped an investigation into the alleged abuse against him. Spurs had insisted that after "extensive reviews" of CCTV and help from lip readers, they'd failed to uncover any chants. "The club and the Metropolitan Police have now exhausted all avenues of investigation," Spurs said. "There is no evidence to corroborate or contradict the allegation and as such neither ourselves nor the police are in a position to take any further action. We are fiercely proud of our anti-racism work and our zero tolerance of any form of discrimination. This is one reason why we have attributed so much time and resource to investigating this matter."

Rudiger was left dumbfounded and sickened by the outcome. He told *Der Spiegel*: "I ask myself, 'How is it possible that nobody of the 60,000 people in this stadium realised anything about it?' So, I stand there [accused] as a liar. I have the feeling that I'm expected to shut my mouth. But I have a message: I won't do that. I felt as if I wasn't a human being, but an animal. A monkey. I think if you haven't lived such situations you can't imagine how I felt. Against Tottenham, I felt incredibly lonely."

The Chelsea player said Tottenham striker Harry Kane had apologised to him afterwards. "I was grateful for the gesture from the England captain. I said, 'It's absolutely not your fault, you don't have to apologise.' But he wanted to do it as a sign that his club doesn't think like that."

Despite the findings, Tottenham have always insisted they "fully support" Rudiger's actions. Many Spurs fans booed him as Chelsea won the Premier League return match 2–1 at Stamford Bridge. Commenting on that, he said, "Yes, I heard it. It's sad. I don't know why they would. Maybe it's because I spoke out about the racism. If you boo me because of that, then you are poor people. This is a sign that we have a very big problem. At the end of the day, I am alone in this case because I am the one who has to swallow this. With the win against Spurs, it makes me feel a bit like, 'Yes, okay,' but it [also] makes me feel like it will always be like this. It shows that these people won because they can go back to the stadium. They won't be punished and at the end of the day I'm the bogeyman. For me, in this case, racism won. For me, it [the case being dropped] was not a surprise, because sometimes they get punished – but mostly, they get away with it. I'm not trying to offend anyone, but you will never understand what goes through my mind at this moment. Or other black players' minds. I am alone. I am totally alone. Authority-wise, I'm alone. People are investigating but I don't want to say they did their job wrong. I hope they tried everything."

While Spurs never discovered who allegedly dished out abuse to Rudiger, a Chelsea fan was arrested for racially abusing Tottenham's Son Heung-min.

Political Moves

Downing Street warned football authorities they must step up efforts to tackle racism. The prime minister's official spokesman welcomed an inquiry launched by Spurs but said it was clear more needed to be done within the sport to address the issue. He said the government would be monitoring the response of the football authorities and was ready to take further steps "if required." The PM's spokesman said, "Racism of any kind has no place in football or anywhere else and we must confront this vile behaviour. Clearly there remains more work to be done by the football authorities in tackling this issue and we are committed to working with them on this to stamp it out. The FA, Premier League and English Football League have significantly stepped up their efforts, but we expect them to continue to prioritise this issue and to consult with both players and supporter groups, and we will be monitoring how the football authorities implement their plans through the season. We will continue working with the authorities on this, including the Professional Footballers' Association and we don't rule out taking further steps if required."

Sports minister Nigel Adams, who was due to speak with the Tottenham directors, described the incident as "depressing". "There is no place for racism or any kind of discrimination in football or anywhere else," he said.

Gary Neville, speaking as a pundit on Sky Sports, called on the PFA to do more in the fight against racism. He said, "We have a racism problem in the Premier League in England. And the Premier League have to step up, they hide behind the FA on this issue. Maybe we have to empower the players to walk off the pitch and stop the entertainment while it is happening. That is the only way I can see it happening. I did not walk off the pitch when Ashley [Cole] was abused 15 years ago, and you might argue that now it's okay for me to sit here in my ivory tower of a commentary box and suggest that players should walk off the pitch. Ultimately I would be ashamed of myself for not doing [it] 15 years ago as I would be absolutely proud of players for doing it now to empower them to think, do something about it and take it into their own hands. The PFA need to act because it's ultimately their job to protect players in their own country and they should protect players if the football associations don't do it."

Neville played in the England team with Cole – who, along with Shaun Wright-Phillips, was subjected to racist abuse during a 2004 friendly against Spain in Madrid. Cole, also speaking on Sky Sports, felt the current anti-discrimination campaigns did not go far enough. "You have a T-shirt in your place [in the dressing room]. They are like, 'Put that on for the warm up, then you can take it off,'" he said. "People don't really care. Why do they wait until something happens in the game to make the announcements? I don't think it is enough – and is it going to stop? It is kind of my fault as well because when I was abused I did not come out, but I just felt I didn't have enough support. Raheem (Sterling) has changed that, he has the people on his side, whereas I did not feel I had that."

John McDonnell, the former Labour shadow chancellor and long-time Liverpool fan, agreed with Neville's calls for players to abandon matches in response to racism. He said, "I fully agree with [Gary Neville]. The Premier League and FA have to start taking more effective action against home-grown racism at matches in this country. We thought we had largely eradicated this scourge but there have been too many new incidences taking place in recent games."

Following racist chanting when England played a World Cup qualifier in Bulgaria, the prime minister branded the culprits "vile" and said such behaviour had "no place in football or anywhere else." Kick It Out's George Starkey-Midha told BBC Radio 4's *Today* programme: "It's imperative that everyone involved in football, on the government, on anyone in any kind of position of authority to really begin to take this far more seriously and look at how we can begin to make inroads, because clearly you've now got a situation where every single week there seems to be another incident and it's a serious, serious problem." Starkey-Midha said there needs to be "far more robust" reporting procedures and "far more comprehensive sanctions," including within football, to respond to racism.

Asked if the Professional Footballers Association was accurate when warning of the "blatant racism that is currently rife in the UK," Mr Starkey-Midha replied, "Yes, absolutely. I think it's undeniable that racism is still a very serious problem in this country. I think people like to look abroad to Italy, Russia and Bulgaria when incidents happen there and I think we're right to criticise when we see it, but there are serious levels of racism in this country still, too. I think unless we wake up to that fact, we won't tackle it properly."

Iffy Onuora, the PFA's equalities coach spoke to BBC *Breakfast*, saying, "First of all, football is only a reflection of society, so we are not saying there is an isolated problem in football. Football is the national game, and we can use football as a vehicle to look beyond football, because what is happening in football is just a manifestation of society, so we can start addressing some of those core issues. What's driving it? That's the starting point, otherwise we will just keep coming back to this same old thing. This is about how we see ourselves as a country. There are people looking at us now. We used to be famous for tolerance, inclusiveness, all those things. We are in danger of losing that. Our values were once about inclusiveness and positivity, and we are in danger of losing this, and for all decent-minded people that should be something to be feared. We spoke about 2012, what a message we sent out with the (London) Olympics – that inclusiveness, that tolerance – and we all thought we were in a really good place. That seems a relic now, 2012. It was only eight years ago. We fast forward to where we are now, it seems such a long time ago. I think most people in this country still want the message that we sent out then, not the messages we are sending out now. All it needs is people in power, in leadership, to take control of this and to provide the leadership and support the players. We have got to use this as a starting point. There is a new government now, there is an opportunity for those to take the lead and really set the tone in a positive way."

Then Chelsea midfielder Willian could not understand why fans racially abuse opposition players when there are black players on their own team. "It's a shame. It's very disappointing, I don't how people can think [like] that," Willian told Sky Sports. "In their team [Tottenham] they have black players as well. I really don't understand what they think or why they do these kinds of things."

Willian wanted football's governing bodies to do more to combat racism. "I think we have to find, together, a way to stop this. It's a shame for everyone. It hurts a lot. They don't need to do it against me, they do it against my teammates, so I feel bad as well. Inside the pitch you cannot think much about this otherwise you are not concentrating [on the game]. We do what we can do, our captain reports to the referee that we had a manifestation of racism and the ref decides what to do. I hope we see more action from the federations, that's what we want."

Two weeks earlier, a man was identified and arrested for an alleged racist gesture caught on TV cameras during the Manchester derby, while Italy's Serie A apologised after an anti-racism campaign featuring posters with images of monkeys was widely condemned.

UEFA chief Aleksander Čeferin pledged European football's governing body was working to tackle the rising problem after a spate of incidents across the continent including the hurling of racist abuse at England players during a match in Bulgaria. Yet, Čeferin accused Prime Minister Boris Johnson of fuelling the problem. "When a politician that calls women with burqas postboxes or mailboxes then says publicly that he condemns UEFA [for not tackling racism] – do you reply to that? Do you believe it's honest? Come on," said Mr Čeferin.

13

A New Low

"The monkey chants started when we went out for the warm up."

– Danny Rose, playing for England

Spurs right-back Danny Rose demanded Serbia be banned from international football when the racist abuse in Kruševac was so bad he could not concentrate on his game. England under-21s secured qualification for Euro 2013 on a night marred by racist chants and a mass brawl at the end. Rose was pelted with stones during the second half.

Rose had been confronted by Serbian players, resulting in an ugly brawl involving players and staff from both sides. Steve Wigley, Stuart Pearce's assistant, was attacked as he attempted to retreat to the tunnel while goalkeeping coach Martin Thomas was headbutted. England goalkeeper Jack Butland had a seat thrown at him.

Rose and his teammates heard monkey chants before the game kicked off and insisted the Serbian FA must be punished by UEFA. Players reported being hit as missiles including coins and pieces of concrete were thrown from the crowd following England's injury-time winner. "The monkey chants started when we went out for the warm up," Rose said. "I asked the lads if they could hear it and they said they could. I went to see Wigs [Steve Wigley] and I told him what was happening, and he just said, 'Try your best to get through it' and people would deal with it after the game. In the first half, I went to get the ball for a throw-in and the fans started with the monkey chanting again. But the first half was nowhere near as bad as the second. Two stones hit me in the head when I went to get the ball for a throw-in and whenever I touched the ball there was monkey chanting. After 60 minutes, my mind wasn't really on the game, I was just so angry. It was just so hard to concentrate and I could've cost the lads the game [...] After 90 minutes of abuse, I expressed my emotions as soon as we scored. The next thing I know, I've turned around and the Serbian players had all run over and surrounded me, pushing me and a brawl broke out. I remember getting slapped twice and then I got ushered away – that's when I kicked the ball and the referee sent me off. I don't understand it, the game had finished. They have to be banned. I don't understand what else they can learn from it; they have to be banned."

Nigel Rose felt powerless watching his son's suffering. "It's hard to take in really. It's almost like a bad dream to be honest [the referee] ought to be ashamed of himself."

A spokesman for the British PM David Cameron called on UEFA to hand out "tough sanctions." "It's not good enough to say that people should shake hands and forget about it. If we're going to stamp out racism from football then it's no good handing out derisory fines as has happened in the past."

Meanwhile, his sports minister Hugh Robertson wrote to UEFA president Michel Platini, demanding severe action be taken. "The scenes at the end of the game last night were disgraceful. Racism in any form is unacceptable and must be stamped out."

UEFA received regular criticism for its disciplinary action on racist incidents, with serious cases often receiving lesser fines than breaches of marketing regulations. England players were regularly subjected to racist abuse and, although fines were handed down to the Slovakian, Macedonian, Serbian and Hungarian federations in 2002, 2003, 2007 and 2011, respectively, fines ranged from just £16,500 to £34,000 – remember, Nicklas Bendtner was fined £80,000 for wearing branded underwear.

Despite Serbia already being on notice from UEFA – following the conduct of its supporters, and in danger of being thrown out of Euro 2012 – following incidents at a qualifying game against Italy in Genoa where Serbian fans threw flares on to the pitch, burned an Albanian flag and fought with police – Serbia's FA launched an extraordinary attack on Rose, accusing him of "vulgar and unsportsmanlike behaviour." In complete denial, they claimed there were no racist chants during the game.

FA general secretary Alex Horne wrote to UEFA to express his "deep concern [at the] shocking and appalling" behaviour of the Serbian fans. "Our players and staff were subjected to racial abuse, violence, as well as missiles being thrown at them throughout the match. What occurred is inexcusable and not acceptable." However, UEFA's promise to highlight and tackle racism looked a sick joke on the organisation's very own website, UEFA.com, which chose *not* to mention, in any way, the racist chanting and post-match violence. Incredibly and hypocritically, UEFA's own anti-racism week was only days away! The very same website claimed, "UEFA's commitment to a European football landscape free of racism, intolerance and xenophobia will be emphasised through a series of activities."

UEFA did go on to announce that they would investigate the racist chanting but also that they would "commence proceedings against the FA for the improper conduct of the England players at the end of the match," subsequently charging the Football Associations of Serbia *and* England.

Platini was embarrassed by the leniency shown towards Serbia, who were fined just £65,900. Gordon Taylor responded that the totally inadequate fine sent "a very poor message out to the football world." He went on to say that he intended to write to Platini to express his dissatisfaction and would be asking UEFA to exercise its powers to appeal against the wholly disproportionate punishments imposed against Serbia. In addition, the FA gave their strong support to Steven Caulker and Thomas Ince in their appeal against UEFA's decision to suspend them.

Horne, too, condemned the sanctions: "Let's be clear, racism is unacceptable in any form and should play no part in football. The scenes were deplorable, and we do not believe the sanction sends a strong enough message."

14

Twenty Years of KIO

"I'm surprised we're still hearing these things in 2013. It's not the first time in my life I've had to hear things like this but I'm 25 and don't want to take this anymore."

– Kevin-Prince Boateng

In 2013, Kick It Out celebrated 20 years of campaigning for equality and inclusion in football. KIO launched a new app, allowing fans to report discriminatory incidents when in a football setting.

"English Football's Inclusion and Anti-Discrimination Action Plan" was introduced by the FA "to address issues and incidents of discrimination in English football and encourage greater inclusion across the game." Meanwhile, with a 99% majority vote, FIFA member countries approved new anti-racism measures at its Mauritius congress.

Also for its 20th anniversary, KIO hosted a dinner that included guests Gordon Brown and Martin Luther King III. Funds from the event went towards the launch of its new education programme, promoting awareness of the positive influence football can have in communities and addressing issues of discrimination and exclusion.

However, 2014 began with yet another controversy, with the FA charging Nicolas Anelka following his anti-Semitic "quenelle" gesture during a goal celebration. Subsequently, the FA imposed a fine and a five-game ban on the player, and he was suspended by his club, West Bromwich Albion.

In April, KIO published research revealing the true extent of football-related discrimination across social media, cataloguing 134,400 discriminatory posts directed at Premier League clubs and players between August 2014 and March 2015. Their research highlighted growing concerns surrounding online discrimination and, in response, they set up a social media expert group that included representatives from Facebook, Twitter, the Ministry of Justice and the Digital Trust. KIO also released the second version of its news and reporting app, allowing media to be attached to reports as evidence, for the reporting of incidents of football-related discrimination on social media platforms. The app also featured Women's Super League grounds for the first time.

Yaya Touré was at the centre of a racism storm on Twitter after KIO reported abusive tweets sent to the midfielder, who had only just returned to the social media site following a five-month absence. Having received complaints of racism directed at the Ivory Coast player, KIO reported it to police and offered him their "full support." The previous season, the three-time African Footballer of the Year had been the target of racist abuse from CSKA Moscow fans during a City Champions League away win in the Russian capital. Touré expressed his disgust at the behaviour of some of the home crowd and called for black footballers to consider boycotting the Russia 2018 World

Cup if the country's authorities did not stamp out racism. CSKA denied racism took place but were nonetheless punished by UEFA with a partial stadium closure for their next European fixture.

Touré alleged that Pep Guardiola favoured picking white players. Guardiola branded the midfielder's comments as "lies." "We were together for two years and he says it now – he never told me to my face," he told Spain's TV3. Touré left at the end of the season following eight hugely successful years but, in an interview with France Football, claimed Guardiola didn't like picking African players. Kevin De Bruyne leapt to Guardiola's defence. "We had the best season ever, so in the end the coach took the right decision to play with the team who played a lot [and] probably thought he wasn't doing enough, wasn't fit enough. I've never saw something racist in the club, ever."

In his final season with City, Touré made just one Premier League start as the club marched to the title in record-breaking fashion. "Pep did everything to spoil my last season. He was cruel with me," Touré told France Football. "Do you really think he could've been like that with Andrés Iniesta? It got to the point I asked myself if it was because of my colour. I'm not the first. Other Barcelona players asked the question. Maybe us Africans aren't always treated the same by certain people. When you see the problems [he] has often had with African players, everywhere he has been, I ask myself questions. He is too intelligent to be caught. He will never admit it. But the day he picks a team with five Africans in it, I promise I will send him a cake."

Another high-profile racist incident involved a selection of Chelsea supporters travelling to an away-fixture against Paris St-Germain in the Champions League. Souleymane Sylla, a black man, was repeatedly pushed off the carriage of a Paris metro train by supporters while racist chants were sung. Banning orders were imposed on all of them.

Kick It Out, meanwhile, condemned comments made by Port Vale owner, Norman Smurthwaite, in which he admitted that the League 1 side turned down the opportunity to hire Jimmy Floyd Hasselbaink over fears of racist abuse from their own fans.

Jamie Vardy faced allegations of racism after CCTV cameras in a casino recorded him calling a man of East Asian appearance a "Jap" and losing his temper during a high-stakes poker game. According to an eyewitness, Vardy accused the man of spying on his hand, before attacking him with a verbal tirade that featured the racial slur. The video footage, obtained by the *Sun on Sunday*, showed the striker, saying, "Jap. Yo, Jap. Walk on. Walk on ... oi, walk on. Yeah you ... Jap. Walk on."

He then gets to his feet and approaches the man, confronting him with an expletive-ridden barrage of insults, before being held back by his teammates. The man then leaves. Vardy, nicknamed "The Cannon" for his explosive temper tantrums, then becomes embroiled in an argument with another casino guest, who points out that his first target hadn't done anything wrong. Launching into yet another foul-mouthed tirade, the Sheffield-born striker squares up to the man, saying, "What the f*** has it got to do with you?" He then asks the man to step outside for a fight, before being held back again by his Leicester City colleagues.

This was the second embarrassing race storm involving the Premiership side in less than three months. Defender James Pearson – the 22-year-old son of manager Nigel Pearson – striker Tom Hopper, 21, and goalkeeper Adam Smith, 22, were all sent home from the club's pre-season tour after they were filmed directing racist and misogynist abuse at three Thai women during an orgy in Bangkok. The video-clip, later shared among friends back in the UK, showed one woman being called a "slit-eye" and another taunted as "minging." The club, owned by Thai billionaire Vichai Srivaddhanaprabha, sacked all three players.

More controversy marred the KIO 20-year landmark, too, and there were deep concerns that, despite the measures being brought to FIFA, the real underlying issues were still being swept under the carpet – measures were still not in place to ban offending nations from major competitions, or impose points deductions in domestic football.

A high-profile incident on the Continent occurred when AC Milan midfielder Kevin Prince-Boateng took the unprecedented step of walking off the pitch in the 26th minute after he was racially abused with monkey chants by fans in the friendly match against Pro Patria. The Ghanaian international, who ripped off his shirt in disgust during the first half was joined by his teammates and opposition players in walking off. His actions resulted in him being asked to join an anti-racism task force set up by FIFA in light of the incident.

"I don't care what game it is – a friendly, Italian league or Champions League match – I would walk off again," Boateng told CNN. During the match, he'd told the referee three times he was being abused. "If it happens again I'm not going to play anymore. The referee said, 'Don't worry,' but I said 'I do worry, it's not very nice.' I was angry and I was sad [...] There were so many negative emotions that came up with me."

Boateng's teammates – M'Baye Niang, Urby Emanuelson and Sulley Muntari – were also targeted by the monkey-chanting. "I think we should not say all the time that we didn't hear it, or go home and say I didn't hear nothing," said Boateng. "We have to stop, look, and open our eyes. It was 100% racist."

Milan club president Silvio Berlusconi, Italy's former prime minister, supported Boateng's stance and warned that the Serie A team would leave the pitch if they were faced with further anti-social behaviour. Meanwhile, the Italian FA said they would investigate. "No sanction or measure can erase the disdain for an unspeakable and intolerable episode," said its president Giancarlo Abete. "We must react with force and without silence to isolate the few criminals that transformed a friendly match into an uproar that offends all of Italian football."

The episode caused Boateng a few sleepless nights, but he promised to carry on his campaign to highlight the abuse despite the fact that he could experience more in the future. "I love the game so much that I would never quit football because of some stupid people."

PFA CEO Gordon Taylor warned players they could find themselves in trouble if they walked off before the referee decided to abandon a match. "Racist abuse should be reported to the match officials by the player and team captain, and then the crowd should be warned. If the abuse does continue then the officials should abandon the game. The warning will also be an opportunity for responsible fans to influence those who are perpetrating the abuse."

However, Boateng, who said he'd complained to the referee three times before the walk-off, received widespread support, including from players Rio Ferdinand and Patrick Vieira. Although former Netherlands international Clarence Seedorf disagreed with the action, believing that it just empowers the racists.

The international footballers' union FIFPRO also offered its support. Their spokesperson on anti-racism Tony Higgins said, "The players of Milan sent a clear message: if racism does not stop, then football will. We have to draw a line. Kevin-Prince Boateng is also a human being. He is entitled to a working environment free of violence, racism and other forms of discrimination."

Seven years later, a mass walk-out involving players and management was considered by the England team in Bulgaria following racist abuse, including monkey chants and Nazi salutes, directed at black players every time they received the ball. Racist chanting was reported to the match officials midway through the first half, the game briefly stopped and a PA announcement was made calling for the chants to stop. However, the abuse continued, and the match was briefly halted for a second time before half-time. Although the match was completed, England winning 6–0, manager Gareth Southgate confirmed his players had considered walking off if the level of abuse continued into the second half. "The referee came across on two of the occasions where we reported the abuse. With the second, we had a long discussion with the players as there was just four minutes until half-time. We were clear that if there was anything at the beginning of the second half we would have walked straight off and, frankly, we wouldn't have come back. But the officials here threw a fair number of supporters out of the ground and in the second half our football did the talking."

Bulgaria was once more in denial, it seemed. Head coach Krasimir Balakov claimed he hadn't heard anything: "I just talked to the English press, and I told them that if this is proven to be true then we have to be ashamed and apologise for it. But, once again, first it has to be proven to be true." Challenged on why his captain, Ivelin

Popov, remonstrated with supporters at half-time, Balakov responded, "*If* our captain spoke to the fans, it was probably because of the way the team was performing."

The FA called on UEFA to investigate the racist abuse "as a matter of urgency." UK Police Football Unit Chief Superintendent Steve Graham told Sky Sports the racist abuse suffered by England's players was "quite simply the worst racist behaviour" he'd ever seen. Graham told Sky Sports, "The fans [sung] songs where they appeared to make Nazi salutes. Whenever Raheem Sterling went for the ball, we were hearing monkey chants and concerted booing and that happened with the other black players [too]. During the pause in the game a flag with right-wing images was displayed as well."

An unnamed Bulgarian player apologised to the England squad, saying that the racist abuse had been pre-planned and coordinated. Kaveh Solhekol of Sky Sports News, who was part of the travelling media in Sofia gave his account of what happened inside the stadium: "Especially in the first half, when any black England players got the ball, they were subjected to abuse, racist abuse, monkey chants, Nazi salutes. By and large a lot of Bulgarians are very well behaved and not racist. Bulgarian police told us they were neo-Nazis, people with balaclavas on, a lot of them wearing all black uniform. [In] the second half, the situation did calm down a bit, but I was very close to the Bulgarian supporters and we still had the racist abuse, we still had monkey noises every time Raheem Sterling got the ball. When Jadon Sancho came on in the second half the first thing he heard were monkey chants aimed at him. It was a disgraceful night for Bulgarian football."

Solhekol also explained that Bulgarian journalists didn't agree that England players had been the target of abuse.

"They were actually quite angry that the English media were asking questions about racism, and that Southgate was talking about racism. It got to a point where the news conference was briefly interrupted by a Bulgarian journalist who was convinced that what we had seen was not as bad. Also, at the end, when Southgate stood up to leave, one of the Bulgarian cameramen standing next to me actually swore at him."

Southgate advocates using educational tools to battle racism. "For me, with the broader discussion around racism, education is key. I think a lot of our players and former players have spoken brilliantly about that in recent months."

Tottenham's Danny Rose says he "can't wait to see the back of football," that racism and politics in the game were making him look forward to his retirement already! "Gareth Southgate was a bit upset after the game because it was the first time he'd been involved in something like that. He didn't know what the right course of action was," Rose claimed. "He said he was fully behind me if I wanted to walk off. I appreciate that, but I just wanted to get the three points and get out of there as quickly as possible. You see my manager (Mauricio Pochettino, Tottenham) got banned for two games for just being confrontational against (referee) Mike Dean at Burnley, but a country can only get fined a little bit of money for being racist. It's a bit of a farce. Obviously, it's a bit sad, but when countries only get fined what I'd probably spend on a night out in London, what do you expect? When the punishment is not as harsh what do you expect?"

Sterling had advice to kids who have also suffered racist abuse. "Don't keep it to yourself, it's one of the worst things you can do; best thing to do is speak to someone you are close with and trust, get your feelings known. I was that 12-year-old kid who didn't like talking. When you're older you realise you [need] to talk to someone in school, your mum or someone else you trust. Don't let them win, get the issue sorted. The longer you leave it, the worse it will be."

15

E-mail Controversy

"Far too much dirty linen has been exposed to the public gaze."

– Vincent Tan, Cardiff City owner

A *Daily Mail* exposé uncovered a series of explicit and offensive texts exchanged between Cardiff manager Malky Mackay and its head of recruitment Iain Moody. Cardiff had been investigating Mackay and Moody concerning eight controversial transfers, scouring 70,000 text messages and 100,000 e-mails before reporting their findings to the FA.

In July 2012, when Cardiff signed Kim Bo-kuyng, Moody had referred to the South Korean attacker and his representatives as "Five of the b******s including the player" in a text to Mackay, who replied, "Fkn chinkys. Fk it. There's enough dogs in Cardiff for us all to go around." Another text said of football agent Phil Smith: "Go on, fat Phil. Nothing like a Jew that sees money slipping through his fingers." Other texts included referring to Israeli club Maccabi Tel Aviv as "the Jews", an official at an unnamed club was referred to as "a gay snake", "the homo", and one French player as someone "who struck me as an independently minded young homo". Another young player, who was represented by a female agent, was told "I hope she's looking after your needs [...] I bet you'd love a bounce on her falsies."

In August 2012, a French agent tabled a list of possible player targets to the club. Moody's subsequent reply to Mackay read: "He needs to rename his agency the All Blacks." Another text read: "Not many white faces among that lot but worth considering." A picture message captioned "Black Monopoly" – every square showing a "Go To Jail" sign – was then sent to a Cardiff employee. Yet another message says of an African player, "Doesn't look like a good C.V. And he's Nigerian."

Mackay was sacked, the club's billionaire Malaysian owner Vincent Tan saying, "Far too much dirty linen has been exposed to the public gaze but, I stress, not by me." Tan said Mackay's dismissal was necessary for the good of the club. "There's been a good deal of publicity generated by, and about, Mr Malky Mackay for the last few months. I have deliberately not responded to this, hoping that the club can be judged on its football rather than personalised arguments about who said what to whom. I have, however, regretfully concluded that it is no longer fair to the club, its players, its fans and the public more generally for this uncomfortable state of affairs to continue. Cardiff City Football Club means far too much to us all for it to be distracted by this."

Mackay responded through the League Managers' Association (LMA), saying, "I leave with my head held high, having gained a level of experience that, upon reflection, I suspect would have been difficult to find anywhere else in British football." Mackay's removal followed a public row with Tan, who had written to the manager on 16 December asking him to resign or be sacked.

Moody – a long-term friend and colleague of Mackay, who'd worked with him at Watford – was replaced by 23-year-old Kazakh, Alisher Apsalyamov, a friend of Tan's son. Mackay apologised for sending text messages that were "disrespectful of other cultures" a day after the FA launched an investigation into allegations of serious misconduct by the pair.

While admitting the existence of questionable text messages, the LMA defended Mackay, claiming that he was "letting off steam to a friend during some friendly text-message banter." Unsurprisingly, the association's statement drew widespread condemnation, with former Reading striker Jason Roberts, a high-profile anti-racism campaigner, tweeting: "LMA actually wrote this. They are actually being serious! Somebody drafted that ... WOW!"

FARE's Piara Powar tweeted, "The LMA defending the indefensible. Why would you put out something so utterly ridiculous? Because you haven't a clue." LMA responded, again defending Mackay, saying that "a couple of one-line texts that were, with the benefit of hindsight, very regrettable and disrespectful [...] were two text messages sent in private at a time Malky felt under great pressure."

Rio Ferdinand tweeted to ask, "Who wrote the #LMA statement???" and described it as "f****** disgraceful".

Together with the London law firm Mishcon de Reya, Tan compiled a dossier including the racist, homophobic and sexist text messages, as well as information on a number of transfers. Subsequently, Moody stepped down from his role as sporting director of Crystal Palace, who also shelved Mackay's appointment as manager. Cardiff also took the LMA to task, reminding them that its members are bound to a code of conduct incorporated into their contracts, which includes: "A Manager shall not use racist or other discriminatory language [and] should demonstrate to Players and other employees under his control that discrimination in any form is unacceptable."

QPR manager Harry Redknapp defended Mackay, saying, "He hasn't murdered anyone, he hasn't raped anyone and he's not a paedophile. Suddenly, everyone is an angel [...] I'm not condoning what he's done but show me someone who has never made a mistake and I will show you a liar."

Redknapp's comments drew scorn from KIO education and development manager Troy Townsend: "[It] shows a lack of understanding about the situation. These are really sensitive issues and you have to respect the reasons behind them. He's almost saying, 'It ain't that bad, is it?' but, unfortunately, for some people, it is."

The FA, meanwhile, chose to take no action against Premier League CEO Richard Scudamore when sexist e-mails from his work inbox were leaked to the press, citing that it had a policy of not acting on private communications.

However, KIO's Lord Ouseley said all governing bodies *should* take action against all proven cases of prejudice and bigotry. "These revelations are further confirmation of how football is tainted with racism, sexism, homophobia and anti-Semitism, and the culture which continues to exist throughout the game and in wider society as a whole. The reality is that these views are most dangerously held by those people in positions of power, and the football establishment knows and condones it."

Ouseley also condemned Dave Whelan after the Wigan owner made offensive comments about Jewish and Chinese people during a *Guardian* interview. Defending his appointment of manager Malky Mackay, Whelan claimed, "Jewish people chase money more than everybody else" and argued that the word "Ch**k" wasn't offensive. Speaking to BBC Sport, Ouseley, referring to Whelan being from an older generation, said, "We must recognise as a diverse society that we have people of all backgrounds, ages and characteristics. Age is no excuse. But people say things that are of a different age [and] we have to help [them] come to terms with modern expectations."

16

Social Media

"For black footballers, being on Instagram is not even fun. You're not enjoying your profile. I don't even have Twitter on my phone anymore because it's almost certain that you're going to get some sort of abuse."
— Wilfried Zaha, Crystal Palace forward

Racial abuse directed at players, and others, through social media has long been a problem. And, today, Crystal Palace forward Wilfried Zaha continues to receive some of the vilest racial abuse directed at him on his social media accounts on Twitter and Instagram. To date, Zaha has reported a total of 50 accounts to police.

Ian Wright
Ian Wright has also experienced racial abuse on social media – it happens "on a daily basis" he says. The BBC pundit shared some of the abuse he'd received after posting on Twitter in support of the BLM movement. Above a screen grab on Twitter of some of the abuse, he wrote: "These aren't isolated incidents!!! It's daily!! This is what I received for posting and talking about

#BlackLivesMatter yesterday. The abuse started a week earlier, the taunting is terrifying. Coming back and back again."

Police contacted Wright after he revealed the vile messages on social media and a teenage boy handed himself in to police.

The messages were all sent from the same account, and contained a litany of sickening remarks: "You are a ****"; "I hate you ... I hate your mom ... I hate your dad ... I hate your brothers and sisters ... I hate all your family"; "You cotton-picking black ****"; " You are a f****** monkey; "C*** c**n monkey n*****"; "Your like 65 years old if I get corona I will cough in your face and give you your death sentence"; "R9 ronaldo will always be better than you ... Just know that ... And he ended his career early with an injury ... But will always be better ... Than you ****".

Wright said: "I know I'm not meant to look at them, but these messages still hit me so hard, man. This is a child!!! He has a direct message to me on IG [Instagram]. This kid [h]as a direct line into me & is able to send this without any worry."

The player turned media pundit quickly received plenty of support, while the Metropolitan Police publicly responded, tweeting: "Hi. If you wish to report this incident, please DM us."

Wright called on others who'd been racially abused on social media to speak up. "Let's show these social media companies how bad this has got, it's ridiculous!!! So easy for them!!" he wrote. "If you or a black friend has had online racist abuse then please post a tweet with the hashtags #NoConsequences and #BlackLivesMatter."

Arsenal fan and *GMB* host Piers Morgan responded: "My God, this is disgusting. Who are his parents? Who are his teachers? So sorry you've had to endure this racist filth, Legend." Fellow TV host Dan Walker also replied: "I'm so sorry you have to see and read that. I'm sure you also know there is an awful lot of love for you out there and 99.99% of people will be disgusted and ashamed that you have received those messages." Meanwhile, Sky Sports presenter Bianca Westwood said: "Absolutely shocking. I'm sorry this happened to you. I don't understand this hatred or where it comes from, especially in someone so young but I hope he is dealt with appropriately! Wrighty, you are much loved."

Wright has often spoken out on racist abuse in football. After black players were targeted in Bulgaria, he said, "Look at that, it says everything you need to know about UEFA. We're looking at a stadium here where half of it is closed with banners that have done nothing. That's the extent of what they feel they are doing to combat racism in this country. The fact is, we've seen a set of people who have got no respect, they don't care, and UEFA are doing nowhere near enough. I'm so proud we're doing what we're doing at the moment. The thing about it is you feel physically sick, but you've got to continue playing through that. What we're seeing now is that you don't and that's what is good.

"It's a terrible day for Bulgarian people and how they are being represented but it's a great day in respects of trying to tackle racism because we can see over in that stand, those banners mean nothing. What we're seeing is a set of fans who do not care and need educating. As a black player, we've heard it for many years about walking off, it's something you don't want to do because you do need your white players to do that for you, so you can go off together, how powerful it is, that will do something."

Wilfried Zaha

Just last year, 2020, Crystal Palace forward Wilfried Zaha shared some of the truly horrific racist abuse he'd received from an Aston Villa fan ahead of a July Palace–Villa match on his Instagram account. Zaha tweeted, saying, "Woke up to this today" above images that included one of the American, white-supremacist hate group, the Ku Klux Klan, and a mocked-up Kellogg's Corn Flakes packet depicting a man with a blacked-up face rebranded as "C★★n Flakes", as well as a message that read: "You better not score tomorrow you black c★★★ or I'll come to your house dressed as a ghost."

West Midlands Police later announced they'd arrested a 12-year-old boy – himself also a victim of a society that continues to show children that black people are inferior – in connection with the incident.

Zaha's manager Roy Hodgson described the abuse as, "cowardly and despicable. There's literally no excuse; there's no excuse at all." Speaking to Sky Sports, the former England boss added that the need to continue to raise awareness of the suffering caused by racial abuse was especially "important at the moment, anyway, with the Black Lives Matter movement and everyone […] making such an effort to eradicate this behaviour."

The posts received by Zaha came just two weeks after the Premier League had launched a new system that allows Premier League players, coaches, managers and family members to report such abuse and pursue legal action on behalf of any recipient.

Describing what Zaha had been subjected to as "completely unacceptable," the Premier League launched an investigation through the new reporting procedure and affirmed that they stood alongside the player "in opposing this, and discrimination in any form."

Meanwhile a statement from Kick It Out chairman Sanjay Bhandari, read: "The most saddening part of this abuse is that it is not surprising. This kind of disgusting targeted racist abuse has become normalised on social media. Twitter, Facebook and Instagram are like the Wild West. To address this, we need social media companies to do more [...] and a concerted and sustained effort between government, law enforcement and the football authorities to prioritise the gathering of evidence and prosecution of online hate."

Aston Villa tweeted support for Zaha and his club and said they were working with the police investigation and that "when the culprit is identified, AVFC will issue a lifetime ban."

Zaha has now reported a total of 50 accounts to police. "Every time I'm scared to even look up my direct messages because it could be filled with anything," he told CNN. "For black footballers for instance, being on Instagram is not even fun for us anymore. You're not enjoying your profile. I don't even have Twitter on my phone anymore because it's almost certain that you're going to get some sort of abuse."

He says social media companies also need to do more. "I got racially abused after the stuff that I got before and it's like, what happens after that account gets blocked? Then they just make a new one straight after. I feel like with everything that we do in life, with everything we register to, we have to give some sort of ID, so why is it not the same with Instagram? Why is it not the same with Twitter?"

And it goes on ...

Alex Scott has discussed how social media abuse made her turn to drink since her retirement from football. She is now a respected pundit on the BBC and Sky and has appeared on *Strictly Come Dancing* following an outstanding playing career for England and Arsenal. In conversation with Troy Deeney as part of the Heads Up campaign focusing on mental health, Scott revealed the extent to which the online "trolling" affected her.

"When I retired, getting trolling, I found that I was turning to drink to try and hide everything, hide what I was feeling. I didn't tell anyone," Scott said. "I didn't tell my mum because I didn't want her to worry or put that stress on her. I was just that person (who thought), 'I can look after myself, I can deal with stuff,' but, obviously, sometimes that's the wrong way. I got to a dark place and it was over Christmas, that's when I was like, 'I can't carry on like this, it's not me, I need to seek help,' and that led me into therapy. I want to take that stigma away from it. Now when I talk about mental health, straight away I'm smiling because I know what it's done for me to leave that place. I'm content. I'm happy, and I've used the tools that I've learned to be in that place."

Chelsea striker Tammy Abraham has been subjected to similarly disgusting online abuse twice during the 2019/20 season – first, following a penalty shoot-out miss during the Super Cup defeat to Liverpool, which left the young player's mother in tears; and, more recently, following Chelsea's shock 0–3 defeat away to Sheffield United. A number of fans – many with Chelsea-related avatars and usernames – branded the England striker "Apebraham". Speaking back in September, Abraham said: "I remember speaking to my mum, she was emotional, she was in tears. It's obviously not nice, seeing your son getting abused. My mum was just thinking, 'Why him?' For me, I am a strong character, it doesn't affect me as much, but it could affect people who don't have my personality."

England's first black player Viv Anderson knows racism is back in the game and has been critical of the punishments handed out to fans who hurl vile abuse.

Speaking on the Saga podcast, He said, "It's a concern for me. I look at the Raheem Sterling thing – he was going to get a ball and then somebody racially abused him – and it went on for weeks and weeks. I think the fines are bordering on ridiculous. When the England team go abroad, it's more prevalent there, and I think the fines are bordering on pathetic. If you said to one of the associations, 'Well, the fine is £6 million,' I think they'd get people out of that stadium very quickly. They wouldn't be welcomed back. The fines have got to be more substantial."

Anderson claimed fellow high-profile former professionals such as Ian Wright had not done enough to support black players and eliminate racism from the game. "I've been to the FA, I've said, 'You have to get these people involved, the people who've been there, seen it, got the T-Shirt.' All these people like Ian Wright are not involved in football – they've been doing stuff on the TV, but they're not involved in helping the next generation of footballers and black footballers. These people have got vast experience of playing at top level, winning things, playing for England – they should be passing their experience onto these kids, but nobody does anything about it."

Elsewhere, *Match of the Day 2* pundit Jermaine Jenas voiced his view that social media companies must do more.

Sheffield United shared an image from David McGoldrick's Instagram account showing racial abuse, with the Blades striker writing "2020 and this is life." "This cannot continue," wrote the club. "Something needs to change."

The disgusting abuse reads: "You f****** dirty n*****. Your n***** life defo doesn't matter. F*** you ya bold c*** WHERE WERE YOU WHEN YOU PLAYED MANURE [Manchester United] YOU F****** S*** APE."

McGoldrick scored his first Premier League goals in a 3–0 win over Chelsea at Bramall Lane to move into the Premier League's top six. Sheffield United added: "As a club we will support David McGoldrick and will do all we can to find the perpetrator of this disgusting message. We will work with the relevant authorities to ensure the person behind this post is brought to justice."

The Football Association of Ireland condemned the "appalling" abuse and offered its support to McGoldrick, who made his international debut in 2014. A spokesperson added: "Such behaviour is appalling and cannot be tolerated by football or society." South Yorkshire Police were in contact with Sheffield United and "will continue to work with the club in relation with this matter."

Sheffield United boss Chris Wilder commented: "David did the right thing straight away [by reporting it]. Hopefully the authorities can take it forward. He'll be deeply disappointed. He has my, the players' and the football club's full support. People can't stay silent. I'm proud that David's flagged it up – and Wilf Zaha. Nobody should have to receive and go through this. They've been very brave in what they're doing and they should have everybody's support, 100%. It's ridiculous that these things are still happening. I'm not the biggest fan of social media. More has to be done by the people in power. We have to work in conjunction with the authorities to punish people who feel they have the right to go online and abuse people. Why should anyone be abused? Zaha and McGoldrick were very brave in what they've done and should have everyone's support."

Zaha called for "action", "education" and "change". He thanked police, and also thanked fans for their "love and support." In a social media message he added: "People need to understand that whatever your age, your behaviour and your words come with consequences and you cannot hide behind social media. It is important that social media companies do as they did yesterday and seek out these individuals and remove them. Very disappointed we didn't get a better result yesterday, but I wanted to come on here to thank you for all your messages of support. I would also like to thank West Midlands Police for their swift action in making an arrest.

Zaha said it was "not the first time" he had received similar messages and said footballers are being racially abused "every day." Zaha tweeted: "It's not enough to be disgusted by these messages I received and move on. It isn't enough to just say #notoracism. We need action, we need education, things need to change."

In response to the arrest, the PFA said: "The posts sent to Wilfried Zaha ahead of today's game were sickening and abhorrent. Players continue to be the target of relentless abuse online. While we're satisfied that the offender has been arrested, the fact a 12-year-old would send such material is deeply troubling. Incidents, such as this, only strengthen the case for tighter regulation of social media companies. We call on the authorities to accelerate the process of appointing Ofcom as the regulator to oversee the online harms legislation."

The PFA held talks with social media companies. Iffy Onuora, of the players' union's coaching and equalities executive, said the talks with Instagram, Facebook and Twitter have been "broadly supportive." Onuora said: "This is just a reminder that there's an awful lot of work that still needs to be done educationally. It is a big challenge, regarding social media. If you compare other media – print journalism has been around centuries – we have got to a stage where they are regulated. Social media is barely out of its teens. It's a phenomenon relatively recent in history.

We're not looking to close down something that has been a force for good but with anything that has assumed the degree of power that it has now, there's responsibility with that. That all comes with regulation. Unfortunately, social media can't be any different from other media and we need to look at how we do that. Colleagues of mine have had conversations with Twitter, Facebook and Instagram. Those conversations have been broadly supportive of what we're trying to say. But maybe there is still a slight difference over how we do it and who does the regulating. I'm sure, like most companies, they'd like to self-regulate but I think it's gone beyond that, given the content is still there and accessible."

Zaha was again targeted with vile racist abuse on social media. This time, he shared the messages in a video, bemoaning the lack of real action from Twitter and Instagram. He called for users on social media to have to verify their identity so they cannot hide when sending anonymous abuse. In the video message, he said: "This is why I don't tend to talk even though I get stupid racist messages every day of my life. But the other day I thought, 'I'm going to out this person.' It happened to be a 12-year-old. How can you have such hatred at 12 and send those type of things? It doesn't make a difference to me how old he is. Anyway, social platforms like Instagram, Twitter – to make a change for people, to not be able to do this stuff and be held accountable for the stuff they send – everyone should put their details in, their proper details, where you live, everything to be able to be able to come on an account so we don't get these messages. Look at these messages I'm still getting." Zaha displayed the horrendous abuse.

The first read: "A n***** bragging about a wee lad arrested, that's a bit sad innit." Another abuser wrote: "Do n** n**** feel any sort of sympathy?"

Zaha continued: "All kind and supportive stuff people have been saying but I want action, I want change. Instagram, Twitter, unless people give their proper full details, they should not be allowed to make an account, because that's all cowards do. These stupid racist cowards, that's all they do, hide behind accounts. And it is going to carry on – we can put it everywhere, we can put it on the news, wherever but it's going to carry on. So yeah until these things are changed, I don't want to hear nothing. Sorry."

Jude Bellingham and Alfredo Morelos

Jude Bellingham received online racist abuse following his final appearance for Birmingham. The 17-year-old, who joined Borussia Dortmund for a fee that was said to exceed £30m, posted a message he received on Twitter, which the Blues described as "appalling." A club statement read: "Birmingham City Football Club abhors all forms of racism. Jude and his family are receiving our full support and we are liaising with West Midlands Police over this matter."

Part of the abuse read, "Black people only think about money." Police were also investigating racist abuse directed at Rangers striker Alfredo Morelos on social media. The Colombian was streaming a live video for fans on Instagram where users could post messages and police were "made aware of offensive comments posted online." Morelos has been with the Rangers squad in France, where they played two friendlies as they prepared for the new Scottish Premiership season.

"I'm not doing this for attention, or for anyone to feel sorry for me," Morelos said. "But these are fans of *our* club. I know it's a minority and I'm not suggesting otherwise, however as a majority who stand by us we need to make a stand to be heard. What I will say is that us players see these comments and they hurt us!"

Rangers backed their players in taking a knee, after defender Connor Goldson called out a minority of fans for "disgusting" comments following his show of support for BLM. Goldson posted a photo on social media of himself and teammates kneeling on the pitch before a friendly in Lyon.

Rangers say any fan "unable to support our players" is not welcome at Ibrox. The club also condemned the racist abuse directed at Alfredo Morelos. Responding to comments on Instagram, Goldson said Rangers players were "hurt" by the backlash as they show solidarity for Black Lives Matter.

17

Highlights and Low Times

"Monday night was one of the highlights of my career with Wycombe. However, what should have been an evening of joy and excitement quickly turned into one of anger and frustration."

– Adebayo Akinfenwa, Wycombe striker

Back in 2006, Kieron Dyer believed he was "used" by Newcastle to defend Turkish teammate Emre Belözoğlu from allegations of racism because he is black. Emre was charged with using racially aggravated language towards Everton defender Joseph Yobo during a Premier League match on 30 December.

Emre was alleged to have called Yobo "a f***ing n*****". Yobo did not hear what Emre said but Tim Howard and Joleon Lescott accused the Turkey midfielder of racist abuse.

Emre always denied the allegations. His agent, Ahmet Bulut, told the *Guardian*: "He is so, so upset because this is the first time in his whole career or life that anything like this has been said about him. He is absolutely distraught but knows these claims are not true."

Emre was joined at the hearing held to investigate the matter by then Newcastle manager Glenn Roeder, chairman Freddy Shepherd, chief operating officer Russell Cushing and teammate Nicky Butt. Match referee Dermot Gallagher had not heard any racist abuse but was informed of the incident and reported it to the FA.

Emre was cleared in March 2007. A statement from an FA disciplinary commission said, "Having heard all the evidence presented, and having regard to the standard of proof agreed with both the FA and Newcastle United, we were not satisfied that the charge was proved."

Dyer, in hindsight, is uncomfortable with how he was used as part of Emre's defence. "There was a time at Newcastle, we played Everton away and we had Emre and there was a massive skirmish with him and Yobo and Joleon Lescott was going f****** ballistic," Dyer told THE KICK OFF. "He was saying, 'He [Emre] has said something racist about Yobo,' and they were trying to get to him in the tunnel. I've never seen Joleon so mad. They reported it to the referee and there was a big, massive FA hearing. Because I was on the pitch and probably because I was black, Newcastle asked me to go as a witness for Emre. I went and I had to tell the truth, which was I didn't hear anything racist. I told my side of the story. The more I think about that – just from Joleon's reaction, he wouldn't go mad for that – and knowing what I do now and maturing, I really regret going to that hearing. Even though Emre was on my team, even though I didn't hear nothing. You don't have that reaction for nothing."

Asked if he felt used by Newcastle, Dyer said: "Of course I was. Of course I was. Emre was a teammate and a friend and I didn't hear nothing, it wasn't like I lied on oath for him. I didn't hear nothing. But knowing what I know and just seeing the reaction, if that had happened the way I am today, seeing Joleon's reaction and the club asked me to be a witness, I'd say no."

Emre was accused of racism three times during his three-year spell at Newcastle but denied them all and was never found guilty by the FA. As well as the Yobo incident, Emre was accused of racially abusing Bolton forward El-Hadji Diouf in October 2006. In March 2007, Emre faced an allegation of racism from Watford defender Alhassan Bangura. Later in his career, Emre was given a two-and-a-half-month suspended prison sentence for a racist insult against Didier Zokora during a match for Fenerbahçe against Trabzonspor in April 2012. The court said the Fenerbahçe midfielder's act constituted an insult crime of "religious, racist, ethnic, sexist or sectarian discrimination."

Dyer does not consider John Terry to be racist for what he said in an on-field exchange with Anton Ferdinand, as he regularly heard racist remarks from white players during his career. "With the John Terry and Rio thing – Ashley and Rio fell out because Ashley defended John Terry in court," Dyer, who played alongside Terry for England and was a QPR player when the incident happened, said. "When people ask me, 'Is John Terry a racist?', I don't think John Terry is a racist, I think John Terry said a racist thing. Anton said, 'You bang your teammate's missus,' he got angry and said, 'You black c***' in retaliation. He said a racist thing which is wrong. But I've seen John Terry, I've been around John Terry, do I think he is racist? No."

Dyer recalled his infamous on-field clash with his then Newcastle teammate Lee Bowyer. "Everyone would bring up, 'Did you fight with Lee Bowyer because he's a racist?' No, Lee Bowyer is not a racist."

Dyer said that the dressing room culture in his era saw white players make "black jokes" in the dressing room. Dyer came through the ranks with Ipswich in 1996 before joining Newcastle in 1999. He joined West Ham in 2007 and had spells at QPR and Middlesbrough, winning 33 caps for England. "There have been times in changing rooms where white players have made black jokes, but I just think it is a dressing room culture – it was then. You could get away with saying certain things. I know they're not a racist so I could take it as a joke. But if I thought someone was being racist I would have them up on it. But hundreds of times there have been times in changing rooms where that has happened. Probably in today's football that doesn't happen so much."

Wycombe's Adebayo Akinfenwa was racially abused during a League One play-off match against Fleetwood.

The striker discovered after the game that he was referred to as a "fat water buffalo" by the opposition. "I believe it dehumanises me as a black man by associating me to a water buffalo, a dark animal, in a derogatory manner," Akinfenwa said in a statement. The FA were made aware of the allegation.

Fleetwood were beaten 6–3 on aggregate after the game at Adams Park finished 2–2, but it was a night of wildly contrasting emotions; the joy of reaching the play-off final soured by feeling "dehumanised".

Akinfenwa took to Twitter to issue a statement: "Monday night was one of the highlights of my career with Wycombe. However, what should have been an evening of joy and excitement quickly turned into one of anger and frustration. Regardless of whether or not there was deliberate racial intent by using that language, if we are to make real and long-standing change then we must strive to educate each other about these issues."

Akinfenwa, who suffered racist abuse earlier in his career while playing in Lithuania, believes education is "ultimately the key" to tackling racial discrimination.

Players and staff across all four top divisions in England took a knee before kick-off at all matches in support of the Black Lives Matter movement. "I have always vowed to stand up and have a voice when it comes to racism," said the former Swansea, Northampton, Gillingham and AFC Wimbledon man. "We must work together to ensure those who have not and do not face racial prejudice understand that what may appear to be them to be a throwaway remark can have such a big and hurtful impact. I feel passionately about raising this because we as a sport and as society must wake up. We must do more.

"Taking a knee, supporting social media campaigns and wearing a logo on our kits is a start, but it is not enough. We must all play our part."

A statement from Wycombe said: "The club fully stands by its players and supports all campaigns to end discrimination."

Rise in Hate Crimes

In 2015, Kick It Out received 402 reports of discrimination, up from 393 in 2014–15. Of those, 135 were in the professional game. The most significant rise in reporting concerned social media, with 194 reported incidents, an increase of 18%. The report came just one day after new figures suggested a 20% rise in hate crimes generally in England and Wales.

Calling once again on sponsors and football authorities to work together, KIO's Lord Ouseley said education projects would help, citing the sport's ability to "bring people of all backgrounds together to play and participate." However, he added this warning: "Young people are vulnerable to the increased levels of prejudice and hate which has been evidenced by increases in reported hate crimes and incidents."

The 402 incidents reported to the organisation represented a year-on-year rise since it first started collating statistics in 2012–13, and:

- of the 135 incidents relating to the professional game, 122 involved fans
- 13 were allegations against players, coaches and managers – almost double the number from last year;
- there was a 2% fall in the number incidents at grassroots level, to 73
- 54% of incidents related to racial discrimination, 20.5% to faith, 17% to sexual orientation and 7% to gender.

"The game is under the microscope and every week incidents of hate are being witnessed [and this] is being exacerbated by the recent worrying levels of hate and prejudice in society that will negatively impact on the sport," KIO said.

Reports are made to Kick It Out through its website, telephone hotline, e-mail, social media and mobile phone app. The FA's latest figures show 902 allegations of discrimination were made last season, a fall of six from last year. The total includes those incidents reported to Kick It Out.

KIO again called for more diversity among football's leaders, pointing to the domination of white men at the top of the game, but it seemed no one was listening, meaning nothing was about to change. Dwight Yorke said of the experience of black players, "Yes, you're doing all your coaching, all your badges but, when it comes to getting a [managerial] job, you're not even getting an interview."

Yorke won three titles under Sir Alex Ferguson at Old Trafford and an impressive 123 Premier League goals in spells at United, Villa, Blackburn, Birmingham and Sunderland. He became assistant manager at Trinidad and Tobago but failed to be handed the top job at any club despite completing all of his coaching badges. He was convinced his skin colour hindered his chances of landing a role in England. He'd wanted the vacant job at former team Aston Villa but could not even get an interview before Steve Bruce was appointed.

"I'm still looking to get in," Yorke said. "I've done all the coaching badges at St George's and the one thing I find very difficult, let alone get a job, is to even get an interview. I'm finding it very, very difficult at the moment. It's often been discussed, no one has really taken it up, but I do have a tendency when I speak to everybody. [Black players are] constantly hitting a wall."

At the time, there were no black bosses in the top flight, with only Jimmy Floyd Hasselbaink and Chris Hughton in the Championship and, although the Rooney Rule in American football required all NFL teams to interview racial-minority candidates for head coach roles, no such regulation existed yet in the English game.

In 2017, Millwall fans subjected South Korean striker Son Heung-min to racist taunts during the FA Cup quarter-final at White Hart Lane. Shouts of "DVD [...] he's selling three for a fiver" were heard every time Son took possession. He answered those bigots with a hat-trick.

"Millwall isn't alone in this [...] with fans at nearly every club [who] think it's still acceptable, it's only a bit of banter," KIO CEO Roisin Wood said. "I've had people come to me and say, 'You're overreacting' – I'm *not* overreacting. These are professionals, playing a game [and] this is the wrong language to be using in 2017."

Kick It Out next accused UEFA of not taking tough enough action against Serbia, after Partizan Belgrade's

Brazilian midfielder Everton Luiz was subjected to monkey chants throughout a top-flight league game against FK Rad.

Troy Townsend said, "They claimed it was only ten fans and they were ejected, but it lasted for ninety minutes; so, if FIFA and UEFA aren't going to take the strongest stand with Serbia, I'd stop them playing in World Cups, Euro qualifiers and everything. Don't give them paltry fines, because they are obviously not bothered. What will bother them is not taking part in World Cup or European Championship."

Stand-up Gone Sour
Roy Hodgson was forced to issue an apology over a joke he made during half-time in England's 2–0 win against Poland, about a space monkey and winger Andros Townsend. His intention was to encourage right-back Chris Smalling to play the ball more frequently to winger Townsend. At least one player was shocked by the remark, believing it could be perceived as racist.

Apparently, the joke was popular at NASA. It goes like this:

After early missions sending monkeys up into space, NASA decide to send a man, too. The intercom crackles …
NASA: Monkey, fire the retros.
NASA (A LITTLE LATER): Monkey, check the solid fuel supply.
NASA (LATER STILL): Monkey, check the life support systems for the man.
Man: When do I get to do something?
NASA: In fifteen minutes – feed the monkey.

Hodgson used the joke to try to emphasise to the England team that Townsend could be critical to the victory.

Hodgson had lavished praise on the impact of Townsend. The FA did not respond to the joke, beyond saying that they'd been made aware of the manager's statement. Stan Collymore said that it'd be ridiculous for anyone to take offence at what he'd said. "Someone leaked it and I bet 100% confident that no player was offended, not one. If they are, do explain why. Racism is hard enough to keep on the agenda as it is, without making everyone think a legitimate space tale should be a cause for offence." West Ham United manager Sam Allardyce agreed. "We're a politically correct country, so we always have to be careful about what we say today, but if we continue to hype it up and promote everything in the press, nobody will be able to say a word very shortly and we'll have to keep ourselves quiet and ourselves to ourselves and not express our opinions."

Hodgson was mortified by the interpretation and apologised for any offence caused. "There was absolutely no intention on my part to say anything inappropriate. I made this clear straight away to Andros in the dressing room." For his part, Andros Townsend said he couldn't understand what all the fuss was about. "No offence was meant and none was taken! It's not even newsworthy!" Wayne Rooney agreed and tweeted "Seen the story on Roy this morning. He done nothing wrong. This is ridiculous."

Reginald D. Hunter
Talking of jokes, PFA chairman Clarke Carlisle had to deliver a huge apology after Reginald D. Hunter used the N-word at its glittering awards ceremony in London. Known for his controversial comedy act, the black American entertainer nonetheless shocked guests by using the phrase several times during the dinner at the Grosvenor House Hotel.

Carlisle said he'd been embarrassed by the decision to book Hunter for the function at a time when the game was embroiled in several high-profile racial incidents. Issuing an unreserved apology, Carlisle said, "We made a really gross error of judgment in who we selected for our entertainment. There are some people who found it funny and some who didn't. Some people found it uncomfortable and some people found it disgusting. I'm embarrassed that we put it up there. After all that has gone on in football over the past few years, with everything that we purport to stand for, his set was inappropriate. It's a really delicate issue and one we've had real problems with, so I really can't understand why we [booked him]. It wasn't a comedy club. I'm not going to lambast Reginald, that's his act, and we should have been aware of that. We simply shouldn't have booked him."

18

Youth Team Players

"I was warming up with a couple of teammates. We were all black and there were monkey chants [...] about ten of them doing it. I didn't know what to do [so] I told my coach [who] went straight to the organisers to tell them what had happened and get the people who were doing it kicked out."

– Rhian Brewster, 17-year-old England junior

The *Guardian* reported that three former Chelsea youth team footballers had launched legal claims against the club after allegations that black players were subjected to racism, physical attacks and one instance when Graham Rix allegedly threw a cup of hot coffee in the face of one of the young prospects.

Rix, youth team coach at the time, was named alongside Gwyn Williams, who'd served at Stamford Bridge for over 25 years. Following a seven-month investigation, the police concluded there was insufficient evidence to take any action, but Chelsea launched its own inquiry – offering in-house counselling to at least one of the players – while the FA's safeguarding team interviewed two of them. Chelsea said, "We take allegations of this nature extremely seriously [and] are absolutely determined to do the right thing, to fully support those affected, assist the authorities and support their investigations."

Behind the scenes evidence submitted to the FA described it as a "feral environment" for some of the black players in the youth team with one allegation being that they were treated "like a race of f***ing dogs." At a Chelsea youth team fixture in Spain, Rix is said to have humiliated one of the black players by substituting him with the reserve goalkeeper. As the player was showering afterwards, Rix is alleged to have shouted, "If his heart was as big as his cock, he'd be a great player that ran more," and that he should've been "the only person in the whole stadium to be able to enjoy the 40-degree heat [because] blacks were always winning the long-distance Olympic events in the heat ... if they weren't chucking spears." There were also allegations of the player being called, among other racist insults, "darkie", "nig-nog", "black bastard", "wog, "midnight" and "jigaboo" by one or other of the accused, and being told by Williams to "F*** off back to Africa [and] sell drugs or rob old grannies." Williams would also punish the player by telling him to "go and clean my office, Richard Pryor – shine my shoes like a good wog" or "Pick up your lip, it's dragging on the floor."

When the player left Chelsea for another team, his new manager wondered why such a talented young footballer from one of England's top clubs appeared to have lost all self-confidence, as part of a written report he submitted that formed part of the legal claim. The player in question is "a good professional who always had a beaming smile," he wrote, "but I always felt behind that smile was a person who clearly had his confidence knocked out of him at Chelsea. Whoever was responsible for that, I don't know.

He never gave me a problem. He was always on time and always gave his all." The player described himself as having "the weight of the world on my shoulders at 16," adding that the distressing effects continued to affect him in his adult life. Every day, he says, he'd walk to Chelsea's training ground, thinking, "Oh, my God, I can't wait for this day to be over [...] I was so low. Even dragging this up now, it really affects me."

In his interview with FA Safeguarding, the player further accused Williams of "flicking my scrotum, flicking my penis, patting my bum" while still a minor. He says he tried to speak on the phone about his experiences years later with FA CEO Graham Kelly but that he wasn't even put through. He accused the FA of having failed him by "not protecting me as a minor." According to his account, the racist abuse started when he joined Chelsea on schoolboy terms. "Even [when I was] 12 or 13," the player explained, "[Williams would say] 'You little black bastard, you coon, you little wog, how are you doing? [...] Hey, look at the fucking blackies here, then. Fucking rubber-lips. Look at their fucking big noses. You black bastard. Been fucking robbing cars, have you?' Let me tell you something – that is the most demoralising feeling you could ever have. I knew it was unacceptable, but I was a minor. When you're in that position, where this guy is a powerful guy at the club, I didn't know how to handle it. I thought it would stop. I just didn't know how to handle it." He says the name-calling and racist stereotyping was constant and that he often wanted to speak to Ruud Gullit about it, but that they didn't act in this way in front of him. The player also told the safeguarding officials that he was physically abused on several occasions. One time he was struck on the back of the head by Rix for asking him to stop "digging me out," and later, in a training session, kicked twice while sitting on the floor, while Rix was singing the Billy Ocean song "When the Going Gets Tough". During a separate training session, he says Rix hurled the ball into his face from a throw-in, leaving him on the floor with a bleeding nose. On one occasion when he decided to stand up to the bullying after the coach asked him if he'd "tried to f*** any of our white girls" at the weekend. On that occasion, Rix allegedly threw a cup of coffee into the teenager's face. The teenager also asked Rix to stop making his sister feel uncomfortable by making suggestive remarks. Allegedly, the coach went red with anger and replied, "I'll do whatever I want and if I fancy a bit of black I guarantee her black arse will get it," then punched the young player in the scrotum.

In 1999, Graham Rix admitted to two charges of unlawful sex with a 15-year-old girl and indecent assault. He was sentenced to twelve months in prison – serving six – and put on the Sex Offenders' Register for ten years. Despite this, he was reinstated by Chelsea immediately upon his release from Wandsworth Prison – he was first-team coach when they won the 2000 FA Cup, served as assistant-manager to Gullit and held a brief spell as caretaker-manager following Vialli's departure, before managing Portsmouth, Oxford United and Hearts, as well as coaching at the Glenn Hoddle Academy in Spain and a brief spell managing in Trinidad. His last managerial job in England was at AFC Portchester of the Wessex League Premier Division.

Gwyn Williams joined Chelsea in 1979 and followed Ken Bates to Leeds United as technical director. His period at Chelsea included spells as assistant manager to Claudio Ranieri and in the scouting department for José Mourinho, before leaving in 2006. Williams was also accused of making homophobic comments to Graeme Le Saux. "He'd wander up to me before training, and say, 'Come on, poof, get your boots on,'" Le Saux wrote in his 2007 autobiography. Williams was dismissed by Leeds for gross misconduct in 2013 after e-mailing pornographic images of women to a number of colleagues, including a female receptionist.

Following the newspaper reports, Eddie Johns, the solicitor acting for Rix and Williams, issued a statement on his clients' behalf denying "all and any allegations of racial or other abuse," adding that the pair had cooperated with the police investigation and the FA. The allegations had not been made directly to his clients, he said, but they would deal with them, if they were.

By May, seven former Chelsea players had accused either Williams or Rix of historical abuse. The BBC spoke to four players, one of whom alleged he'd been subjected to an "exhaustive list" of racial slurs. Another player described Chelsea as "institutionally racist." Their claims were supported by two white witnesses – former players Gary Baker and Grant Lunn. Baker, who played for the Chelsea youth team from 1981 to 1985, told BBC Sport that "somebody should be accountable and answerable to the things that were said." All four players claimed their football careers and personal lives had been affected by the abuse and the inability to report it. "The behaviour was appalling but [we] had no way of challenging [it], which made it even worse." Another of the players believed the abuse was "psychologically engineered" to cause conflict between the players, black against white. Another said he'd feared going to the training ground, and believed race had a part to play in him being released by the club, which, he agreed, was "institutionally racist at the time."

Renu Daly, a specialist lawyer in supporting victims of abuse at Hudgell Solicitors, thought the claims could be the tip of the iceberg across football, and thinks further claims will emerge. "I think [players] should come forward because I don't think these people should suffer in silence." Asked whether seeking compensation was a factor, Daly said, "Money is the last thing on the players' minds. The main reason they're coming forward is they've never had their distress addressed." Confirming this, one of the accusers said, "Compensation doesn't come into the matter; you can't turn back time and money is certainly not going to bring back the old me [...] The two characters that have moved on and have had successful lives, they are walking around confident that it never happened." They want to give other players the opportunity to realise that, if they do make a claim about racial abuse, that, similar to the Windrush generation or the #metoo movement, they'll no longer be ignored. "It's also about allowing younger players coming through to have a platform to say, 'Hang on a moment, I'd like to question that. Can we have a conversation?'"

Rhian Brewster

Everton's 17-year-old England junior Rhian Brewster won universal praise for talking out about his experiences of racism in an interview with the *Guardian*. Brewster recalled seven times he'd been racially abused or witnessed the same happening to a teammate. Five of the incidents occurred within seven months, two while playing for England and one occurred during the World Cup final.

Brewster detailed the racial abuse he'd experienced on the pitch since the age of 12 and called on football authorities to hand out "more severe punishments." On one occasion, in 2015, an opposition player *was* punished following an incident at a youth tournament with Liverpool in the Czech Republic. "He admitted he'd said it and they banned him from the rest of the tournament," Brewster recalls. "After the game, he tried to apologise but I wouldn't shake his hand." Brewster was only 15 at the time, *but* he was even younger – just a 12-year-old boy – the first occasion he was racially targeted, in Chelsea's junior system at a tournament in Russia. "I was warming up with a couple of teammates. We were all black and there were monkey chants [...] about ten of them doing it. I didn't know what to do [so] I told my coach and he went mad. The game was still playing and he went straight to the organisers to tell them what had happened and get the people who were doing it kicked out."

Another incident occurred in Croatia, during a match against Ukraine in the European Under-17 Championship. England won 4–0, Brewster scoring the second goal. He'd angered a Ukraine player after chasing the ball into the penalty area and colliding with the goalkeeper. "I didn't mean to hurt the goalkeeper and I said sorry – just left it there. But then there was an incident [with the same outfield player] later in the match. It was a bad challenge and I pushed him. We got into an argument and he called me a n*****."

He was abused during the Under-17 World Cup final held in India, too, in which England beat Spain 5–2 and for which he won the Golden Boot. The incident related to Morgan Gibbs-White, another 17-year-old, from Wolverhampton Wanderers. "Something happened in the box," Brewster says. "As Morgan was running away, [a Spain player] called him 'a monkey'." The FA lodged an official complaint but UEFA, with no video footage, concluded there was not enough evidence for disciplinary action.

The next incident happened during Liverpool's under-19s UEFA Youth League tie at home against Sevilla. "We were on a break. A ball came down the left. I was trying to get up with play when one of their players started running across me, trying to block my line and stop me running. I grabbed him and he fell over, theatrically [and] said something to me in Spanish. We were arguing and then he [said] the N-word [...] I was going to walk off the pitch and go straight down the tunnel, I was that angry. Steven [Gerrard] grabbed me and said, 'What's happened?'" However, the Sevilla player denied any wrongdoing and UEFA eventually ruled there was insufficient evidence, yet none of their staff was interviewed to establish if there were witnesses.

The teenager said he'd also been racially abused by Leonid Mironov, during a UEFA Youth League Liverpool–Spartak Moscow game – but European football's governing body said it could find no conclusive evidence of the allegations, leading Kick It Out to state it was "deeply disappointed." "I got fouled. I was on the floor and I had the ball in my hands. One of their players started saying stuff in Russian to the ref. I said, 'It's a foul, man, what you playing at?' [Their] player leaned over me, right down to my face, and said, 'Suck my dick, you n*****, you negro.'"

Five players from each side plus the match officials were all questioned about the incident, but none confirmed hearing any discriminatory language. Mironov admitted swearing at Brewster during the Russian club's 2–0 defeat but denied using racist language. Consequently, in concluding their investigation, UEFA said it found "no evidence to corroborate the allegations" and, therefore, no legal sanctions would be applied to Mironov.

Following the findings, KIO issued a statement saying it believed "there are issues with clubs, such as Spartak Moscow, who have been involved in several alleged racist incidents in recent years, receiving little or no discouragement by national and international football authorities in response to [those] allegations." While accepting Liverpool UEFA's decision, the club praised Brewster's "courage" in speaking out, saying it was "very proud of the maturity, dignity and leadership Rhian has displayed in bringing focus to this issue and he will continue to receive our full support."

The FA, meanwhile, echoed KIO's disappointment, but vowed to "continue to work with UEFA on how to best tackle incidents of discrimination in the future."

"My mum and dad are unnerved because this is not the first time," Brewster said. "They're angry and they don't want it to keep happening [and because] nothing has been done about it." His dad adds that they're doing it because "they can't get to you – they have no other way. They've tried to tackle you and it's not working, so the only thing they can do is try to get into your head." Mike Gordon, Liverpool's co-owner, contacted Brewster several times to let him know he had the backing of the people at the top of the club. KIO education manager Troy Townsend is in regular contact, and Liverpool's academy director, Alex Inglethorpe, has also offered support.

Despite the racist abuse he's received, Rhian Brewster says he won't give up the sport he loves. "I love the game. I'm never going to stop loving it. It's just disappointing to know it's [racism] still in the game. If it wasn't in the game, it would be so much better. You wouldn't have to worry about playing abroad, worrying about what the fans [or] another player [are] going to say. I wouldn't have to worry that if I score they are going to call me all types of names. I don't think UEFA take this thing seriously. They don't really care. That's how it feels, anyway, like it's been brushed under the carpet."

19

A Profusion of Controversial Incidents

"Urgent action is needed to halt the rise of the far right at British football grounds."

– Len McCluskey, *Daily Mirror.*
GENERAL SECRETARY OF UNITE

Mason Holgate accused Liverpool striker Roberto Firmino of calling him the N-word during an incident at a Friday night Merseyside derby. Holgate, accompanied by manager Sam Allardyce and director of football Steve Walsh, went to see the referee Bobby Madley after the FA Cup tie at Anfield. *Sunday Mirror Sport* used a lip-reader, Tim Reedy, to look at TV footage of the incident that erupted when Holgate pushed Firmino over advertising hoardings in front of the main stand. The players then squared up to each other – and it is then that Holgate claimed he was racially abused. Reedy said that "Fermino, in retaliation to the push, confronts Holgate, shouting some words at him, to which Holgate doesn't react […] because Firmino is speaking in Portuguese. My findings are that Firmino did *not* use racist language [but] says the words '*Es maluco, filho da puta?*', which translates as 'Are you crazy, you son-of-a-b★★★★?'"

Consequently, the FA took no action. "Having considered all of the available evidence, we consider it's not sufficient to raise a charge against Firmino. However, we are completely satisfied that the allegation was made in absolute good faith by Holgate and that there is no suggestion of this being an intentionally false or malicious allegation. We continue to take all allegations of discrimination extremely seriously and would encourage all participants who believe that they've been the subject of or witness to discriminatory abuse to report this through the appropriate channels." Following the judgement, Firmino released his own statement: "As difficult as it's been to remain publicly silent, given the serious and damaging nature of what it was claimed I said during the game, I did so to demonstrate my respect for the process and to allow the issue to be investigated in the most thorough way. It's critical for football that tackling racism and all forms of discrimination is taken extremely seriously. As someone who has experienced racist abuse during my life, I know how damaging and hurtful it can be. Now the process is concluded, I would like to place on record, for the avoidance of any doubt, I did not say the word, or a variation of the word, that was claimed and subsequently reported in the media. I did not use any language that referenced race. I did not – and would never – reference a person's skin colour or culture, by means of insult, during a dispute or an argument."

Jay Rodriguez
West Bromwich forward Jay Rodriguez successfully contested his FA charge for the alleged racist abuse of Brighton and Hove Albion defender Gaëtan Bong. Rodriguez submitted his appeal against the FA's misconduct charge to avoid a five-match ban, imposed following an

incident where the player appeared to pinch his nose after the pair clashed and Bong complained to the referee.

In his evidence to the FA, Bong said he was "100% certain" Rodriguez said to him, "You're black and you stink." Rodriguez, in his evidence to the investigation claimed he'd said, "Breath fucking stinks," and submitted character statements from players and managers at several Premier League clubs, including Tottenham manager Mauricio Pochettino, Bournemouth manager Eddie Howe, Liverpool midfielder Adam Lallana, Southampton striker Shane Long, defender Maya Yoshida and Saints goalkeeper Kelvin Davis.

Speaking on SFR Sports in France, Bong said, "[Rodriguez] said certain things of a racist nature and I took it badly […] I reported it to the referee and I hope there's a punishment. He said something in reference to my colour. You see very clearly he pinched his nose in relation to what he said. I asked him to repeat it. I think at the moment he repeated it he realised what he'd said."

While accepting that Bong's complaint was "made in absolute good faith [with] no suggestion that this was a malicious or fabricated complaint," the FA found the charge "not proven," explaining its verdict thus: "The essential issue for us boiled down to one question: Are we satisfied the player [Rodriguez] probably said to GB [Gaëtan Bong], 'You're black and you stink'?" Two lip-reading experts engaged by the FA were unable to confirm or deny what had been spoken as "the player's mouth was obscured."

Stan Collymore
A long-running feud between former England internationals Stan Collymore and Ian Wright was reignited when the former sent a foul-mouthed tweet containing a racial slur.

Collymore, who was working for the Russian broadcaster RT, accused Wright of being an "Uncle Tom" – a black person who is subservient to white people. In an interview with the *Guardian*, Collymore also suggested, "To be a black pundit, you either need to be a comedian like Chris Kamara or Ian Wright – guys who have big pearly-white smiles and everyone loves laughing at – or Jermaine Jenas and Alex Scott, who are completely inoffensive. What you're not allowed to do is call out the status quo, which is what I do." Wright posted a picture of himself and Kamara, laughing together, to which Collymore replied, angrily: "You know what you are, Ian, and always have been, which is why only you are employed by every British broadcaster. The epitome of a Tom. C★★★."

Wright, a regular analyst on BBC's *Match of the Day* and a World Cup pundit for ITV, responded: "Representation matters. Opportunities matter. I feel sorry for you, but you have to let the chip on your shoulder go and take some responsibility for why broadcasters and brands won't be associated with you. Everyone should have the opportunity to fight for their case but the fact that you have to do it at the expense of others speaks more about you than all of us." The pair are rival red-top names: Wright for the *Sun*, Collymore the *Mirror*.

Their feud started in 2015 when Wright refused to work alongside Collymore on a Channel 5 Football League programme, Wright's son Shaun Wright-Phillips having been the target of criticism from Collymore. "I don't do mischief, Stan," Wright wrote. "I said f★★★ Channel 5 and f★★★ Stan Collymore! How's that? Now, if you don't mind, I've recorded myself on Premier League legends! Wanna watch it." They clashed again because Collymore believed Wright should have taken a stand over an article in the *Sun* in which Kelvin MacKenzie insulted Everton midfielder Ross Barkley. Their exchange included taunts from Collymore that Wright was being subservient while Wright brought up Collymore's assault on former partner Ulrika Jonsson. Collymore, who has spoken openly about his history of mental health issues, was a broadcaster with talkSPORT for eight years, until the station decided not to renew his contract in 2016.

Len McCluskey

In a *Daily Mirror* news article FOOTBALL 'HATE MOB' IS ON RISE, Unite union leader Len McCluskey warned of the far right's infiltration into football, a throwback to the bad old days of the 1980s. The article stated that, "Urgent action is needed to halt the rise of the far right at British football grounds, says union leader Len McCluskey. The Unite general secretary speaks out after warnings that members of the Football Lads' Alliance (FLA) are trying to infiltrate fans." McCluskey called on his union to back a motion at its annual policy conference in Brighton for clubs and supporters to take a stand against the far right, fearing that elements of the FLA and other groups including the English Defence League (EDL) and Britain First were exploiting austerity to whip up working-class anger.

The *Mirror* also reported that the Premier League had warned clubs about the FLA after some supporters were seen trying to spread anti-Muslim hate at games. The FLA flag was banned at some grounds. Ex-EDL leader Tommy Robinson joined the FLA on a march, saying "football supporters were coming together to oppose the Islamisation of Britain." Its supporters were later filmed chanting support for Robinson after he was jailed in May 2018 for contempt of court.

McCluskey – who'd worked with Show Racism the Red Card "to keep bigotry away from our kids" – said, "It started in the 90s to combat hate merchants infecting our grounds since the 70s. We cannot go back to those days. The trade union movement needs to tackle this head-on. I call on all members to become part of the opposition to the rise of this new far right street movement. Let not the peddlers of prejudice win."

20

Personal Views

"What will be the outcome? A few more black people on TV, more black agents, steering committees and other elite black groups set up in a few visible industries. But, nothing will change nor demands made for 99% of black people, our communities in the inner city."

– John Barnes

Garth Crooks

"The racist abuse from some football fans in the early days can only be described as horrendous. What many of them didn't understand then was how their bigotry became my greatest motivating force to succeed. Being the best I could be was partly in response to racist abuse. In those days, the football pitch was the only place I could express myself. I was in control and no one could do anything about it and the freedom that came with it was exhilarating."

Garth Crooks played for Stoke City, Tottenham Hotspur, Manchester United, West Bromwich Albion and Charlton Athletic. Throughout his career, he was an active member of the Professional Footballers' Association and was elected the first black chairman of the union.

Currently, he works for BBC Sport as lead pundit on *Final Score* on BBC One on Saturday afternoons. Here, he talks of the marriage between the Professional Footballers' Association and Kick It Out.

"The relationship between the PFA and KIO has been like a long-standing marriage. The oldest football trade union in the world became entwined with a fantastic idea: "Let's Kick Racism Out of Football". This emotional cocktail reminded me of the classic movie, *Guess Who's Coming to Dinner?*, the story of two people from very different cultures whose affection for each other was so powerful it cut through society's norms like a laser-beam. Like many mixed marriages, it seemed like a brave collaboration at the time but one that would prove to last the test of time.

"The PFA had created a reputation for itself under its commander-in-chief Gordon Taylor. The former Birmingham City and Blackburn player had proved to be just as formidable in the boardroom as he was as a winger and, when the time came for Lord Herman Ouseley, to pop the question and ask for Gordon's assistance to help them launch KIO in 1993, it was the beginning of a important relationship. Of course, such forces coming together took the game more by the throat than by surprise. It needed the calming influence of luminaries like Arsenal's Director of Football David Dein and FA Executive David Davies – who, along with Herman and Gordon will always be regarded as KIO's founding fathers – to explain the merits of the campaign.

"In the early days, it was the players that provided the oxygen for KIO and were the driving force behind the launch. While some fans were vocalising much of the hate and bile that was coming from the terraces throughout the 80s, KIO needed the players to make a statement and grab the attention of decent football supporters across the country with a firm NO to racism in football – and KIO was it. It was a bold move by the association because it knew that fans, like players, occasionally get cross with each other and say things that are meant to hurt but not necessarily wound. Footballers get the chance to shake hands and apologise when an incident gets out of hand – fans seldom do. Nevertheless, there have been moments in this marriage when the relationship between KIO and the PFA has been severely tested. When players fall out with each other, KIO has been forced to rebuke the behaviour of a high-profile PFA member because an incident is splashed across the front and back pages. But, like all good marriages, both organisations have continued to look to the things that united them and not what divided them.

"During the years, we have seen some remarkable changes in the way KIO have helped the PFA address issues around discrimination thanks to this unique relationship. The PFA's Equality Department has a role in ensuring that players throughout the leagues are regularly versed in what is considered to be "acceptable behaviour and language" in a constantly changing world. When there are disputes between players on the field of play, however uncomfortable, the association no longer insists on withdrawing in line with its previous dictates but represents both parties in finding a resolution. The three-step protocol that protects black players from experiencing racial abuse during a match has had a significant impact, while the introduction of female players on to the PFA Management Committee has been groundbreaking. The associations voice has also been loud and clear in relation to LGBT issues and their gay members being discriminated against. The PFA will not tolerate such behaviour and will support the strongest possible sanctions against the perpetrators.

"These are just some of the landmarks that the PFA & KIO have jointly presided over since they've been together. They have not been easy introductions and in some places they've left their scars. Nonetheless, the marriage has survived, and the parties continue to look to each other for inspiration. And long may it continue."

Bill Kenwright

"It was clear we didn't have many black faces in our crowd, and that needed to be urgently addressed, and I think I did something positive to do just that."

Born in the Wavertree area of Liverpool, Bill Kenwright transformed Everton from one of the last bastions of the "all-white" dressing room into a modern multicultural club during his near 30-year association with the club.

I've known Bill ever since he became an Everton major stakeholder and member of the board, and I have never come across a more genuine, passionate and likeable figure in football. He rarely gives interviews but, for this book, he's willing to discuss the transformation of his beloved Everton in terms of inclusion and diversity. His efforts deserve a knighthood!

While football has always been Bill's passion, it was in the arts that he made his name. His first break in acting came at the age of 18, when he landed a part in Granada TV's *The Villains*. Further parts followed, including one in *Z-Cars*, the theme of which is still played to this day to accompany Everton on to the field.

Bill also appeared in several West End musicals before he joined the cast of *Coronation Street* in 1968 as Gordon Clegg. At the end of his 12-month contract, he stunned producers by asking to leave the series – the first time a young actor had made such a huge decision. Since then, he's produced hundreds of shows all over the world, including Willy Russell's long-running hit *Blood Brothers*.

His company, Bill Kenwright Ltd, is now the most prolific theatre production company in the world. As a director, Bill has been responsible for Tim Rice and Andrew Lloyd Webber's *Joseph and the Amazing Technicolor Dreamcoat*, *Jesus Christ Superstar* and *Evita*. He also directed Andrew Lloyd Webber and Jim Steinman's *Whistle Down the Wind*, was nominated for a London Theatre Critics' Award for *West Side Story* at the Shaftesbury Theatre and a Tony Award for *Blood Brothers* on Broadway. His films include the Stephen Frears-directed *Cheri*, starring Michelle Pfeiffer, *The Day After the Fair*, *Stepping Out*, *Don't Go Breaking My Heart*, Sundance Festival award-winner *Die Mommie Die* and *The Purifiers*. He co-produced, with Elvis Presley Enterprises, the phenomenally successful national arena tour of *Elvis – The Concert*.

He holds an Honorary Fellowship from Liverpool's John Moore's University, is an Honorary Professor of London's Thames Valley University and has an Honorary Fellowship from Nottingham Trent University. He was made a CBE in the 2001 Queen's New Year's Honours and, the following year, received the Variety Club Bernard Delfont award for his contribution to the entertainment industry.

His success as a renowned producer and his passion for Everton came together in 1989, when he was invited to join the club's board, rising to the position of deputy chairman a decade later when he launched his successful £20m bid to buy a 68% majority share from Peter Johnson. In 2004, he was appointed chairman in place of Sir Phillip Carter and, just one year later, saw the Blues secure a place in the Champions League qualifiers under manager David

Moyes, ending an almost ten year wait for a return to European competition.

Today, Everton looks much like any other Premier League team, packed full of players from around the world, and it's impossible to imagine it was not always that way. Everton fans became notorious in the 1980s for singling out John Barnes during his first appearance in a Merseyside derby, when scores of bananas were thrown onto the pitch.

Being mixed-race, Everton player Mike Trebilcock – who played in the 1966 FA Cup Final – was not generally recognised as being black. "I remember people were quite surprised when they heard he was mixed-race," recalls Bill.

Cliff Marshall, a boyhood Blue, who was signed in 1974 after showing promise as an schoolboy, would go onto become an Everton trailblazer – was the first black player in the royal-blue shirt. Bill recalls, "I genuinely think he was one of the first black players to play for a top team and, like a lot of our previous players, he also benefitted from the support of the Former Player's Foundation, which at the time was unique to Everton."

He managed just seven starts in two seasons. "I didn't see it as any different [being the first black player to represent the club], if you're good enough, you'll play. Although there were chants and sometimes bananas thrown on to the pitch in the early days, it didn't affect me," Marshall says. "I just got on with it and played the game." This was an era when famously racist *Love Thy Neighbour* was one of the most popular TV programmes!

When I interviewed John Fashanu about racism in football for the *Daily Mirror* in the late 80s, he stated that Everton were one of the clubs who didn't at the time have *any* black players. He made no further comment! The *Mirror* series of articles highlighted the depth of anger among players such as Fashanu about the way fans treated black players. EVERTON IN RACE HATE FURY was the headline, when Goodison fans taunted Arsenal's David Rocastle, Michael Thomas and Paul Davis. The paper followed up with THANK YOU EVERTON, when Davis praised the club for taking a firm stand against the bigots.

Twenty years later, in 1994, Daniel Amokachi signed, after it was widely suggested that Everton, through the 1970s and early 80s, were regarded as a "white" club. There were unsubstantiated rumours as to why the club didn't go ahead with a deal to sign Dion Dublin – the official line was that the transfer broke down over the financial terms, but Bill is clear, this was nothing to do with race. "The deal on Dublin was definitely nothing to do with colour!"

Another unsubstantiated rumour was that Curtis Fleming, an Irish full-back playing for St Patrick's Athletic was called up for a trial after an Everton scout gave rave reviews. When he arrived, the club discovered he was black and sent him home. Earl Barrett was also one of the tiny group of black players to filter through for Everton.

Racial abuse aimed at black or foreign players at football grounds was still rife in 2000, according to university researchers who carried out a survey of 33,000 fans. Fans from Everton, Rangers and Celtic topped the league table for the largest number of racist comments heard, the survey found. Arsenal, Charlton Athletic and Wimbledon won praise for reducing racism through campaigns inside their grounds but, according to Sean Perkins of the Sir Norman Chester Centre for Football Research at Leicester University, racism overall remained much the same as it was in the last survey, for the 1996/97 season. Fans were asked: "Have you witnessed racism aimed at players this season [1998/99]." The percentages were: Everton, 38%;

Rangers, 36%; Celtic, 33%; West Ham, 32%; Newcastle, 31%. Best in the ranking were: Wimbledon, 11%; Charlton, 12%; Derby, 14%; Southampton, 16%; and Arsenal, 16%.

As a result, Everton sent club stewards to away games to sit with undercover police officers in an attempt to identify ringleader supporters. The Merseyside club expressed their disgust that racism had resurfaced and resolved to overcome the problem. Club secretary at that time, Michael Dunford, said, "A number of covert initiatives will be implemented in the coming weeks, of which undercover officers and stewards travelling with our away fans will be merely one. They will work closely with the local police forces at the grounds we are visiting, but other measures must remain secret. We are determined to ensure that Everton Football Club does not suffer from the awful taint of racism."

A minority of deranged Everton supporters' songs sung at away-fixtures were published by the *Liverpool Post*: "Trigger, trigger, trigger shoot that nigger"; "Hou, Hou, Hou, Hou's had a heart attack"; "Gerard Houllier is dying, what a wonderful way to spend the day, watching Gerard Houllier pass away". Manager Walter Smith issued a statement: "Quite simply, there's no place for either racism or violence at Everton FC and we shall do everything within our power to root out the culprits. We know that 99.9% of our club's supporters are honest and honourable and we know that they will back us in this fight against a pernicious evil." Talking of "the foul-mouthed and dishonourable actions of what we know to be a very small minority," he said, "The Goodison Park switchboard and e-mail system has been inundated with messages from loyal, right-thinking supporters, who wish to condemn those involved in Saturday's disgraceful, unforgivable events." Mark O'Brien, editor of the website fanzine *When Skies are Grey*, observed, "The only way it will stop is if the police kick them out of the ground. If you travel all of the way to Fulham but are kicked out for singing racist songs, you won't do it again."

For Bill, the accusations about Everton make his skin crawl; he would certainly not tolerate any discrimination based on colour. "I'm amazed and appalled at the percentage figures you give about the Everton crowds abuse levels." Bill was also clearly taken aback by the mere suggestion that black players might have been blackballed at Goodison. Not under Bill's watch. "Certainly not since I've been on the board," he commented. "I don't think there was any real problem and I certainly know of no policy since I've been involved of barring black players. I never think of colour. We've had lots of black players in our team, but it has never occurred to me that my club had once been thought of as 'all-white'. In fact, that shocks me."

Bill did act to rectify the issues around the Everton fan base, though. "When I started the Community Programme at the club towards the end of the 80s, I brought in a lovely guy, Alan Johnson, who was black, not only to help me address issues with the crowd, but also to get some more black faces in the crowd. I remember we looked at crowd photos and could see none. We worked at this deficiency and many other problems that Everton shared with all of the other top clubs. It was clear we didn't have many black faces in our crowd, and that needed to be urgently addressed, and I think I did something positive to do just that. Ever since I've been associated with Everton, I've viewed the club as multicultural. Nothing else crossed my mind, not even close."

As with Yorkshire cricket, there was a time when football clubs attracted players from within their own catchment area. The foreign players came from Scotland, Wales and

Ireland. Bill recalls, "You thought then that if they didn't come from Merseyside, they weren't really part of us! Football was a much more insular game in those days. A different era, a different way of life. As an eight-year-old boy in love with Everton, I never thought of anyone from the south of England playing for us! Don't forget, those were the days when players went to games on the bus – sometimes you might find yourself sitting next to them – and they took a packed lunch the wife made up! You thought then that if they didn't come from Merseyside, were they really one of us? That was a different era, a different way of life. Today, it's European football, the Premier League, new owners, foreign managers and players – and Everton is the same as any other club, casting the net as wide as possible to find the right players, whether from Brazil, and whether they cost £50m."

Paul Elliott

"The Rooney Rule needs to be now applied across the whole of the game inclusive of all of the stakeholders in every job. In the Premier League it should be applied at academy level so there is a proper supply chain and accountability process."

Paul Elliott was appointed chairman to the FA's Inclusion Advisory Board (IAB) in 2017, in recognition of his 30 years in tackling racism in England and Europe. His capacity as chairman means that he also represents the IAB on the main FA 12-man Board. He also sits as an FA Council member and represents the FA on UEFA's Football and Corporate Social Responsibility committee.

A much-liked, cultured centre-half, with Charlton, Luton Town, Aston Villa, Pisa, Celtic and Chelsea, he was Chelsea's first black captain and, in 1987, the first black English player in Italian football (Serie A). He was also the first black player to win Scottish Player of the Year while at Celtic.

The former England B captain advised the European Parliament and UEFA on how best to fight racial prejudice. After being awarded an MBE for services to youth football and anti-racism initiatives, Paul was the first modern-day player to receive a CBE from the Queen in 2013. He's one of KIO's founding fathers.

Elliott was heavily involved in the Kick It Out campaign adopted for Euro 2008 by UEFA's president Michel Platini, at a time when the Frenchman was regarded as UEFA's forward-thinking president, destined to succeed Sepp Blatter.

Back in 2008, in an interview with Henry Winter in Zurich, Elliott made the point that Paul Ince had to work even harder to get a top managerial job, that the Continent was "twenty years behind the UK" in combating discrimination and that a glass ceiling existed for black managers at the highest level.

"If you look at his [playing] peers, Gareth Southgate and Roy Keane, they've come straight in at management top level, haven't they? I've got no problem with that [but] if you compare Ince's CV with theirs, he's just as impressive head-to-head. There's a dinosaur mindset which shouldn't be in existence. He's a pioneer as a manager with what he achieved at Macclesfield Town and MK Dons. He's been outstanding," Elliott said. "Thirty per cent of players in the game are black but there are only two black managers: Paul Ince and Keith Alexander. We have lost a generation of potentially good managers. Look at the multicultural country we live in, and the diversity within the game, and that has to be reflected in the boardrooms and administrative worlds. It isn't. [People] feel disillusioned, disenfranchised and they walk away. Paul Ince is a role model. It will breed confidence in others. When Laurie Cunningham, Cyrille Regis, Brendon Batson and Viv Anderson came into the game, they were key role models, and that created confidence. They showed the stereotypical managers at the time they could do a job at the top level."

Ten years after that interview, Elliott can see a day when England appoint a black manager. "Frank Rijkaard has managed Barcelona and Holland. Ruud Gullit has been an excellent role model. We all know the positive contribution black players have made to this game. In England, on the field and in the terraces, there isn't a problem but in the early 80s, it was horrific with the banana-throwing, monkey-chanting and the BNP."

Speaking of Europe, Elliot says, "Italy and Spain [lack] integration. It's them and us. Immigrants are marginalised from mainstream society. In Italy, there was booing and monkey chants when I was in possession of the ball. I take my family to Sardinia every year for holidays – Italy is one of the most beautiful countries in the world, but discrimination is still very prominent there. The Ultras bring that extremism. In the UK, we're 20 years ahead. Luis Aragones is still there [as Spain coach, despite his racist comment about Thierry Henry]. The Manchester City boy, Nedum Onuoha, in the England Under-21s got abuse in Serbia. There's a big problem in Eastern Europe [but] Platini has a zero-tolerance mindset to discrimination and inequality."

Back in 2002, in an interview with the Scotsman, Elliott discussed being the first English black footballer in Italy. "It was difficult – there was monkey-chanting and booing, and a banana thrown at me. Actually, it's one of my funniest stories. I remember I was having a terrible time in the match, and somebody threw a banana, which hit my leg. I actually picked [it up], peeled back the skin and ate it, then threw it back at the offender. I remember talking to journalists afterwards, and they said, 'Paul, why did you do that?' I told them I was having a bad time, I had a much-improved second half and that was because of the nutritional value from the banana!"

Back in 2011, when Sepp Blatter said racism could be dealt with by a simple handshake, Elliott spoke of being "terribly disappointed on a personal level" and went as far as to suggest the FIFA president had been guilty of a criminal offence. "If you make racist remarks in the street, you can be prosecuted under the Public Offences Act. If you do the same thing on a football pitch, the 1992 Football Offences Act facilitates that eventuality. Not even the president of FIFA is above the law. It's not right that such a powerful man harbours these narrow views on racism. [Racism] keeps going, evolving, as we now have challenges with homophobia, anti-Semitism, etc., so all of us as adults, parents, teachers, coaches etc. have responsibilities to work against it with whatever capacity we can."

In 2017, anti-racism campaigner Derek Ferguson said Scottish football had come a long way since bananas were thrown at Mark Walters 30 years ago, but progress can still be made. Ferguson uses his recollections in his work with Show Racism the Red Card. "We're in a better place, but we've still got a bit to go," he said. "Thirty years ago, it was horrendous but, with education, things have got a lot better." Ferguson visits schools as part of his work with the campaign group and believes that football can play a role in eradicating racism from society. "I talk about Mark, I talk about that incident. There are certain areas I go to where it's rife. From my football point of view, it will get through to [young people] about having that respect and treating people the way that you would like to be treated. You've got to be really careful with the terminology and that's why we're in the schools, to pass on that message.

"The same thing happened with Paul Elliott as well [...] It was horrible to witness, and it didn't just affect Mark, it affected his teammates. When I look back, I get angry with myself. I was a young guy at that time. I wish I'd challenged it, but I didn't know any better. The games should have stopped, but we just carried on. I was embarrassed. Mark might have thought, 'Are all Scottish people like that? Do they have a hatred for black people?' Now, things have got a lot better, and it comes down to education."

Unfortunately, Paul Elliott was forced to resign in 2013 from all KIO roles following reports of a racism row. FA Chairman David Bernstein said, "The use of discriminatory language is unacceptable, regardless of context. It has made Paul's position untenable. I wish to thank Paul for his dedicated and unstinting work, particularly in the area of anti-racism. I am saddened by this turn of events and it is with regret that we accept Paul's resignation."

Elliott's undoing was the result of a text message dispute over a business venture with former Charlton player and close family friend Richard Rufus, in which the N-word was used. In a statement, Elliot said, "I regret using it. It is inappropriate and not part of my everyday vocabulary. As an advocate of high standards of public behaviour, and integrity in public life, I know the use of this word sends out mixed messages and contradicts my position as a Kick It Out trustee. I believe I did the right and honourable thing [by resigning and] will continue to be active in other projects in what I believe to be a true and just cause."

Elliott, whose football career had been curtailed by injury in 1992, had been a Kick It Out trustee since 1996. At the time of the offending comment, Football Against Racism in Europe executive director Piara Powar believed his comments were not racially offensive. Powar told *Telegraph Sport* "I understand the concern over the use of the N-word, whoever uses it, in whichever context. However, I cannot accept that it is racist to use it between two very close friends and business colleagues in a private text, when both are black, from almost identical ethnic and social backgrounds, and there's been no allegation of racism. Racism and other forms of discrimination are not simply about words. It may be difficult for some to accept the difference between those words used with discriminatory intent and those that are not." Powar was sure Elliott would recover from the saga. "I know Paul very well and I know the skills that he has, the understanding of the game that he has and its politics, and I have no doubt that Paul will be back and fighting. In the end, what Paul does is seek to represent those who are disenfranchised in society and perhaps in football as well. I think he'll continue to seek to represent those groups and, in time, his skills will bring him to the fore again."

Thankfully, a year later, Elliott resumed his career tackling discrimination and promoting inclusion in football after being offered a role on the FA's Inclusion Advisory Board. The appointment was welcomed by Lord Ouseley: "Paul has dedicated his life to fighting discrimination, and his contribution throughout Kick It Out's history is immeasurable. We're delighted English football will benefit from his expertise once again."

Looking to the future, Elliott identified the challenges ahead in our Internet-mediated age. "It's provided a cowardly platform for much negativity. The upside is the vigour applied by the authorities with the power to apply sanctions when necessary. This is not just football, it's within society. Technology is great but the downside is that the abuse of social media can give people an unacceptable voice to abuse whoever they feel they want to target, whenever they feel like it. There are many challenges for the whole game, especially in terms of the modern day players, and the question is whether there is the progress being made in terms of mental illness and gambling. Education is critical. We know football is far more diverse, the whole demographic of society has changed, and the stakeholders, boards, councils, committees, employment, have to reflect football and society. If you now go to football stadiums, they are very good at self-policing. However, one of the biggest current challenges is still that while the number of players is close to 30%, there's still less than five black managers in the game. That historical imbalance has to change. A real positive change we've seen is the governance reforms, the implementation of the Rooney Rule, which is a huge game-changer. An important scheme I'm prominent in is a coaching programme to develop the current and future generation of black coaches.

"My own personal and professional journey started in the very challenging societal times in the late 70s. Racism was overtly prominent and began to have a dominant presence in football stadia across the country. At that juncture, the National Front held centre stage on the streets of London and that visibility was prominent in stadiums like Millwall, Chelsea, Leeds, Everton, Burnley and Blackburn. Black players were the prime target for their vitriolic, vociferous abuse. Those dark, ugly days coincided with the activation of my career at Charlton Athletic and, thereafter, Luton Town, Aston Villa, Pisa, Celtic and, finally, Chelsea.

"My proudest professional legacy landmarks were [being] the first black English defender to play in Serie A, the first modern day black defender to play in Scotland, the first black Scottish Player of the Year and becoming Chelsea's first black club and team captain.

"Education, respect for equality, diversity and cohesion, were all intrinsic values within the KIO model. The truth is that, to start with, the footballing stakeholders were not entirely convinced about its sustainability and their support was given with trepidation and cautiousness. However, they soon realised it was one of the best investments they could ever make. No one could envisage such evolutionary growth, given KIO is a charity with no statutory, enforcement or regulatory powers, but it challenged football stakeholders and held them to account in a way that no other campaigning organisation could and set an example with the primary focus on their responsibilities, leadership and their duty of care to serve and govern the game.

"With formal legislation activated through the Football Offences Act, the demographics of our society has changed beyond recognition, the Bosman ruling (meaning players who reached the end of their contract were free to move on without their club receiving a fee) – being a massive game-changer. We have Jean-Marc Bosman to thank for helping to create more diversity and inclusion on the field, in dressing rooms and stadia, with more BAME, women and people with disabilities in attendance. The game evolved unintended positive consequences but, simultaneously 21st century challenges emerged as other forms of discrimination – homophobia, xenophobia, anti-Semitism, Islamophobia – crept into society and football.

"The 30,000 visits players have made to schools, prisons, hospitals etc., embracing their social responsibility, is unparalleled in the world game. KIO has been the most effective campaigning organisation, in my opinion [...] a positive catalyst for change in impacting football and society."

Andrew Cole
"I was recently approached by a very good friend of mine, an ex-player, he phoned me to ask if I'd apply for a vacant job in management just so that the club could have its full quota of ethnic applicants!"

The 'Rooney Rule', brought in to specifically ensure greater advancement for black managers and coaches, is not the answer, according to Andy Cole, now a respected ambassador for Manchester United and TV and radio pundit.

In an interview for this book, he told me he believes that the landmark initiative for the benefit of ethnic minorities, modelled on the successful formula used in the States, doesn't work here in the UK where he feels exclusion is still prevalent, and racism is alive and kicking, and in some aspect has got worse.

"There is not going to be a big change in the foreseeable future," is his damning indictment. By that, he means there won't be a big hike in more black coaches and managers, and there won't be any fundamental shift towards greater representation with the game's ruling bodies that would precipitate change.

"Take the Rooney Rule, for example. It doesn't work. I've spoken to some black guys who feel it has been an important change, but I've disagreed with them. My view is that you can have as many BAME candidates as you like applying for the job, they might even be the best candidates for that job, but it doesn't mean they will get that job, and I suspect that they won't.

"It grieves me to say this but I was recently approached by a very good friend of mine, an ex-player – he phoned me to ask if I'd apply for a vacant job in management just so that the club could have its full quota of ethnic applicants! No, I didn't give him the instant response you might expect! He's a good friend of mine, a black coach who I respect as well as get on with. However, we did exchange a few words. I told him that the club was mugging him off, and that there was no way I was going to make such a bogus application just so the club can fill the quota under the Rooney Rule.

"The trouble is that racism is still thriving within the world, and as sport reflects society, it's still there in football, and I have to say in some ways it has gone backwards."

Speaking in 2011, Cole commented that he'd been discouraged from pursuing a career in football coaching and management because of the dearth of opportunities for black ex-players. He said English football was facing a "lost" generation of potential managers because black ex-players would "walk away" from the game.

His view hasn't changed. "I respect black coaches and managers who do it, because I know how hard it is for them to get where they are, to even get a job. There are 92 clubs and about five black managers, with Chris Hughton the only black manager in the Premier League. He does a phenomenal job, and I know Brighton have stood behind him, but he seems to get sacked at other clubs even though he was doing a good job. Chris is a gentleman, a shining light, an inspiration for all aspiring black coaches and managers, who are thinking of getting into it after finishing playing.

"I've been asked many times before and, as I get older, I think more about putting something back, more so to the younger generation, and I think I could do a good job teaching strikers the art of goalscoring. But management? It doesn't resonate with me."

From a personal perspective, he suffered "bits and pieces" of racism during his illustrious playing career. "I'm a great admirer of Cyrille Regis. Players of his generation took all the flak so that players of my generation had to put up with just bits and pieces of racism. People like Cyrille gave me my opportunity, so I have nothing but respect for him and those players of his era.

"These days, we still have problems and we do need Kick It Out, but they cannot solve the problems alone. It's often said that KIO ask the players to wear T-shirts once a year – some do, some don't and not all the clubs sign up to it – but once a year – it's a bit of a novelty. Of course, KIO are active all the time, but the big names, the top players, need to speak out to get the message across."

One of the "bits and pieces" of racism Cole refers to involved two men who were jailed after they racially abused him during an Aer Arran flight in 2014. Travelling from Dublin to Manchester, Gregory Horan and Lee Byrne were already drunk before boarding the 9.30 a.m. flight. They began pestering Cole, calling him "Mr Blackman". "Where I'm from," Byrne had said, "it's politically correct to address you as Mr Blackman," one of them told the player. Cole told Byrne to "just leave it" but the abuse continued with Byrne now calling him a "spook". After the trial, Cole took to Twitter to thank his followers for their backing.

Not long afterwards his son Devante was subjected to racism, too, while playing a youth match in Spain for Manchester City in 2014. Devante was racially abused and spat at by players and fans of Atletico Madrid, in a UEFA Youth League game representing City's Elite Development

Squad, managed by Patrick Vieira. In a statement, UEFA said, "Disciplinary proceedings have been opened [which] will be dealt with by the UEFA Control and Disciplinary Body on March 20."

Brendon Batson
"It's only the colour of the shirt that counts."

As a former Deputy Chief Executive of the PFA and now a trustee of the association, Brendon Batson's tireless work led to him being awarded an OBE for services to football in the Queen's 2014 Birthday Honours.

Two years later, Batson was contacted by the former West Ham United striker Clyde Best, who was writing his autobiography, and was gathering insight into what it was like for a fellow black player striving to make his way in the early 1970s. "It brought it all flooding back," Batson says. "Clyde was a star when I was coming through the junior ranks at Arsenal, there were John and Clive Charles at West Ham (John was the first black player to represent England at Under-18 level) and Ade Coker from Nigeria. The abuse they all used to receive was incredible but, outwardly, they never appeared to let it affect them. There were a sprinkling of black players in the 70s and when Viv Anderson won his first England cap in 1978 – the year I joined West Bromwich Albion – it seemed as if there was an explosion and that we were going to be freely accepted."

These days he runs Batson Sports Consultancy Ltd, and says, "We should be proud of what football has achieved. If you look back to those dark old days – the offensive graffiti and chanting – clubs took it on and the environment is much more family-friendly now. My family didn't come to see me play football – you don't want your loved ones and friends being subjected to abuse. While we should be proud of the steps taken, it will always be a struggle but in terms of the presence of black players on the field of play, the outbreaks are less frequent and at least people know what they can do about it if they hear it. I was subjected to some abuse, maybe three times, twice with the same player, but it was seldom. Players are only interested in whether you can play. In the heat of the moment, things are said and, as long as they can be dealt with (and sadly not all of them are), on the whole, it isn't a problem among the players.

"In early 1993, I was Deputy Chief Executive at the PFA when a young lady called Louise Ansari came to see me with an idea – from Herman Ouseley, who, at the time, was CEO at the Commission for Racial Equality – of using the power of football to help address issues of racism in society. It was like a lightbulb going off. I went straight to my boss, Gordon Taylor, and said it was something that we needed to run with. I was very enthusiastic about the idea but it was also clear to me that rather than just being a one-off campaign that would run for a year and then end, it needed to be more than that, it needed longevity if it was really going to work. I'm not sure that even I envisaged it would still be going [now] though! Perhaps the surprise is that it didn't start even earlier [...] I kick myself for not thinking about it 10 or 20 years before.

"When we launched it, it was with people like Ian Wright, Gary Mabbutt, Paul Elliott, Pat Nevin and Garth Crooks on the platform because we didn't want to make it purely a black issue, we wanted to show there was support for the work across the spectrum, and looking back, that was an important decision because I think it helped legitimise it. People couldn't marginalise it as just a little protest group."

"Let's Kick Racism Out of Football" launched with what Batson says was a great slogan: "It's only the colour of the shirt that counts." Initially, the CRE and the PFA set it up and the Football League quickly came on board. Supporters groups bought into it and, from there, it built gradually, accumulating support from around the game – that process is still going on both within the organisation or by inspiring and supporting other campaigns, be they national, international or on a local level. Clubs got on board early on, which was important. They ensured that their stadiums were cleaned of racist graffiti [...] which were a big thing in my time as a player and set a tone throughout grounds that made it intimidating not just for players but for supporters, too.

"In 1997, it became an independent organisation [which] gave it a stronger voice and, within two years, they instituted a hugely significant change to the Football Offences Act. Where in the past, if a person was chanting racial abuse on his or her own, it didn't constitute an offence until they did it in unison with others, the law changed so that any racist abuse or behaviour by an individual was now an offence. That was a landmark moment. Not only did it improve the atmosphere in football grounds, it emboldened the decent majority to stand up against those involved in racism. It gave them a voice and gave them support.

"We see football in this country now as such a melting pot of nationalities, ethnicities, religions [...] and they are not willing to accept any forms of racism. Players are prepared to speak out about abuse when they are targeted. They are willing to make a stand.

"Kick It Out has had to be flexible, it has had to change over time, but it has never lost sight of its core values or the job that it is there to do. When you think back to the 70s and contrast that with grounds today, it's tempting to become complacent and think the battles have been won.

We know that's not the case and that there's still work to do.

"Kick It Out is as relevant today as it [ever was], albeit that the challenges are different and widening to take in abuse of other kinds beyond the race issue. I'm sure it will still be doing work that's just as important when it celebrates its 50th anniversary!"

Leroy Rosenior

"I'd been abused, had monkey chants, 'black this, black that' during my career. From my managers as well: 'You black this, why don't you this and that?' That was the normal language then, you just got on with it. If you wanted to have a career, you had to. If you reacted, people said you had a chip on your shoulder that you weren't part of the team [and] I wanted desperately to be a professional footballer."

Leroy Rosenior advocated life bans for racial abuse, publicly declaring his controversial views in the wake of the John Terry and Anton Ferdinand case. "The FA have let down the whole of society, not just black players. A lot of people are ashamed of what's gone on, no matter their colour. It's fine for the FA to say it was an independent inquiry, but it didn't get the proper result. It depends how good a player you are what type of punishment you get – [Terry is] still Chelsea captain. We need zero tolerance. We need people to know that if you do this you're banned for life. Do that a couple of times and people will sort their life out."

Rosenior's career began at 17 and he was quickly subjected to horrific racist abuse. He and Paul Parker were chasing down a ball when a crowd of 15,000 fans gave them a Nazi salute, a vile pattern repeated throughout the 1980s, a period when it wasn't uncommon to be spat at, too. Even his own coaches sometimes spoke to him in racially derogatory terms and, while that was one of the closely guarded dressing room secrets of the time, it's since emerged as being commonplace.

Now a campaigner for Show Racism the Red Card, Rosenior visits two schools a day, five days a week, coaching and delivering education programmes and workshops to 60 kids at a time. What he's heard demonstrates that the underlying issues that fuelled the racism he suffered still remain. "They'll say, 'I call him Chinky and he doesn't mind.' But, if he seems all right with it, it's because he's in the same situation as I was in. He wants to be a part of something and he doesn't want to be seen as not having a sense of humour. This is where it starts. We go into the schools and we show the kids a thing called the Pyramid of Hate. It starts with racist labels and then leads to fights. Not all the time, but [...] because you're alienating someone [...] it can lead to people getting hurt. It can lead to murder. This is what we saw with Stephen Lawrence. With those people in the Stephen Lawrence case, they thought it was acceptable to call people names because in their community nobody ever pulled them up on it. I just wanted to change the way adults deal with things with kids. The message I hear from adults when a kid has a go at them is, 'Oh, just ignore them.' But, if you [do] you're condoning it and they do it to someone else.

"You need to deal with it but in a positive way. They need to go and tell the teachers, so the teachers know that bullying isn't acceptable. The saying I was brought up with as a boy, 'sticks and stones may break my bones, but names will never hurt me' [is an] awful saying. I wanted to go and smash them in the face. These things stick with you for a long time and they affect you. Since

I've been doing this, so many players have been wanting to engage in it, wanting to talk about it, because they understand.

"The great thing now is seeing lots of white players getting involved. It gives players the confidence to talk in front of the kids. It's not something they'd have done otherwise and it's great for their future careers. They come out of Show Racism the Red Card and they go into other roles, like broadcasting or administrative roles, where they've got the confidence to go up and talk in front of people. It's a two-way thing and the impact it's had on the schools – how they act, how they behave – is incredible."

Ruud Gullit

"The more you stand up for your rights, the bigger a player you are, the more hostility you will face. I just said to myself during these trying periods, 'OK, Ruud, when you stick up for yourself you know what'll happen' [but] I've always done what I felt had to be done, what was right."

Netherlands captain Ruud Gullit led his country to victory at Euro 88, became 1987 European Footballer of the Year and World Player of the Year, achieving the latter accolade again two years later. He also achieved a number three hit in the Dutch Top 40 with the anti-apartheid song "South Africa", a collaboration with the reggae band Revelation Time. During his spell as a Euro 96 BBC pundit, he coined the term "sexy football".

Appointed Chelsea player-manager in 1996. Ruud led the club to FA Cup triumph in 1997 (the club's first major trophy in 26 years), becoming the first non-British manager to win a major trophy in England.

Born in 1962 in Amsterdam to a Surinamese immigrant father, Gullit grew up in one small split-room at the top of an apartment building. He formed his football skills on the streets and signed for a junior side at the age of eight.

Gullit has consistently shown his commitment to campaigns against racism, not only in football, but also in his vehement support of South Africa's struggle against apartheid – hence the pop song. He dedicated both his World and European Footballer of the Year awards to South Africa's future president Nelson Mandela, who, at the time, was still imprisoned for his humanitarian fight against apartheid. In 1996, the Dutch Sports Ministry honoured Gullit with the role of European Ambassador for the campaigns against Racism and Violence in Football.

Ruud spoke out about his own experiences during Euro 2012. Writing in his *Mail Online* column he said, "The monkey sounds that greeted the Holland team at their training session this week were an embarrassment to the Polish authorities. The problem of racial abuse of footballers is now on everyone's radar and it has to be dealt with. There is no place to hide here at Euro 2012. I was in Poland on Friday and, walking around Warsaw, you could see that UEFA are trying to educate people on racism. There are fans' parks everywhere, with information on tackling racism. But it is the responsibility of governments to act, too – it can't all be down to UEFA, even if football is such a powerful medium."

He said that Holland captain Mark van Bommel was correct to speak out and draw attention to an incident where racial abuse was thrown at Gullit on the pitch. "When I played, I received racial abuse, but I was just one of a few black players and we weren't backed up by the authorities. Now there are so many at the top of their profession and they have the backing of important people. I used to ignore the abuse and felt powerless to change attitudes. My only weapon was my performances on the pitch and I'm proud to have played for some of the biggest clubs in the world, as well as winning the European Footballer of the Year and World Footballer of the Year awards. Players won't take that type of abuse any more. We had to because we had no backing. I used the racist abuse in a positive way. I thought people were afraid of me so I used it as my motivation."

Pat Nevin
"I've made my views clear in Parliament, at a Hammersmith Council event, but, in reality, I've been saying the same thing for a long time now – we've come a long way, but we still have a long way to go."

Pat Nevin received an Honorary Degree of Doctor of Letters from Abertay University in 2012. It was in recognition of his contribution to the field of sports in a football career spanning 20 years, his work as CEO of Motherwell Football Club, as a football writer and broadcaster, and in recognition of his work as patron of Show Racism the Red Card and anti-apartheid campaigner.

Nevin has been a huge supporter of the campaign for many years and has a place in the Show Racism the Red Card Hall of Fame along with John Barnes, Shaka Hislop, Gary Lineker and Ian Wright.

He played for Clyde, Chelsea, Everton, Tranmere Rovers, Kilmarnock and Motherwell. The height of abject and blatant racist abuse occurred during his hugely successful period at Stamford Bridge. Pat routinely intervened when teammate Paul Canoville, the first black player in Chelsea's history, was subjected to racial abuse during matches. "Canners" forged a close bond with Pat after the Glaswegian remonstrated with and publicly condemned supporters who racially abused him.

Speaking at the Football Firsts' Black History Month event in association with the Paul Canoville Foundation,

Nevin disclosed that he received death threats, yet still felt compelled to speak out. "I couldn't not intervene," he told Sky Sports News. "The accepted thought in football [at the time] was ignore the racism, maybe the club would do something about it or maybe the FA will do something about it. The black players were being told to shut up about it when a lot of them wanted to talk about it. Me speaking about it may have sounded brave, unusual – maybe I was the only one at the time, but it was my background. Paul Canoville didn't know my background, which was quite political. I was a student doing a degree in Glasgow and us students got a wee bit involved in politics. I spent time at anti-apartheid marches. I come from an Irish background and ten years before my time there were signs outside bars saying, NO BLACKS, NO DOGS, NO IRISH, so there was kind of something there as well. It was just about being brought up thinking there should be equality and equal chances for everyone. I just wanted to make sure that for other people, it wasn't made difficult for them to do the things they should be able to do, live a normal life, work and be treated with respect. When I saw those biased viewpoints being brought into football stadiums it was like, 'I won't bring my politics if you don't bring your politics. You've brought yours, I'm bringing mine, it's back on you.'"

In 2012, Nevin elaborated about the extent of the threats on a special edition of BBC Radio Scotland's *Off The Ball* football chat show, broadcast from the Edinburgh Fringe. "I got a few [death threats], two different sets of them. I got them early on in my career when I was at Chelsea, from the far right, when I was starting up the campaign against racism in football. I've had a few more recently, over the last couple of years, for the anti-sectarian stuff I've been standing up for. Some people don't seem to agree with that." Asked whether the threats had come from Celtic or Rangers fans, he replied: "Amazingly, they don't sign it! I'm just trying to say to people, 'Try to live together, be friendly.' It's not that complicated."

Nevin spoke at a Hammersmith Town Hall event, supported by the FA, PFA and Kick It Out, ahead of a panel discussion with Chris Ramsey, Paul Elliott, Ricky Hill, Andy Impey, Hope Powell and Howard Gayle. Canoville was in hospital after complications following a bowel operation, which left him in an induced coma for a week, but he managed to send a video message, which was played to guests in attendance. Elliott said he was thrilled to be part of the occasion. "It's lovely to have such an assortment of quality players, who have all made a huge substantial positive difference to the game," he said. "Canners is a top man and together we have seen some of the most challenging of times. He was an outstanding player and his contribution to the game was fantastic. He's been a bit poorly, but we have sent out our good thoughts to him and I'm delighted that he is on his way to a speedy and efficient recovery." Just back from the World Cup in Russia the much-in-demand media pundit felt it was important to gather together a wide range of opinion about the big issues of racism and discrimination in a book to commemorate KIO. He wanted to re-open a debate that needs to be reviewed, and there was no better time than now.

Nevin said, "As a student in Glasgow and while playing with Clyde we were a renowned bunch of lefties, so I was involved in all sorts of anti-apartheid and anti-racism marches and movements long before Kick It Out was formed. But coming to Chelsea was certainly an eye-opener, I couldn't believe what was going on. I'd been used to sectarian bigotry, but nothing like this.

To say I was disappointed in what I came across is an understatement. I was shocked. We had nothing like this in Scotland. It was pretty intense in a game with Crystal palace in 1984, and I felt compelled to talk about it. It wasn't long after that, together with Gordon Taylor and Herman Ouseley, we were suggesting there needed to be a campaign to combat it. It was particularly entrenched at clubs, even my beloved Everton and we got involved in Merseyside Against Racism when I signed there even before KIO was formed. But KIO brought it all together at a time that it was becoming a touch political with a small 'p'. Perhaps I was just naïve at the time, but I thought that the black players shouldn't be putting themselves up to combat this, it ought to be done on their behalf. But, as time went on, and the problems were being faced head on by the likes of KIO then you know the black players had to speak out as well, which they did. It was important for players to have rights, and that meant all players. It meant that people like myself didn't need to be at the forefront of the campaign, but I was always there in the background if needed to speak out about it. I've made my views clear but, in reality, I've been saying the same thing for a long time now … we've come a long way, but we still have a long way to go. In the land of perfection, there would be zero racism, but that's never going to happen, it will never disappear entirely, but it does need to be controlled.

"There are still places where the message has failed to get across, some areas of Eastern Europe, for example. We all thought it would be bad in Russia at the World Cup, but it wasn't, and that was refreshing. The important point is that you should not be subjected to discrimination in any shape or form anywhere or any time, but certainly not at your place of work.

"The famous biblical phrase 'The poor are always with you' could easily apply to racism. Although FIFA and UEFA have woken up to the problem, the game's leaders haven't quite got to grips about how to sort it out – the kind of punishments needed. Fines are pitifully small. If you raise your shirt to show a political message on your T-shirt, you'll be hit with a massive fine, but only receive a tiny fine for racial abuse. Clubs and, indeed, national teams have no control over supporters who attach themselves to them, but they can take steps. Fines need to be much more robust. For too long, and even now, it seems to be two steps forward and one step back."

Nevin likes my suggestion that KIO should be funded by the FA to take over disciplinary procedures in relation to racism. "Yes, I do like the morality of it, but having studied law for a couple of years, I can see all the obstacles that would be put up to avoid it!"

Greater representation at the highest level is a constant theme running through this book, and Pat is no stranger to the discrimination that exists. "I've never seen colour, I never saw it when I was a chief executive and had to appoint a manager. We had 50 applications and I can't remember if there was more than one black applicant, but it never crossed my mind that I should make a choice based on colour. Football is about tiny margins, and if you pick someone for such a vital role for tokenism then that is wrong – it has to be the right person for the right job. Not the wrong choice for the right reasons."

Again, as I have throughout this book, I pose the question of whether we might ever see a black chairman of the FA. "Yes, I think we will. The problem is that the old boys' network exists everywhere, not just in football, it exists in every structure of society. In football, we need to apply pressure that it is the right man for the job, not the wrong choice for the right reasons. To get there, there must be equal opportunity for everyone. I've real confidence that that will happen. Football is a huge business and as such if the right man comes along to run this industry, it won't be determined by whether he is black or not; if he's the right man or indeed woman for the job, he or she needs to get it."

Jermain Defoe

"I played for England against Spain in a friendly at the Bernabeu in 2004 and it was well documented that me, Ashley Cole and Shaun Wright-Phillips were among the black players who received monkey chants. It was a huge international match and it shocked me that this was happening. But that was probably the last time I experienced any kind of racism, and every year it seems to be improving. Maybe I've been lucky, but I haven't experienced much of it directly towards me. I've obviously heard stories, especially from years ago."

With 57 caps and 20 goals to his career, Jermain Defoe, OBE, started out with Charlton Athletic, joining their youth team aged 14, before moving to West Ham United at 16, making his first team debut in 2000. After a season-long spell on loan at Bournemouth until 2001 he was established in the West Ham line-up. After relegation in 2003, he moved to Tottenham in January 2004 and, after four years, was sold to Portsmouth. He had one season at Fratton Park before returning to Tottenham in the January 2009 transfer window. Leaving for Toronto FC of Major League Soccer in 2014, he returned to England in January 2015 to sign for Sunderland, before returning to Bournemouth.

In an exclusive interview for this book, Defoe says, "John Barnes came into the England camp once to give us a talk about what it had been like for him in his early Watford days but, since then, massive steps have been made in this country and I believe things are heading in the right direction. Attitudes are changing on and off the pitch and people are trying to get it (racism) out of the game completely. Racism and discrimination shouldn't be happening anywhere, whether that is sport or society in general.

"I can't speak highly enough of Kick It Out and all the initiatives they've put in place over the years. Kick It Out has been so important to this country. All the things they've done show people they are serious and that whatever goes on – or used to go on – will not be tolerated.

"Football is such a powerful tool. It brings people together. It unites them, educates them and helps break down boundaries. We saw that with the World Cup in Russia, and we see it every weekend around the country. It can have a huge impact on making sure discrimination is no longer part of our society, and that is what Kick It Out have been working hard to achieve.

"Footballers are role models and when we go into schools, it is a chance to help educate young people, to show them what is right and what is wrong. The kids we are speaking to are the next generation and we have the opportunity to help mould their views and beliefs. It's been great to be involved with Kick It Out and I would recommend any player to do the same."

Jermain received an OBE in 2018 for his work setting up the Jermain Defoe Foundation. This was just under a year after the tragic death of six-year-old Bradley Lowery. Jermain formed a strong bond with the little boy, who was repeatedly picked to be a mascot for his beloved Sunderland while he battled neuroblastoma. He said, "I've got great memories of Bradley in my head but it wasn't easy seeing someone that you love suffer like that, especially a young kid, where he didn't really understand what was going on and you have to remain positive."

Defoe's foundation was launched in 2013 after a hurricane in St Lucia, the Caribbean island his grandparents came from. The charity provides support for abused and vulnerable children there and has expanded to help children in the surrounding islands and the UK.

Defoe's brother Jade died from head injuries sustained after he was attacked in the street in 2009. He lost his grandparents at around the same time and, in 2012, his father died of cancer and a cousin died in an accident at a swimming pool.

Defoe became the ambassador of the E18HTEEN project – endorsed and supported by the PFA among others – which aimed to mentor kids between the ages of 16 and 19, who either had been, or were, in care. The primary objective was to get those in care into training, education, apprenticeships and full-time employment. Such was the success of the project that it won the London Beyond Sport Award.

Defoe is an ambassador for the Prince's Trust – one of the PFA's long-standing partners – which provides opportunities for young people who need that extra support in life to gain employment, education or training.

In an interview for a PFA tribute magazine, he said, "I came from East London, a massive family and I just remember clearly when I was younger playing in a park with my mates and I don't feel like I've changed in any way. You have to acknowledge you're blessed – where you've been to, where you've come from and to be able do something that was my dream. When you're in a position like I am now, it's important to give back. It's all very well saying it, but it's doing something for the community. I know how important it is to the kids, they love it. I remember being at a local club in the East End, we were told that a professional player would come to do the presentations and the night before, you couldn't sleep. We had Kevin Campbell of Arsenal one year and, though I was a huge Ian Wright fan, it was incredible to see Campbell in the flesh and be able to hear him speak. Little things like that, to understand the feeling I had. If you [as a player] just turn up for an hour, it's unbelievable.

"I lost my brother in 2009 and I spoke to some of the people at Tottenham and we came up with an idea of doing my own thing," recalls Defoe. "We thought of 18, my special number. We wanted to help get kids who were in foster care, kids on the street, kids without families to have a better life and we came up with the E18HTEEN project. One day, Sky TV came to film a session we had with the kids and I sat at the top of the class, Geoff Shreeves [the lead Sky TV interviewer] asking me a few questions. There was a group of ten who were about 17, 18 years of age and he said I should stop talking and let's hear from the kids. He asked them what they thought of me and they said, 'He's changed my life.' You don't ever expect anyone to say that. They said they'd be on the streets if it wasn't for the positive message I had. I got emotional. I started to cry a little. It meant an incredible amount to me. You think that going out on a Saturday afternoon and scoring the winning goal is the greatest feeling ever, but this is on another level."

Paul Canoville
"I didn't want to come out on the pitch. I would warm up inside the changing room and go out just before. I hated being a sub. When I warmed up, it was, 'Sit down, you n*****.' At the old Stamford Bridge, I used to stay behind the goal. It was a long way to the crowd at the old ground."

Having played for Chelsea and Reading, Paul Canoville founded the MTC (Motivate to Change) Foundation in 2009. Honorary President of ICA Sports Football Club and an ambassador to the Guy Mascolo Football Charity/ Goal Getters, he's also the author of the award-winning 2009 sports book *Black & Blue*.

"Thank you for wishing to include me in this project; it's a subject that is very close to my own heart especially in my era." So began Paul Canoville, one of the footballers most associated with the worst excesses of extreme racism.

In an exclusive interview for this book, Paul commented, "I champion Lord Ouseley and herald Kick It Out, as it is now known, 100%. Not only do they acknowledge racism that goes on within football, they work hard to be recognised as the official body to go to – be it a fan or a footballer experiencing racism, on or off the pitch.

"I wish it could have been there when I was playing but I'm delighted that Kick It Out is there now. It shows players of today you don't have to shoulder it alone. KIO will take it seriously, look into the matter but, most importantly, give support.

"While statistically, incidents being reported are increasing, it also shows the success of Kick It Out being viewed in the eyes of the new generation of fans and footballers, as a recognised anti-racism body, and that these incidents are being reported, rather than being kept under the radar."

Canoville was the first black player for Chelsea. That should be something to savour, and in a way it was then, and remains so now. However, it came at a price. A very heavy price: in the form of vile, racist abuse from when he made the breakthrough in the early 1980s. Much of that abuse from the club's own "supporters".

Dealing with such adversity has become second nature. He has battled drug addiction, successfully fought cancer on three occasions, seen his baby son Tye die in his arms and coped with a "seriously complicated" personal life, fathering eleven children with ten women.

Let's start with the good things. "Winning the Division Two title in 1983/84 was amazing. We had a good, good team. Personally, there are three highlights. Scoring a goal against Fulham that got us a draw and played a big part in helping avoid relegation when we were in a mess in 1983. Also scoring a hat-trick against Swansea. But the one that everyone loves to talk about is the Milk Cup game against Sheffield Wednesday (4–4 in quarter-final replay in 1984), when I scored, about ten seconds after coming on as a sub, and then got another in an amazing game."

Now the bad things: monkey chants, bananas being hurled at him and being threatened with physical violence.

"I remember scoring a goal and hearing that some fans wouldn't have it because a black player scored. It didn't count, so they said we had lost not drawn. How do you live like that? I had to control my anger so many times so outsiders couldn't see. I had to see the bigger picture."

Canoville's mother dealt with racism after coming over to England from the Caribbean. He credits her with giving him the strength to deal with the excessive abuse and now uses his experiences positively, working part-time for Educate Through Football. His work with the Motivate to Change Foundation, sees him visiting primary schools around the country and abroad and he has recently started a new project called Motivation4Change. "It's brilliant doing what I do. I go into schools, telling them how important education is, as well as telling them what I went through – the racism, bullying, the problems, following your dreams and the good times – everything. My new venture is working with ex-offenders and youngsters with behavioural problems, giving them the life skills to get back into the community. I share my story."

When Canoville was plucked from his hometown, non-league club Hillingdon Borough in December 1981, there were few black players. He was booed and had all sorts of racist abuse hurled at him by Chelsea fans as he warmed up before his debut in an away game against Crystal Palace.

At the same fixture two seasons later, on 14 April 1984, the abuse was just as bad. His teammate, the now respected pundit Pat Nevin, scored the only goal of the game and came out in support of Canoville afterwards, calling the abuse disgusting. "I respected Pat and was honoured when he came out and said what he said. I was getting hardcore abuse. But he scored, and he made that statement and, boy, did people take notice. It eased things for me. I had family members saying, 'Why are you playing for them?' But that helped massively."

Former Chelsea defender Frank Sinclair also praises Canoville's strength: "My first memory of going as a nine-year-old was the racist abuse the players suffered. It was so intimidating and being in the minority and seeing the abuse players like Paul got was terrible. I was a Chelsea fan and then I joined as a schoolboy and was also a ball-boy. It was really difficult. I got to the point thinking maybe I didn't want to stay. I was a young black player aspiring to play for a big club, but the verbal abuse and chanting at the black players was scary. Paul acted with such dignity. He never responded and proved people wrong with his ability. He just took it on the chin and how he dealt with it was fantastic. He undoubtedly paved the way for black players to come through."

Viv Anderson

"It was a lot easier for me than, say, Laurie Cunningham or Cyrille Regis. They were flamboyant forwards so they were identified much more. Cyrille got a bullet through the post with the message, 'This one's for you if you play for England.'"

Viv Anderson, the young Nottingham Forest substitute decided to retreat back along the touchline and retake his place alongside Brian Clough in the dugout. "I thought I told you to warm up," said the manager. "I have done, boss," replied Viv. "But they're throwing bananas, apples and pears at me." Clough stared back. "Well, get back out there and get me two pears and a banana!" Viv recalled the incident at Carlisle in the mid-70s during an interview with the *Daily Mail*. "It was Cloughie's way of having a bit of fun with what was a racist act, but he also meant that there was no point me sitting next to him cowering. He pulled me over afterwards and said, 'If you let people like that dictate to you, I'm going to pick somebody else because you're going to be worrying about what the fans are going to say.' I was 19. After that, I made sure there was nothing, whatever people shouted, that would have a bearing on what I did."

Racists first targeted him twelve months earlier as he was preparing for his second game for Forest in a League Cup tie at Newcastle. "Dog's abuse. Really vicious. 'Black this, black that.' I went back in and told the manager, Dave Mackay, I didn't want to play. He just told me to get myself out there, and it's a good job he did. I remember getting knocked onto the track by the Newcastle striker John Tudor and everybody cheering. It was quite hard. I was 18 and there were 50,000 people in those days for a cup-tie. I had to get on with it. There were times when I wondered if I wanted to be in this but sometimes you have to go through these things. There's a black face in most football clubs now and, hopefully, I've done my little bit to make it easier for them to forge a career."

The former Forest, Arsenal and Manchester United full-back still has the telegram from the Queen that was waiting for him in the dressing room that night, and an MBE followed many years later, even though he didn't fully appreciate the significance of his achievement at the time. "As soon as I became the first (black player for England), it was always going to be an issue. I was honoured and privileged, but it was finished as far as I was concerned. It was absolutely the last thing on my mind at the time. All the stuff that went on the day before and the day after went in one ear and out the other. Someone said to me the other day, 'You're a walking piece of history,' but I don't think of it like that until somebody else says it."

He never experienced racism growing up in Nottingham as the son of Jamaican immigrants. "When I started, there weren't many black faces and they were all forwards like Clyde Best, Laurie Cunningham and Cyrille Regis. They used to say black lads couldn't play in the cold weather. Then I came along and loved it. I was a black man who liked short-sleeved shirts and it was my job to kick the winger. Basically, that was it. Anything else I did was a bonus. I broke the mould there."

In his autobiography, *First Among Unequals*, Anderson describes going to the launch of England's bid for the 2018 World Cup as a guest of a company he represented. He was shocked the FA had failed to invite a single black person, yet still found room for a member of the BNP. He said at the time, "It's 2010, we're a multiracial country trying to get the World Cup and there was no John Barnes, no Emile Heskey, no Ashley Cole. The FA realise they made a mistake that day. Slowly but surely, they're getting it right."

Anderson played at Sheffield Wednesday under Ron Atkinson, another of football's big personalities later caught on air making ill-judged, racist comments. He said at the time of Big Ron's sacking as a TV pundit, "I can't condone what he says, not for a minute, but if you ask me if Ron Atkinson is a racist I would say, no. Ian Wright would say that he is, but we've all got a personal view. He bought me and I never heard any racist terms whatsoever. He said the wrong thing and he's been punished for it."

As KIO approached its 25th anniversary, in an exclusive interview for this book, Anderson looks back with huge pride and fondness at his record of being the first black England player. "When I come down to London, the cabbies still ask me about certain games and playing for England, but it does seem a long time ago, and all those cabbies are getting old now! While that record can never be taken away from me, it's not about living in the past, it's about the next generation.

"For the next generation, there needs to be greater incentive, especially for the black and [other] minorities who are still lagging behind when it comes to [the] senior level in this game. You see plenty playing the game, but still so few coaches, managers and those in the boardrooms.

"Gareth Southgate did really very well in the World Cup and made us all proud of England again, but there's still a lot to do to reach the next stage of equality in English football. We are a multicultural nation, yet that is hardly reflected in our football, not when you look at the upper echelons of the game. The Rooney Rule might be the solution, it might not [...] I just think we need more ethnic people at the elite level to give young ethnic boys and girls some hope that they can achieve as well.

"Having said all of that, I still think KIO has done a marvellous job. I recall being approached about it when I was at Middlesbrough and Bryan Robson and myself were keen to be involved from day one. I am sure that, over the years, KIO has helped to change the mindset of everybody in football, and that has been good for football, but we all recognise that there's still a lot to do."

Keith Alexander

"I've been very lucky to have a chairman and a managing director to whom colour doesn't matter. We've had a lot of support from the local council. It's a liberal-minded club. The fact that I am black is immaterial. I must have been the best person to have applied for the job, or otherwise I wouldn't have got it."

Keith was the first full-time black manager in the Football League in 1993, the very year Kick It Out was born.

When Keith was growing up in Nottingham in the 1960s, he used to run errands for a local hairdresser called Mrs Cunningham. In an interview with Simon O'Hagan, published in 1993, Keith recalled: "She had a dog, and one day she asked young Keith if he could go across the road to the corner shop to buy it some food. So, I went in the shop and said, 'Can I have a can of dog food, please?' And the woman behind the counter said, 'They tell me it's very nice stewed.' I thought nothing of it and I just said, 'Oh, yeah, very nice' or something and it wasn't until years later when I heard people talking that I realised what the woman had meant. She thought we ate it. She actually thought we ate dog food."

Keith made history when he took over as the manager of Third Division Lincoln City. The first black manager in the League was Tony Collins in 1960 at Rochdale, but Keith was the first full-time black manager and the first of the generation born to those 1950s immigrants, which provided English football with some of its most exciting and talented players.

Racial abuse of footballers was still routine, even though every team in the League bar Everton had at least one black player. Keith recalled a time in his playing days with non-League Kettering when he scored the winning goal at Fisher Athletic, in south London, "and was nearly lynched." Acknowledging what high-profile black players went through in the early years "must have been appalling," Alexander says, "We've moved on a lot since then but, the fact remains that, if you're black, it's still twice as hard to get on in any walk of life. I've been very lucky to have a chairman and a managing director to whom colour doesn't matter. We've had a lot of support from the local council. It's a liberal-minded club. The fact that I'm black is immaterial."

He feels black players generally had the courage to rise above the abuse. "I think it's because they haven't made a fuss that it's died down. But there will always be some people who go to matches just to pick on players. That's all they are there for, and I don't think they'll go away."

John Barnes

"It's happened before [...] a limited amount of elite people benefitting from a movement designed to help the majority ... the #metoo movement, Colin Kaepernick taking a knee ... Tarana Burke started #metoo years ago to highlight the sexual abuse of young black girls in inner cities."

John Barnes, sounding pessimistic, asks, "What will be the outcome? A few more black people on TV, more black agents, steering committees and other elite black groups set up in a few visible industries ... but, nothing will change nor demands made for 99% of black people, *our* communities in the inner city.

"I've been told this time it feels different – the conversation debate won't die down. Well, it seems to be over. The only visible sign we will now see, once again, is footballers taking the knee and talking about racism in football. Oh, yeah, and actors and singers.

"I was going to wait till the end of the week to see if *GMB* (ITV's breakfast show) continues 'the conversation and fight against racial inequality,' as they claimed we need to do but, so far, it seems to have stopped."

One of the most gifted footballers of his generation, Barnes has also been one of the most articulate. He believes banning fans who are found to have racially abused players is not the long-term answer to a problem that has plagued football for generations. "Racism exists, education is the only way. Just banning people is not the answer because they will always find ways of letting you know they are racist without it being illegal."

John Barnes called for "systematic racism" to be challenged and more to be done to rid society of the prejudice. He had to endure horrific abuse and has used his profile to campaign for more to be done to stamp it out.

When he signed for Liverpool in 1987, he was only the second black person to play for the club. He became a legend among Reds fans but suffered abuse from opposition supporters and, at times, even players throughout the 80s and 90s. An iconic image shows him backheeling a banana, which had been thrown on to the pitch. In 2020, Barnes again clashed on social media with *GMB* host Piers Morgan, who'd been outspoken about the decision of the Duke and Duchess of Sussex (Prince Harry and Meghan

Markle) to step down from their royal roles. His comments had infuriated Barnes, who responded on Twitter: "Piers Morgan racist [sic] racist remarks swept under the carpet... *GMB*. Don't have topics on racism unless you're willing to truly discuss the topic when something is right in your face!!!"

He went on to say: "A real topic of racism to be discussed on GMB... piers [sic] language is IGNORED... but one topic because it can't be proved... racism towards Meghan is done to death because u can't prove it... not even a denial from piers not important ... wonder why?? Hmm."

Barnes further tweeted: "Message to the BLACK COMMUNITY. GMB and piers Morgan isn't concerned with the fight against racism. They try to convince u they are by criticising weak scapegoats who get caught but do nothing when the powerful get caught. DON'T BE FOOLED."

Born in Jamaica, Barnes moved to London with his family when he was 12. Joining Watford at seventeen, he made his England debut in 1983, signed for Liverpool four years later, and stayed with the club for a decade, scoring 108 goals in 407 appearances. In April 1989, after the Hillsborough disaster claimed the lives of 96 Liverpool fans, Barnes attended several funerals and visited the injured in hospital. He pulled out of an England international friendly in order to fulfil these public duties.

Twice in his career he was voted Football Writers' Association Footballer of the Year and also won the PFA Players' Player of the Year. He was inducted into the English Football Hall of Fame in 2005 in recognition of his contribution to the English game.

Today, having retired from football, Barnes mostly works as an ESPN pundit. In 2008, he launched the *Daily Mirror*'s anti-racism "Hope not Hate" bus tour, paying tribute to murdered black teenager Anthony Walker, the 18-year-old killed with an ice-axe in a racist murder in Liverpool in July 2005. Standing alongside Anthony's mum, Gee, he said, "Whatever racist abuse I went through as a player, is nothing to what this family have been through. Mrs Walker [...] has felt the real tragic effect of racism, and no sports player's experience comes near to it."

During a South America tour, Barnes, Viv Anderson and Mark Chamberlain were racially abused on a flight to Santiago by National Front activists posing as England fans. It is one of many sordid tales he exposed about racism in his 1999 autobiography. "They [the NF] kept saying, 'England only won 1–0 because a nigger's goal doesn't count'," Barnes wrote.

In an interview with the *Independent*, in May 2013, he was quoted as saying, "Last week, I was with Gabriel Clarke from ITV and he brought all the back pages about my goal and the tour. Looking through the newspapers, there was not one mention of the incident on the plane to Chile. The good old days. The issue I have is that they have journalists around then who are around now who now feel just like you (about the incident). They champion the cause that racism is wrong. Then, they never said a word. Have they changed their mentality? Would they have got sacked if they wrote it?"

Barnes's views on race, and the incidents are very different to what he calls "the party line." He admits that he will never be offered a role by the PFA or KIO because he does not believe in zero tolerance, quotas, the Rooney Rule, and forcing people to give a black man a job "and all that kind of rubbish." Instead of legislation, Barnes asks people to confront what he says is the "unconscious racist" in everyone, including himself.

When he arrived at Anfield in 1987, he received letters telling him to "go back to Africa and swing from the trees." Kenny Dalglish stood up for him in public but, in those days, the dressing room jokes knew few boundaries.

In a 2011 *Daily Telegraph* interview, he agreed with people criticising Sepp Blatter, but added, "If you want to have a South African-style Truth and Reconciliation Commission, get in every manager and player who is over-40 and ask them, 'Say you have never used the N-word.' Most won't be able to. Much more than 75% of people back then in the 80s would have. We are all racist to a certain extent. We all make presumptions about other people based on their colour, culture or ethnicity, in variable degrees. We judge people even on their accents. When Eric Cantona said what he said about trawlers and seagulls, he's a philosopher because of the French accent. It sounds intelligent. If Paul Merson said it in his Cockney accent, we'd say he was talking rubbish."

Barnes believes that "until black people are regarded as intellectually and morally equal, we will never be equal. That is why I don't like the idea of black, sporting role models. What we are saying to our black kids is, 'You don't have to worry about education, you can become a boxer, you can become a runner.' Now, it's okay for white sporting role models because white people also have role models to show the kids who can't do sport they can be prime minister or whatever. What role models do black kids have? John Barnes? Yeah, but what if you don't like football?"

Barnes, referring to Alan Hansen's use of the outdated word "coloured" – which caused quite a storm of controversy – points out that the use of language changes and suggests we should be looking at "intent" when judging people. He says, "In the 1970s, people were afraid to call me black because they thought it was an insult. They would say 'coloured.' Now it has gone full circle. It's not an issue. The intention is the most important thing."

He's been told many times that people don't see him as black. "If you don't see me as being black, what do you see me as being? Normal? Is black not normal? And secondly, if you don't see me as being black, what is your impression of what black is? Because I may well speak well and I am okay, that's not the impression of what you have as black? What I say about myself, black footballers or black pop stars, is that we have been 'elevated out of blackness.' Because when people see us, they don't see us as being black. These are the issues that we should address."

Harry Redknapp
"In my playing days it was pretty tough being a black player, but that era has long gone. People are different, the game is vastly different, and thank god for that. That evil in the game is no where near as bad as it used to be, and you have to say that Kick It Out has played a massive part in making that happen, as they have helped to open people's eyes to it."

Harry Redknapp has been around the block and back again as one of football's most experienced and knowledgeable managers, so his views on racism, dating back to the days of Clyde Best, are worth listening to.

"Clyde was one of the first black players to come over to English football and he experienced some difficult times for sure, the noises from the crowd, he got almighty abuse," recalls Harry.

"It's hard to imagine it was 50 years ago. No one could possibly dislike Clyde, he was such a lovely fellow. The West Ham fans loved him, but he got dog's abuse when we played away. Yet, it didn't bother him, it went right over his head, he thought they were idiots and he actually felt sorry for them."

Redknapp believes KIO has "opened peoples' eyes" and changed perceptions in this country, but he points out that it's more evolution than revolution: "Yes, there has been an amazing improvement, and much is to be applauded in what Kick It Out have achieved, there is certainly more black lads playing in this country than ever before, virtually as many as English players."

Redknapp has a contentious view about why there are so few black managers but has every confidence that will change. "I don't subscribe to the notion that black coaches and managers are being excluded due to race or colour. If they are good enough they will get the job in my opinion. It just doesn't cross my mind that chairman and directors would pass by a good candidate because he is black, I just don't believe it. My view is that as more and more black players make the progression to coaches then they will become managers. We have had successful black managers with Ruud Gullit and Chris Hughton and we now have more and more foreign owners.

"It isn't a question of you don't see any black faces in the board rooms of English clubs, you could argue you don't see many English faces! Look at the clubs these days, especially the biggest clubs in the land – Chelsea, Manchester City, Arsenal, Manchester United, Liverpool, Everton – they are all owned by overseas investors. It used to be the butcher, baker and candlestick maker, but these days you need to be a multibillionaire to afford a club, not just a millionaire."

Les Ferdinand

"How can it possibly happen that I don't see any black people in a prominent position within the FA?"

Les Ferdinand is Director of Football at his former club Queens Park Rangers and is in a unique position to assess in real terms whether there are genuine opportunities for black and ethnic minorities to wield authentic power in the game's governing bodies.

Ferdinand's playing career included spells at Queens Park Rangers, Beşiktaş, Newcastle United, Tottenham Hotspur, West Ham United, Leicester City, Bolton Wanderers, Reading and Watford. He earned 17 caps for England. Ferdinand is the eighth highest scorer in the Premier League with 149 goals and became affectionately known as "Sir Les" in his spell playing for QPR for his inspiring character as well as his goalscoring power as a centre-forward.

Les faced the racist wrath of Everton fans in 1996. "What does anger me is when you see parents doing it in front of their kids. When Newcastle played at Goodison on the opening day of the 1996/97 season, I picked up an injury and needed treatment on the perimeter track. As I sat by the touchline, dads in the stand were hurling all kinds of abuse at me, much of it racist, as their sons sat beside them. Those kids will think it is perfectly normal to carry on like that."

Ferdinand is one of the few to have progressed into a football club's boardroom, which makes his views even more potent. He accused the FA of "covert racism" following a 2014 report detailing an alarming lack of BAME coaches. The study, carried out by the Sports

People's Think Tank, found that there were 19 BAME coaches in the 552 top coaching positions at professional clubs in English football at that time and Ferdinand argued that the figures confirmed the presence of institutional discrimination within the game's governing body.

Just a year later, Ferdinand believed English football remained inherently racist. Speaking to Sir Trevor Phillips as part of a Channel 4 documentary on race, QPR's director of football claimed the fact that he has only once been offered a route into football management since retiring as a player did not reflect well on the game in this country either.

Today, "Sir Les" has less-than-positive views about the issues facing the game: "I still feel that there's a long way to go. On the surface, it all looks like there is great progress, and it's all heading in the right direction, but I'm able to look much deeper into the boardrooms of the clubs and within the FA and I can so no person of colour or ethnic origin in any prominent position."

Can he foresee a black chairman of the Football Association? "Not in my lifetime! How can it possibly happen – I don't see any black people in a prominent position within the FA. Everyone keeps telling me how much progress has been made, how much has been done, but I am afraid that much of it is just lip service.

"You're made to believe that things are going in the right direction because of the existence of KIO and other similar organisations that have grown over the years. People have somewhere to go if they are experiencing problems or have grievances, and KIO will be there for them to kick up a stink. But, for all of that, there's still no one at the top of the game representing the minority interests, the representation at the top level is totally disproportionate.

When you look at teams in the English game right the way through all the age groups to the senior levels, there will be 60–40 representation, but it is nothing like that in staff, coaching or management."

21

KIO Equality and Inclusion

"I feel honoured to have the opportunity to build on the team's great work over many years and look forward to setting out my vision for equality in football in the months ahead."

– Sanjay Bhandari, Kick It Out Chair

"Everyone keeps asking why our players are not interacting on social media. [It is] Because they're being driven away from it."

– Troy Townsend, KIO Education Manager

"It saddens me that current players both black and white continue to use racist, sexist and homophobic language and accept it as normal through many mediums."

– Marcus Gayle, KIO Education Manager

Kick It Out continues its journey with a brand new head and an ever-expanding education programme. Here, Troy Townsend, Marcus Gayle and Chair Sanjay Bhandari talk about the future.

Kick It Out works jointly with the Premier League to deliver equality and inclusion training for clubs' academy players, staff and parents. These workshops aim to raise awareness on current issues including discrimination, underrepresentation and stereotypes. Each workshop is delivered by Kick It Out and involves discussing topics such as racism, homophobia, sexism, faith, disability, social media and the impact of acceptable and unacceptable banter in a changing room environment. In August 2016, Kick It Out and the Premier League announced the launch of the Equality Inspires Award, presented to Premier League clubs who successfully complete the required number of workshops with their academy sides throughout the relevant age categories, as well as with parents and club staff. Clubs have a two-year timeframe to complete these workshops and gain the award. Any club that undertook workshops throughout the 2015/16 season are able to include these to gain the Equality Inspires Award. In May 2017, Watford were the first club presented with the award in appreciation of their outstanding work as part of the Equality Inspires programme. The award was presented by former Hornet and Equality Inspires tutor Marcus Gayle before their Premier League clash with Liverpool at Vicarage Road. The award recognised the academy's impressive record in embracing and arranging equality and diversity training for all its players as well as staff and player's parents and guardians. Troy Townsend, KIO Education Manager said, "The club has embraced the concept of Equality Inspires over the last two seasons, by ensuring that those connected to their academy structure have received the appropriate training to support their understanding of equality, diversity and inclusion within their working environment." Liverpool FC were presented with a trophy in recognition for their continuing excellence as part of the Equality Inspires Academy programme in 2017. On behalf of KIO, Townsend and Gayle visited the club to acknowledge their commitment to equality and diversity training and to deliver the final sessions of the season. On receiving the award, Liverpool's Academy Director Alex Inglethorpe said that KIO had "really challenged our thinking with the workshops that they have hosted throughout the season and it is a real privilege for the club to work alongside them on such a regular basis."

Troy Townsend
Townsend had surprised England manager Gareth Southgate ahead of the 2018 World Cup with a presentation on the racist abuse that leading black footballers experience on social media. Townsend, who runs workshops introducing academy boys and professionals to diversity and equality across race, gender and sexuality, worked closely with Liverpool before and after their recent trip to Spartak Moscow, where Rhian Brewster was racially abused in the UEFA Youth League tie.

In an interview with Sam Wallace of the *Guardian* a few months before the tournament, he revealed it's an open secret many leading black players avoid social media interaction because of the racial abuse.

Townsend called on social media companies to do more to regulate users and said he hoped black players would come together to speak out about the effect the abuse has had on them. He was speaking in Amsterdam at a press conference ahead of the friendly against Holland. Southgate said that English football should get its own house in order.

Townsend – father of Crystal Palace winger Andros Townsend – made his presentation to leading figures at the FA, including Southgate, women's senior team manager

Phil Neville, technical director Dan Ashworth, Under-17s World Cup-winning coach Steve Cooper and women's coach Mo Marley. "I included some of the comments in the presentation to show the impact of winning the game but also what the players have to deal with when they are active on social media. In the picture, were seven black players and four white players. The comments included: 'Is this the England squad or the Senegal squad?': 'It looks like Nigeria's team'; 'Everyone else sees four white players, I see seven black players'; 'Seven out of eleven are non-English, what's happening to this country?'; and 'Where are the English lads?'

"These kinds of comments are absolutely par for the course. Everyone keeps asking why are our players not interacting on social media. Because they're being driven away from it. We need to use the power of the player's voice; I don't think we use it enough. I know Yaya Touré has spoken up a bit and I have a video of him talking about the impact that abuse had on him. I would love to see a powerful video made by players about the hatred being spouted towards them. Ultimately, the power is with the social media companies."

Townsend announced publicly that he'd "lost faith and trust" with the FA's anti-racism policy after they dismissed a discrimination charge involving his grassroots team in 2015. The FA delivered a unanimous verdict of "case unproven" after Townsend alleged three players from his Redbridge Under-17 team were racially abused. The youngsters said they'd been subjected to monkey taunts and gestures by the parents of opponents AFC Hornchurch during a game in the Eastern Junior Alliance League. His decision to go public with details of the incidents brought the FA's commitment to educating and eradicating racism from the sport into question.

Troy quit as manager at Redbridge and, in an interview with the *Daily Mail*, said, "Racial abuse is degrading, you question yourself, you question whether you're a good person and I don't think anyone, particularly kids of 16, 17, should be subjected to this. I had a decision to make: ignore this or take a stand. I decided to make a stand and I hope people understand the reasons behind it. If the FA are serious about challenging discrimination, they should start administering punishments that are in line with the seriousness of the offence."

The sackings of Chris Powell and Chris Ramsey in 2015 were "disheartening", according to Townsend at the time. Powell departed Huddersfield and Ramsey left QPR to leave four bosses of black and minority ethnic and Asian backgrounds in the top four leagues. "To lose both managers sends out a really strong message to those aspiring to get on this journey," he said.

However, Frank Sinclair, who coached Brackley Town in the National League North disagreed with Townsend, and was convinced there *are* opportunities for black coaches in England. "They [Powell and Ramsey] are both terrific lads who've given me advice in the past, and you're disappointed that they lost their jobs, but you've got to be realistic," he told BBC Radio Northampton. "To make a statement that more or less says, 'Is it because of their colour that they've been sacked?', is something that I had to make a response to because I totally disagree. It can be damaging. I don't question a chairman's integrity."

In 2016, Kick Off, a sport's facility in Dewsbury, Yorkshire, where members of the Muslim community play football, had the word "Paki" sprayed on its window. Townsend said at the time, in an interview in the *Sun*, that he never thought he'd see such a thing. "These are young Muslims who want to play football. Yet, they get that sprayed onto their facility. This is the kind of stuff football must challenge on a daily basis now." Following the Brexit referendum in 2016, there was a spike in hate crime, where vile extremists targeted ethnic minorities or foreign nationals. Townsend feared a minority element hijacked the result to bring back racist behaviour into the game. "With the country leaving the EU, we now have more issues. Every day, people are being victimised. Even with stuff said like, 'Get out of my country' – that's hate. When you're in an unpoliced environment such as grassroots football, it can be open to that kind of nature, which we thought we'd long left behind."

Marcus Gayle

Marcus Gayle is an English-born Jamaican, most recently in post as manager of Staines Town. He starred for Wimbledon and Watford before finishing his playing career at AFC Wimbledon. A member of the Brentford Hall of Fame, he made 230 appearances in two spells with the club. Winning fourteen caps for Jamaica, he played in the 1998 World Cup. He is now focusing on his role with KIO, where education is a key component on battling discrimination in all its forms.

Marcus tells me: "Young players now are different to when I was their age. There was no Kick It Out when I was coming through the ranks in football. I had to tough things out, build up a resistance and endurance to achieve where I wanted to be in the game without any safeguarding or support. You couldn't report anything to a third party. Academy players today are now equipped and feel they can express if anything untoward is happening. These players can articulate very well given the chance. They feel they can trust Kick It Out and we would never put that at risk."

Marcus recalls his times growing up within the dressing rooms of "hard knocks." "From the beginning, leaving school at 16 and entering the football industry, there was a culture that had to be accepted to fit in. Racist, sexist, homophobic language was part and parcel of every football club. And to be honest, I was to become part of that culture by giggling along with it – I'm not proud of it but I was using it at times. It was almost as if you had to accept the culture to progress in the game which I don't agree with but being so young it became the norm. Personally, I was never racially abused to my face on the pitch. But have been socially. I've had teammates refer to opposition players of colour racially but would turn to me and see my frown and say, 'You're all right, you're one of us." Over the years as a player, I've had a sense of awareness that treating people differently because of the colour of skin or background is something not to be tolerated.

"It saddens me that current players both black and white continue to use racist, sexist and homophobic language and accept it as normal through many mediums. As an ex-player, I now have zero tolerance and will continue to help combat any forms of discrimination.

"There has been a positive impact with Kick It Out, an organisation that has brought an awareness of many issues within the domestic game here in England. And here we are today in a better place but still dealing with a lot of the same issues regarding equality for all that take part in the game.

"Today, we have an Equality Inspires educational workshop for academy players from Under-10s to the Under-23s which I'm part of along with Troy Townsend. The workshops consist of having discussions on various topics such as banter, music and social media within the game. We get such a positive response after the workshops that it has enabled academy players to be better equipped in tackling forms of discrimination. Clubs and players now feel the importance of having these workshops. We offer support and guidance along their journey.

"What the players are unhappy about is the governing bodies not doing enough to combat racism and discrimination."

Sanjay Bhandari

Kick It Out appointed equality expert and avid football fan Sanjay Bhandari as the organisation's new chair, succeeding founder, Lord Herman Ouseley, who led the challenge on racism and discrimination in football for 25 years.

An active and recognised leader on equality, diversity and inclusion practice, Bhandari was a member of the Premier League's Equality Standard Independent Panel for four years and is part of the government-sponsored Parker review into the ethnic diversity of UK boards.

Prior to his KIO appointment, Bhandari had a 29-year career in professional services, spending 15 years as a lawyer specialising in fraud and white-collar crime at a leading international law firm. He then held a number of leadership roles at KPMG and EY, where he was a partner for 12 years, before taking up a portfolio career as an independent board member, adviser and charity trustee.

For three consecutive years from 2017, he was named as one of the *Financial Times*' EMpower 100 ethnic minority leaders and, in 2016, as one of the top 100 most influential BAME people in business in the inaugural Upstanding Executive Power List.

Bhandari wants to build and expand on the hugely important work Kick It Out has been doing to campaign for equality in football for more than 25 years. "I am absolutely delighted to join the board of Kick It Out as its chair. I have been a football fan all of my life and a vocal advocate for inclusion. I am passionate about helping football to be a game where people of all backgrounds feel welcome and included from the terraces to the pitch, to the boardroom.

"I feel honoured to have the opportunity to build on the team's great work over many years and look forward to setting out my vision for equality in football in the months ahead."

Bhandari faced slurs of "Paki" from social media trolls within minutes of the announcement. He held a series of summits with Facebook and Twitter as part of a three month strategic review into the charity's work and pledged to listen to some of the campaign group's fiercest critics.

He took over during a turbulent period for the charity after it was found to have governance failures following concerns raised about safeguarding, bullying and harassment.

He declined to take questions about the regulatory compliance case, commissioned by the Charity Commission, instead setting out his vision for the future. He also described how he had experienced the feeling of being unable to report racism on the terraces. He said he had been called "Paki" twice at Wembley.

Bhandari wants, over the next three to seven years, to see a game where "a black player can play in any stadium and be confident that he will not be abused" and "supporters wearing a hijab, kippah or turban can attend a game without receiving stares or abuse."

The Manchester United fan would also like a professional player with a same-sex partner not to be news and expressed a desire for aspiring BAME coaches to feel they will get the same opportunities as their white counterparts, a young girl should have the same chance as her brother to be a professional.

Bhandari said, "Over the last 30–40 years, there has been significant progress. Undoubtedly, the level of overt and abusive discrimination in English football, as in society, is not as prevalent as it was in the 1970s and 80s. But in the last few years, we have seen a definite spike in reported incidents which again reflects society at large."

Football's problem with racism reflects society and could continue to get worse he warned: "This is a societal problem, not just a football problem, but football has a unique ability to influence social attitudes and can affect positive social change. What I believe is that, for football, the answers will lie in collaborating and diving into the detail where the devil resides. As an industry, we may need to tone down the finger-jabbing and proffering of silver bullets. There are none. We need to get people around a table and focus on the current mechanisms we have to prevent, detect and react to incidents."

Three new trustees joined Bhandari: Chris Paouros, Cindy Butts and Kevin Miles, together with Katherine Allen, John Nagle, James MacDougall and Iffy Onuora.

Bhandari lead a strategic review into KIO with all staff and trustees alongside the entire football community, and urged those vocal against the anti-discrimination body to get in contact with him. "I will learn just as much from our most ardent critics as from our most loyal advocates."

In 2015, he was in the away end at Arsenal with his beloved United 3-0 down at half-time. A fellow United supporter pointed towards him and his nephew. "How have they got tickets?" the man shouted, using a racist term to describe Bhandari. He turned on other black and Southeast Asian fans sat nearby. There was no retaliation or condemnation from other fans.

Bhandari has been a United season ticket holder for more than 30 years. He was abused twice at Wembley in the mid-1990s, where on one occasion he was confronted by rival fans outside the stadium. "I think racism has got worse over the last few years," says the former lawyer, who has worked with prisoners on death row. "As a United fan, I've noticed it more at away games where there is this resentment about the difficulty of getting away tickets.

"This 'tourist racism' is a new manifestation and Asian fans are often seen as an easy target because there is this stereotypical perception that we're passive and won't fight back. Now I'm seeing that apply to Southeast Asian fans too when there are large groups of fans coming from overseas. They aren't always welcomed with open arms."

He has faced criticism from former board member Garth Crooks for not being an ex-player and therefore not understanding the trials recent professionals have experienced. Bhandari responded: "While I won't have had the experience that a player will have had of racism on a pitch, I've had my experience of racism in life and on the terraces. I definitely want to work with the players, the likes of Raheem Sterling or Ian Wright, because I think they're the catalyst for change."

Wolverhampton-born Bhandari believes that his "completely different professional experience" means he can be "helpfully naïve" in how KIO looks for different ways to tackle discrimination. "I can ask the questions like: why do we do it like that? Have we always done it like that? Or can't we do it differently?"

KIO received £800,000 from the FA, Premier League, EFL and Professional Footballers' Association the previous year and while it continues to be funded by the organisations that run the game, its independence and impartiality is always going to be questioned. "When I experienced that kind of racism, especially when I was with my nephew, it made me feel angry but also powerless because I'm doing the calculation of whether I can complain about this person. You're thinking about your personal safety and the first instinct is that you hope it goes away. I want to advocate for people to report incidents but also understand the mechanics that it's quite difficult sometimes."

Bhandari wants football to be "a zero tolerance place and a beacon of hope for the rest of society." He wants white players and fans to become activists.

"All of the attention in football is on the high-profile incidents in the Premier League but mercifully, they're relatively few and far between compared to grassroots football where anecdotal evidence tells us that something happens every week. We need to deal with both sides of the equation. It was Martin Luther King who said that ultimately 'What we remember is not the words of our enemies but the silence of our friends.' The message to fans and players is: be those friends and don't be silent; be activists. It's one thing being Raheem Sterling, he's a really powerful voice, but it's equally or more powerful if Harry Kane or Harry Maguire speak up. In the same way for fans, if I complain about racism, people expect that. But if a white middle-aged man complains about it, people stand up and listen a little bit more. It isn't just my responsibility as a member of an ethnic minority to address that. Anyone can complain because discrimination corrodes society. It doesn't hurt just me, it hurts all of us."

22

The World Cup

"Racism has no place in Parliament."
— Dawn Butler, MP

Before the tournament got under way, Raheem Sterling was the centre of constant criticism of his lifestyle, convincing the then-23-year-old that "they hate what they don't even know".

Sterling received negative media coverage over his allegedly "lavish" spending habits, including when he bought his mother a house in 2016 – and the tattoo of a gun on his leg, which was a symbol to mark the death of his father at a young age, was misinterpreted by the media, according to the Manchester City and England forward. "It's sad that I even have to say this, but I'm going to say it, anyway," Sterling wrote in a column for *Players' Tribune*: "There's a perception in certain parts of the media that I love "bling." I love diamonds. I love to show off. I really don't understand where that comes from. Especially when I bought my mum a house, it was unbelievable what some people were writing. I think it's really sad that people do that. They hate what they don't even know."

Sterling talked of his struggles growing up, cleaning hotel bathrooms with his mother at the age of six, and the sacrifices his family made. "If you grew up the same way I grew up, don't listen to what certain tabloids want to tell you. They just want to steal your joy. They just want to pull you down. I'm telling you right now, England is still a place where a naughty boy who comes from nothing can live his dream."

Provocative TV presenter Piers Morgan tweeted, "Get that gun off his leg." The front page of the *Sun* ran with the headline, RAHEEM SHOOTS HIMSELF IN FOOT, describing the tattoo as "sick." Anti-gun campaigners criticised him for sharing a photo of himself with the tattoo of an M16 assault rifle on his leg. The image was branded "totally unacceptable" and "sickening." Sterling responded, saying it reflected a vow he made to "never touch a gun" after his father was shot dead when he was a boy. (Sterling's father was killed in Kingston, Jamaica.) The young player revealed his tattoo in a photo posted to Instagram of himself in training with teammates at St George's Park.

Lucy Cope, who founded the group Mothers Against Guns after her son was shot dead in 2012, said Sterling should not play for England unless he gets rid of the tattoo. "This tattoo is disgusting. Raheem should hang his head in shame. It's totally unacceptable. We demand he has the tattoo lasered off or covered up with a different tattoo. If he refuses, he should be dropped from the England team. He's supposed to be a role model but chooses to glamorise guns."

Sterling, who joined City from Liverpool for £49m in July 2015, responded on Instagram saying that he is fiercely anti-gun because his father was murdered when he was just two years old, and that the FA supported him.

"We all support Raheem Sterling and acknowledge the honest and heartfelt account he gave via Instagram last night," an FA spokesperson said. "He and the rest of the squad are focused solely on preparing for the forthcoming World Cup."

Oliver Kay of *The Times* said the media should "give him a break." "I like Raheem Sterling," he said. "A talented, determined footballer, role model for a lot of kids, a great success story. A gun tattoo doesn't look like his greatest idea ever (and, yes, I read his Instagram post, which was very sad), but who actually cares? It's a tattoo. Give him a break." The *Manchester Evening News* insisted that "the real Raheem Sterling is very different from the public portrayal." *MEN*'s Stuart Brennan wrote: "He is portrayed as a vacuous, shallow, egotist with too much money, little sense and no morals. Those of us who have taken the time to meet him know that to be the opposite of the truth." Gary Lineker, meanwhile, stressed that the player was an outstanding talent with a brilliant work ethic," and called the *Sun*'s treatment of him "disgusting."

Ahead of the World Cup in Russia, enormous pre-tournament hype suggested it would be infested with racism. Danny Rose advised his family against travelling to watch him fulfil a lifelong ambition to participate in the World Cup. Having been verbally abused in an Under-21s match in Serbia in 2012 which resulted in a huge furore over the lenient punishments, Rose had "no faith" in the football authorities. The Russian Football Union had already been fined £22,000 for racist chants by fans in a friendly against France.

England's players held a team meeting over the situation and Gareth Southgate said, "I sympathise 100%. He has had experience of that (racism). I was not aware of the conversation Danny had with his family. He talked to us about it. We had a meeting with the players a few nights ago. I had asked him, for the benefit of other players, [to share] experience in Serbia – and to share some things. What is clear is that he felt let down by the authorities and was not the only one who had experience of that, which is sad to hear. He is part of our team and our family for the next few months. We tend to support our players. It is sad. None of us know what will happen in Russia and it is sad he feels there is a possibility that there could be something he does not want his family to experience. It seems the fines are not making any difference. But Welbeck had an experience with Arsenal in Russia and it was really good. All of these problems are down to a lack of education. It is something we might not want to talk about, but it is something we should talk about."

The families of England's players were staying in Saint Petersburg, 40 kilometres away from the national team's training base in Repino, and Rose did not want his tournament preparations distracted by concerns for their safety. His father Nigel was particularly upset. Rose described how his father had followed him throughout his career and regularly watched him play for Tottenham at Wembley, even though he did not get back home to Doncaster until 3 a.m., and had to be up for work four hours later.

Russian football had been marred by racism at club and international level for several years. But it was not a problem during the 2018 tournament and Rose changed his mind and said he was was open to his family being there. "If I manage to get in the team at some point, I may change my mind." He said: "It's the first time I've been in Russia. It's different to what I've expected and I am having a great time."

Sexism, rather than racism, marred the 2018 World Cup as broadcasters were ordered to stop cameras zooming in on "hot women" in the crowd as FIFA's diversity committee acted. Federico Addiechi said FIFA needed to help tackle sexism. "We've done it with individual broadcasters. We've done it with our host broadcast services," he said. Anti-discrimination group, the Fare Network noted that sexism was the biggest problem at the Russia World Cup after monitoring games. The organisation "documented more than 30 cases." Asked if the crackdown on cutaways of female fans would become official FIFA policy, Addiechi said, "This is one of the activities we definitely will have in future – it's a normal evolution."

Spanish football journalist Gemma Soler, who covered the 2014 World Cup in Brazil, said the incidents of harassment did not surprise her. "It makes me sad but at the same time I feel happy because this kind of misbehaviour, that has existed forever, is receiving more attention from media and a general reprobation from society now."

Colombian correspondent Julieth Gonzalez Theran, meanwhile, was reporting live from Moscow when a man approached her, put one arm around her, grabbed her left breast and kissed her on the cheek, before running away. Elsewhere, Brazilian reporter Julia Guimaraes dodged a kiss by a passer-by while on air from Yekaterinburg. "This is not polite. This is not right. Never do this to a woman. *Respect!*" she shouted, pointing her microphone at the man, before turning back to face the camera. Many other female reporters endured similar treatment. "Something that might look like fun in sport's frivolity is actually problematic behaviour because these are professionals doing their job and they're being harassed and assaulted in some cases," said Courtney Radsch, director at the

Committee to Protect Journalists, a US-based advocacy group.

Videos of female fans being asked to repeat vulgar phrases and words with sexual connotations in a foreign language did the rounds on social media. In the first few days of the tournament, a group of Brazilian men filmed themselves as they surrounded a Russian woman, urging her to chant about the colour of a woman's genitals in Portuguese. In another video, a couple of journalists from Paraguay asked a woman to say a phrase related to her vagina in the indigenous Guarani language. Mariana Linhan, Fare Network's media officer, said, "The sexist, offensive nature of the incidents is much wider than football. I think its worrying and derogatory and it's clearly a trend that leads to the fact that women still have to fight for their place in football."

Before the tournament there were concerns that homophobia and racism would be the major areas of concern, but Fare Network executive director Piara Powar said sexism was the main focus of the discrimination logged by his team – who reported multiple incidents mainly of Russian women being "accosted in the streets" by male fans. Powar believed the real number of incidents was likely to be "ten times this," adding that there had been several cases of female reporters being grabbed or kissed while on air.

FIFA, meanwhile, warned the FA about fan behaviour after "political chants" were heard during England's semi-final defeat to Croatia. Its disciplinary committee issued charges and, having studied footage, determined a small minority of those in attendance at the Luzhniki Stadium were guilty of misconduct. Chants of "No surrender" were heard during the national anthems, though no details were given of the infringement. FIFA "considered all factors."

While football authorities dished out paltry fines for racism, the FA were fined 70,000 Swiss francs (£50,000) after Dele Alli, Eric Dier and Raheem Sterling wore "unauthorised" socks, ignoring a FIFA warning to stop. The players wore branded ankle support socks over official Nike ones, "breaching media and marketing regulations and the FIFA equipment regulations. FIFA had previously requested the Football Association to cease the activity that led to the breach and had in fact imposed a sanction on 10 July for the same infringement that had been caused by a higher number of members of the English national team."

The FA condemned the "disgraceful conduct" of a group of England fans making Nazi salutes and anti-Semitic comments in a video, filmed in Volgograd, where England beat Tunisia. The men in the video were taunting Tottenham fans, the London club that has an historical association with London's Jewish community. "We strongly condemn the actions of the people in this video," the FA said. "We are working with the relevant authorities, including the UK Police investigations team, who are making enquiries to identify the individuals involved and take appropriate action. The disgraceful conduct of the individuals in this video does not represent the values of the majority of English football fans supporting the team in Russia." British police tracked down the individuals involved and one was served with a five-year ban from attending England matches abroad. Two others appeared at a special magistrate's hearing in Leeds for a "football-related offence." A fourth man detained on a train from Moscow to Volgograd ahead of England's first game, was served with a three-year banning order after a court case in Oxford.

Diego Maradona issued a statement after making a racist gesture to an Asian fan during Argentina's opening tie with Iceland in Group D. ITV broadcaster Jacqui Oatley witnessed the incident, and tweeted, "Maradona not so cool now. Some South Korea fans just shouted 'Diego' and he obliged with a smile, kiss and wave. Then pulled his eyes to the side in a clearly racist gesture. All of us who saw it are stunned." Fellow sports presenter Seema Jaswal backed Oatley's claims – made inside the Otkrytiye Arena where Argentina were surprisingly held at 1–1. She said, "I'm sat right next to Jacqui and saw Maradona's gesture. He should know better. The lads filming him were so excited to get a picture of him and that was his response. Very disappointing."

Maradona played down the incident, insisting the media were looking to make a story out of nothing. In a Facebook message, Maradona – paid £10,000 a day by FIFA – wrote, "I understand better than anyone in the World Cup [that] people are looking for news everywhere, but I want to be clear with this. Today, in the stadium, among so many demonstrations of affection from the people, I was struck by a group of people around a fan who filmed us. I saw an Asian boy wearing an Argentina T-shirt. I, from afar, tried to tell them how nice it seemed to me that even the Asians cheer for us. And that's all, guys, come on."

FIFA opened disciplinary proceedings against the Mexican Football Federation after thousands of supporters repeatedly yelled "puto" – the Spanish word for a male prostitute – during their victory over Germany in their opening game at the Luzhniki Stadium. The chanting, directed primarily at Manuel Neuer, was filmed by the governing body's independent anti-discrimination observers and reported to those responsible for policing the stadium. The abuse was the first major test at the

World Cup of FIFA's "three-step process" for dealing with bigotry from the stands. The first step involved the referee stopping the game so a warning could be issued over the public address, which, if ignored, the match is suspended and eventually abandoned. In the event, FIFA did not initiate the three-step process. Asked why, a spokesman explained, "A public announcement was prepared, but the chants ceased. After the match, and as an important step for further action, the incident was duly included in the match report, as well as the evidence produced by the anti-discrimination observers. Based on those reports, FIFA's disciplinary committee has opened proceedings against the Mexican FA."

World Cup referees were under orders to follow the three-step process if they heard discriminatory chanting and the chairman of FIFA's referees' committee, Pierluigi Collina, insisted match officials would not hesitate to do so. "The referees know it very well and, of course, they are ready to go through it when needed." The FMF (Mexican Football Federation) was repeatedly fined for its fans' "use of the word 'puto'" during World Cup qualifying games but avoided a stadium ban, a sanction that had been imposed on other Latin American associations for persistent homophobic abuse by supporters. The Court of Arbitration for Sport cancelled two fines issued to Mexico in November, ruling the chants on those occasions had been "insulting" but not intended to offend. It allowed other fines imposed on the FMF to stand, though.

FIFA finally took action over the "puto"-chanting after being condemned for failing to punish Mexico for it at the previous World Cup in Brazil. During qualifying matches for Russia 2018, it punished homophobic abuse on 56 occasions, with Mexico accounting for 12, Chile 10, Argentina 6, and Brazil and Honduras 5 each. Chile and Honduras ended up with stadium bans, sparking calls for FIFA to increase the severity of its punishments for homophobic chants.

Unlike "race, colour, language, religion or origin," sexual orientation is not mentioned in Article 58 of FIFA's disciplinary code, which punishes acts of discrimination. Breaches of Article 58 incur a minimum fine of 30,000 Swiss francs, with "serious offences" punishable by matches being played behind closed doors, the forfeit of a match, a points deduction or expulsion from a competition. All 56 cases of homophobic chanting during the 2018 World Cup qualifying games were dealt with under Article 67 of the code, which covers "insulting words," and for which there is no minimum tariff.

Piara Powar, the chief of Fare, which helped FIFA administer its anti-discrimination monitoring system, said in November that "harsher punishments" were needed for homophobic abuse, highlighting the current loophole in the regulations.

Senegal attracted worldwide attention in Russia, not just because of their win against Poland – the only one for an African nation at that point – but also because they had the only black manager in that World Cup. Aliou Cissé was the Senegalese coach. The former Birmingham City and Portsmouth defender commented on the eve of the tournament: "I am certain that one day an African country will win the World Cup. It was some 25 years ago that African countries regularly came just to be a part of the World Cup. I think that things have developed but it's more complicated on our continent – we have realities that are not evident in other continents. We trust our football, we have no complex, we have great players, now we need African coaches for our football to go ahead."

Cissé was aware of the lack of black managers across world football, even in Africa. Nigeria, Morocco and Egypt were led by coaches from Germany, France and Argentina, respectively. Abdoulaye Thiam, president of Senegal's Association de la Press Sportive, spoke to *The Times*, telling the newspaper that the coach's wife was from Rwanda, that he had lived and played in England and France, and wanted all African coaches to work hard and succeed, emphasising that "my skin colour is not important" – it even annoyed him when it was brought up. "This is a coach who is very strong on tactics and the technical sides of football," Thiam added, "and that is what he wants to talk about."

Lord Alan Sugar' made a "joke" on Twitter about Senegal's World Cup squad which backfired spectacularly. The entrepreneur and host of *The Apprentice* had tweeted a photo of the Senegal team, adding, "I recognise some of these guys from the beach in Marbella. Multi-tasking resourceful chaps." The UK Peer apologised after comparing its players to people selling bags and sunglasses on beaches, as if they were selling counterfeit goods. His tweet was described as "seriously misjudged" by the BBC.

Osasu Obayiuwana, the British-Nigerian associate editor of *New African* magazine and contributor to the BBC's *World Football* show, was not impressed. He wrote on Twitter: "Dear @Lord_Sugar, I'm afraid no Senegalese or African will see this as funny. What you wrote was hurtful and plays to a racist stereotype. If you really don't see what's wrong with what you've written, you have a lot to learn still. You should know better!"

Sugar subsequently took down the image, saying, "Just been reading the reaction to my funny tweet about the guy on the beach in Marbella. Seems it has been interpreted in the wrong way as offensive by a few people. Frankly, I can't see that, I think it's funny. But I will pull it down, if you insist."

Actress Kelechi Okafor went on Twitter to vent her displeasure, tweeting, "Let me tell you why @Lord_Sugar is a wasteman. He's one of those wilfully ignorant people who thinks he can't be racist because he grew up poor. The tweet is overtly racist, but he has said with his chest that he has nothing to apologise for."

An hour and 20 minutes after posting the initial image, Sugar then returned to Twitter to issue a further apology, stating, "I misjudged me [sic] earlier tweet. It was in no way intended to cause offence, and clearly my attempt at humour has backfired. I have deleted the tweet and am very sorry."

BBC World News anchor Babita Sharma said Sugar's tweet was "Shocking, vile [...] [the sort] that you take a screen grab of because you know it will soon be deleted." Replying to Sharma, Sugar rudely hit back: "If it [sic] so vile why have you retweeted it. You make me sick." The BBC's press office also said in its statement that Sugar was "in no doubt aware about our view on this."

Labour MP Dawn Butler said she was "very troubled" by Sugar's tweet. Referring to the fact that he sits in the House of Lords, the UK's upper governing chamber, she said, "Racism has no place in Parliament, or society," and demanded that "swift action must be taken." Butler promised to write to the House of Lords' Commissioner for Standards. She also called on the BBC to cut all ties with Sugar and told *This Morning*: 'He is a Lord. He's not just a punter down the pub, having a bit of a joke. He runs *The Apprentice*; can you imagine if you're a black man going on that show, what you would think? In the back of his mind, we all know what he thinks now. His line, 'You're fired!' should be hanging over his head like it does his contestants. The BBC should suspend him while they investigate. Why on earth did he feel empowered enough to send out a tweet like that? Why try and denigrate a team of black men? He's in a position of power. He works for our state broadcaster. I fail to see the joke. It was offensive and his response was also offensive. What an arrogant man. I know plenty of old people, who fought in the war, who would never say these things. We thought the racism would come from Russia, who thought it would come from the House of Lords? He's made more than one mistake, he didn't really apologise. He is in a position of power, has five million followers, he has responsibilities."

Piara Powar, Executive Director of the Fare Network, waded into the controversy, too, issuing the following statement: "Alan Sugar has deliberately and with racist intent sought to demean a World Cup football team in the middle of a global celebration that Africans have as much a right to be a part of as any other continent. And, as if the words were not damaging enough, he has illustrated the point with a graphic. This ignorance and stereotyping of a whole race, a continent of over 1.3 billion people, is disgraceful. It is particularly damaging coming from a prominent public figure, a member of the House of Lords. It shows the attitudes that people continue to hold and how they see football as the space through which to air them."

"This lazy, stereotypical and bigoted kind of attitude belongs to a bygone era," educational charity Show Racism the Red Card told BBC Sport. "The World Cup is a celebration of different cultures and brings people together from across the globe. Lord Sugar's unhelpful and ignorant comments go very much against the spirit of this unique occasion and are probably best kept to himself."

Ndongo Ndiaye, a former basketball player, now adviser on youth and sport to Senegalese President Macky Sall, spoke to *The Times* from the team base in Kaluga, two hours south of Moscow, suggesting the comments were "ignorant and hurtful." He said, "Everyone here is talking about this tweet, it has made headlines in Senegal, too. I think it is very ignorant from someone in his position. Of course, there must be freedom of speech, but this was wrong, and it is hurtful to the players and people from Senegal. If I was his boss, if I was responsible for him, then I would fire him."

Grime icon Lethal Bizzle said, "If anything, it's taking us back in time to a culture and society that we've moved on and evolved from. "The "Pow" hit-maker continued on Twitter: "Mr @Lord_Sugar with all due respect, this is disgraceful. It's probably funny in your circles. But this is not banter, it's racist. Big man like you, u should know better." Later, following up on his tweet, the East London musician told *Metro* that he didn't hold any animosity towards Sugar – he actually respects him – but that he needs to understand why it wasn't a joke. "In 2018, just being a black person, it's hard to overcome certain barriers. I think of the challenges I faced and defeated to get myself into the position to challenge the stereotype [...] I just think that a man in such a powerful position should know better. It's disappointing, because I respect this guy – he seems like a people person – I just think he got this one terribly wrong. To mock that (what they're doing for their country), and to make a joke out of that it's disgusting, it's disgraceful. And to use the Senegalese team like that, it was uncalled for. I know some people may see it as light-hearted banter, but being black [...] quite frankly, we are up against it in society. There's no place for this. As a black person, I'm trying to be in the position you're in, Lord Sugar, and you're just belittling us by saying things like this – it's uncalled for. It's all good apologising, that's all cool […] but you have to understand that you saying things like that is not helping us. It's taking us back. It's putting the perception out there that it's okay to say things like that, when really it isn't."

Lord Herman Ouseley was appalled. "This coming from one of Britain's most respected business leaders, a man who was born into an East End Jewish family and is proud of his roots, and a former Tottenham Hotspur chairman. Someone, in other words, who ought to know about racist stereotypes. It shows we have a long way to go. Any assumption made about somebody based purely on their race is racism. There's no getting away from that. Even when the perpetrators think they're being funny – or with the misguided aim of being supportive even – it's unacceptable. When some Manchester United fans sang songs about Romelu Lukaku (the song made reference to Lukaku having a large penis) they thought they were being that – supportive – despite the offensive words. 'It was banter, it was good-natured,' those fans said, but it wasn't, and we wrote to the club to ask them to take action and to their credit they did. Both the club and the player asked the fans to stop, in public and with social media statements, and that minority of fans did. Son Heung Min was subjected to chants "DVD" while playing at Millwall in the FA Cup and was abused in the same way by a West Ham fan who pulled up alongside the South Korean international at a junction and filmed the episode. When he scored a brilliant goal against West Ham at Wembley last season he went over to the away fans and gave them the 'shush' gesture. Both Millwall and West Ham condemned the incidents.

"Some of the stereotypes are racist, some are just lazy. A common one still heard is that foreign players are 'soft' and that they cheat. We know neither is true, but they persist. But they all need to go. We at Kick It Out are working hard in this area. Our education manager, Troy Townsend, runs a project called Equality Inspires, in partnership with the Premier League. He goes into Premier League academies, schools and colleges and works with the clubs and the players to challenge received views and unconscious biases. These deal with racism and homophobia but also they are designed to raise awareness of the number of footballers of different faiths in the game and to be aware of making harmful and offensive assumptions.

"Even during this World Cup, the former Manchester United defender Patrice Evra was upbraided by many on social media for appearing to patronise his fellow TV panellist Eniola Aluko for her football knowledge – which, based on her 102 caps for England and all the trophies she's won at Chelsea, is considerable. So, Lord Sugar may be one of the highest profile figures to say or tweet something offensive – but he isn't alone. It's our job at Kick It Out – and indeed everyone in the game – to challenge and re-educate those offenders so that football can be enjoyed by everyone regardless of their faith, gender, sexual orientation, disability or ethnicity."

Rather predictably, Lord Sugar received the backing of his long-term verbal sparring partner, Piers Morgan, who defended him against allegations of racism. "I've known @ Lord_Sugar for 25 years," tweeted the journalist and *GMB* TV presenter. "He can be a halfwit of biblical proportions, and prone to terrible 'jokes', as we saw today. But he's not a racist."

One of the stars of the first series of *The Apprentice* declared it "absurd" to label him a racist. Saira Khan posted on Twitter, writing, "I can state categorically that @Lord_Sugar IS NOT A RACIST! His tweet showed that he is of a generation that has not quite got to grips with what is acceptable in today's British civil society. To brand him racist is absurd!"

Sugar also faced criticism for a tweet that pictured the then Labour Leader Jeremy Corbyn alongside Adolf Hitler. Unrepentant, in that instance, he later responded: "It's a joke, but the angry brigade like to moan." The last words on the subject of Alan Sugar's tweet go to Stan Collymore: "As I said. Ingrained in every level of British society."

During the same 2018 World Cup the Swedish FA complained to police about racial hatred and threats aimed at winger Jimmy Durmaz following his late mistake against Germany. The substitute gave away the stoppage-time free kick that led to Toni Kroos's late winner in the Group F clash. Reaction on the 29-year-old's Instagram account began almost as soon as the goal was scored. The Swedes began their next training session in Gelendzhik by uniting behind Durmaz as he read a statement from his cell phone. "I am a footballer at the highest level, being criticised is something we live with, but being called a "f****** immigrant" and a "suicide bomber", and having death threats made against me and my children is completely unacceptable," Durmaz said. "I am Swedish, and with pride, I wear our shirt and our flag. I want to thank the fine, wonderful people who spread joy. It warms us all. We stand united, we are Sweden." The entire squad shouted, "F*** racism!", before applauding and jogging out to their workout. General secretary Håkan Sjöstrand said that the Swedish FA reported the abuse to police on behalf of the player. "A number of complaints have been made with the Swedish FA as the plaintiff so that Jimmy can concentrate on what he is here to do – play football.

But Durmaz is fully behind the complaints," Sjostrand. said in a statement. "We do not tolerate a player being subjected to threats or abuse. It's uncomfortable and very upsetting to see the treatment that Jimmy Durmaz has had to put up with. Completely unacceptable."

No sooner was the World Cup over than Russian third-tier side Torpedo Moscow cancelled plans to sign defender Erving Botaka-Yobama, denying that they had done so because he was black. Torpedo faced fan protests after announcing the signing of Botaka-Yobama, who is of Russian and Congolese descent. The club said the deal for the 19-year-old, a former Torpedo youth player, had been cancelled for financial reasons. "Skin colour is never a criterion when selecting a player," the club explained. "Racism has no right to exist. We adhere to this point of view." The club added that Lokomotiv-Kazanka Moscow, who the player was joining from, had demanded a transfer fee, causing the deal to be called off. A group of fans known as the Zapad-5 Ultras wrote the following on Russian social media site Vkontakte: "Black may be one of our club's colours, but we only want whites in our ranks." Those comments were condemned by Alexander Zotov, head of the All-Russian Union of Footballers, "There have been changes in the minds of people after the World Cup but there is still a group of idiots. I read a lot of statements about the football player. Some were openly racist. These people with limited horizons exist in any country. We saw how open our society and people are [during the World Cup]. There are fans of Torpedo who are normal, and do not welcome the behaviour of that group in relation to Botaka."

Arsenal's Mesut Özil quit international football over the "racism and disrespect" in Germany over his Turkish roots. He was photographed with Turkish president

Recep Tayyip Erdoğan at a London event in May, and he immediately received hate mail and threats. Germany's football association, the DFB, was among those to criticise Özil. He was blamed for Germany's disappointing World Cup, their worst in 80 years. "I am German when we win, but I am an immigrant when we lose, he said."

Özil met Erdoğan with fellow Germany international İlkay Gündoğan, the Manchester City player who is also of Turkish descent, and Everton striker Cenk Tosun. Özil says he and Gündoğan talked about football with the president. Özil, who has always been proud of his Turkish heritage, presented Erdoğan with a signed Arsenal shirt during the meeting. Photographs were released by Turkey's governing AK Party in the build-up to elections in the country, which Erdoğan won outright. Many German politicians questioned Özil and Gündoğan's loyalty to German democratic values. Özil's meeting caused controversy in Germany with their team manager Oliver Bierhoff suggesting he should have been dropped from the squad. Özil said he would have been "disrespecting his ancestors' roots" had he not posed for photographs with the Turkish president. "In May, I met President Erdoğan in London, during a charitable and educational event. We first met in 2010, after he and Angela Merkel watched the Germany vs Turkey match together in Berlin. Since then, our paths have crossed a lot of times around the globe. I'm aware that the picture of us caused a huge response in the German media, and while some people may accuse me of lying or being deceitful, the picture we took had no political intentions. For me, having a picture with President Erdoğan wasn't about politics or elections, it was about me respecting the highest office of my family's country. My job is a football player and not a politician, and our meeting was not an endorsement of any policies." Özil's treatment, he felt, made him "no longer want to wear the German national team shirt."

He posted three open letters to social media, the final confirming his retirement from international football, in which he condemned the "racism and disrespect" he had been subject to. He did not feel accepted in German society despite paying taxes, donating to good causes there, and being a World Cup winner. "It is with a heavy heart and after much consideration that because of recent events, I will no longer be playing for Germany at international level while I have this feeling of racism and disrespect. I used to wear the German shirt with such pride and excitement, but now I don't. I feel unwanted and think that what I have achieved since my international debut in 2009 has been forgotten." Germany is home to three million people of Turkish descent, and immigration and the rise of far-right parties are key issues. Özil questions in his statement why other dual-heritage teammates have not been subjected to the same treatment. "Is it because it is Turkey? Is it because I'm a Muslim? I think here lays an important issue."

Germany's Social Democrat Justice Minister Katarina Barley said, "It's alarming if a great German football player like Mesut Özil no longer feels wanted in his country."

Özil added, in his statement, "Certain German newspapers are using my background and photo with President Erdoğan as right-wing propaganda to further their political cause. Why else did they use pictures and headlines with my name as a direct explanation for defeat in Russia? They didn't criticise my performance, they didn't criticise the team's performances, they just criticised my Turkish ancestry and respect for my upbringing." Germany's football association "emphatically rejected" allegations of racism but admitted it could have done more to protect him from abuse.

Kick It Out condemned Özil's treatment, pointing out that it was part of a wider problem, similar to those involving black players in England and France. "Following Germany's exit from the World Cup, the racist treatment Mesut Özil has faced by elements of their media, supporters and wider society is extremely disappointing – but is also reflective of the experience of a number of footballers across Europe from mixed heritage backgrounds," KIO said. "Immigration has transformed modern life and modern football for the better – the success of the Premier League is due to the contribution of footballers from around the world, while the World Cup has been enriched by players of dual heritage such as Özil. However, Özil is right to suggest that for elements of society, 'when we win, I am German, but I am an immigrant when we lose.' Unfortunately, black players in England, France and beyond have been treated in a similar fashion for a long time.

"We understand that football is a results business and inevitably there will be criticism of players when a leading nation such as Germany is knocked out of a tournament at an early stage. But the singling out of Özil by parts of the German media, discriminatory comments made by supporters, the lack of support from some sponsors and the alleged treatment by DFB President Reinhard Grindel (Özil had accused Grindel of "belittling" him and advancing his own political agenda), has gone far beyond any reasonable analysis of his performances. Footballers must always be wary of their status as role models being exploited for political propaganda, but no player should ever have their loyalty to their country questioned because of a dual heritage. The mere fact that Özil decided to represent Germany should be enough to demonstrate his commitment, but clearly in some circles that is not enough.

"Mesut Özil has been treated disgracefully and we have contacted Arsenal to offer our support to him at this time. Those who have driven him to consider international retirement should be ashamed of themselves and his case should encourage all of football to reflect on how the game treats footballers from mixed heritage backgrounds."

ITV commentator Clive Tyldesley summed up the 2018 World Cup tournament for this book: "There was no repeat of the violent hooligan clashes we saw in France during European Championship games involving Russia and there were no reports of racist abuse of players. LGBT supporters were allocated 'safe spaces' to gather in and, although that in itself sounds sinister and decidedly unsafe, it was a concession of sorts. Even the domestic flights all landed safely. Most doomsday predictions proved unfounded. Does that prove Russia has purged itself of all of its moral sins? I doubt the Pussy Riot pitch invaders on World Cup final day have seen much of the blue skies over Moscow since. Just days after the tournament, Torpedo Moscow cancelled plans to sign a black defender following a social media protest by Ultra-fans. FIFA recently fined the Russian Federation for racist chanting at a March international. The show of best behaviour during the tournament has even aroused rather than calmed the suspicions of some.

"So, did President Putin call all of Russia's 'mafia' leaders in to arrange an armistice for the duration? Or has he simply been misunderstood? The truth is probably somewhere in between and, in Russia, the 'in between' stretches thousands of kilometres between the borders with Finland and China. I enjoyed the World Cup in its setting. Whether that setting was the real Russia or some FIFA version of Disneyland, I cannot judge.

"I got the impression that if the leaders could just leave it to the people to sort any differences of culture and politics then the Cold War might just melt. But then England reached the semi-final [...] I could have been dreaming it all."

23

BAME Football Managers

"It is quite shocking and the more we speak about it, and reflect on it, the more it hits home that there's an incredible imbalance. The game has a responsibility to redress the balance."

– Chris Hughton, LMA board member

"It is a priority of the LMA to support and encourage BAME coaches to develop their skills and equip themselves with the knowledge and experience to build long and successful careers in the game."

– Richard Bevan, LMA chief executive

(From a report by the League Managers' Association (LMA), June 2018)

Arguably, the focal point of discrimination in the English game revolves around the staggering inequality that currently exists. The LMA is at the coalface of the fight for equality in management and coaching.

The LMA's declared relationship with Kick It Out is "focused on KIO building a strong and professional relationship directly with the LMA and its members," according to the LMA statement regarding their up to date analysis of the coaching and management structure in the English game. It continues: "KIO attend all the manager pre-season meetings with the LMA and the LMA facilitates a programme of club visits and one-to-one information meetings between KIO and the managers during the season. The LMA is a visible presence at all key KIO conferences and events and the LMA actively engages its members to attend. The LMA helps provide mentors for KIO's programmes and has provided LMA members to support KIO with their external communications, providing ongoing visibility for all KIO activity through its own publications including the *Manager Magazine* and members' *Touchline Journal*. The LMA is committed to equal opportunities for all candidates who wish to become professional football managers and coaches.

"The statistics within the professional game clearly identify that there continues to be a significant under-representation of BAME individuals in coaching and management roles, especially relative to the number of BAME players. This is an issue that the LMA takes extremely seriously. We want to see more BAME individuals progressing through the coaching and management ranks and taking up senior positions with clubs. We are certain that there will be significant benefits to the game with a more diverse coaching and management workforce, and that there are many BAME individuals that can, and should, build long and successful coaching and management careers.

"There has been some progress in addressing the game's weaknesses in this area over the past two years as the game has embraced a more joined-up approach, but there is still much more that can be done. This is an issue that requires tangible and practical game-wide interventions if significant change is to be realised. The LMA continues to take a positive approach to all initiatives that seek to proactively influence this issue and we continue to work with all the relevant stakeholders in the game to move this issue forward.

"The game must develop a unified approach to proactively identify BAME individuals, both players and those in the amateur game, with the potential to develop coaching and management skills for the professional game. These individuals need to be encouraged and supported to view coaching and management as a viable career option through which they must be supported by coaching and assistance with other necessary qualifications.

"Continued investment in education for any BAME individual to realise their potential and to build a successful career in the increasingly competitive international coaching and management market, it is imperative that the game provides them access to world-class education and training opportunities. It is vital that the game takes a more unified approach in the provision of coaching and manager education, delivering a consistent approach across the various coaching levels including in-career learning and development. Education programmes must also adapt to the specific requirements of working in the professional game, including a focus on subjects that will have a positive impact on career and personal development and drawing on the practical insights and experiences of those who have gone before. The LMA will continue to expand its targeted and vocational qualifications and education offering delivered through its Institute of Leadership and High Performance with continued encouragement for uptake and attendance of BAME candidates across all its programmes.

"The LMA is an advocate for significantly more open and transparent recruitment processes in the game. The game is currently too reliant on informality in its recruitment processes with a strong influence of private networks that can create a recruitment environment that is at risk from the impact of unconscious bias – to the detriment of BAME individuals. The LMA is supportive of interventions that ensure BAME individuals are afforded interview opportunities. The LMA will continue to be supportive of all BAME individuals in encouraging and supporting preparation for job applications and persistence.

"The issue of shortening role tenure for managers and coaches, especially in the lower leagues, is one that impacts across the whole employment market, including BAME candidates. The short-term hire and fire approach, which is endemic across the game, as well as a perceived lack of opportunity, act as a disincentive to those considering coaching and management as a career option. Clubs will derive more stability and more long-term progress and success if they retain, work with, and develop their talent. In turn, individuals will build more viable careers thus enhancing the attractiveness of the profession. The LMA will continue to advocate for a more long-term, strategic approach to recruitment and retention across the game.

"Undoubtedly, BAME role models can, and will over time, have a significantly positive impact in encouraging BAME individuals to consider coaching and management careers. The game needs to be proactive in using role models, acknowledging their achievements, and, where possible, engage them in well-structured formal mentoring programmes. In addition, the game can and must do more in funding the provision of in-career guidance and support services for all those in the professional game, especially BAME candidates. Appropriate investment in quality career support services, designed for the specific requirements of the profession, will have a positive impact on individuals' career development and the retention of talent in the game. The LMA will continue to engage and champion its BAME members and, where appropriate, work with them to act as mentors for the next generation of BAME managers and coaches. In addition, we will continue to invest in and expand our programme of career support services delivered through the LMA Institute of Leadership and High Performance.

"The game as a whole must address the significant lack of diversity across leadership in the game, not just from a BAME perspective – but for all under-represented groups. Increasing diversity in the boardroom will have a lasting and positive influence on decision-making, recruitment and performance across the game. The LMA will continue to proactively and openly work with all stakeholder groups that look to positively influence diversity across the game.

"The under-representation of BAME individuals within coaching and management roles is an issue that cannot be addressed effectively using the silo mentality that so often dominates thinking in football. There has been some progress in attempting to unify various stakeholder groups and coordinate an approach and the FA's 'English Football Inclusion and Anti-Discrimination Action Plan' has been a positive step. However, more can still be done to bring all parties together for the benefit of the game as a whole and the LMA will continue to advocate for a more unified approach to this issue.

"Suggestions that the 'situation will naturally improve over time' are hugely detrimental to delivering a positive outcome for BAME coaches and managers. The game must continue to assess and evaluate the progress it is making across this issue and where required resolve to increase investment and positive interventions. The LMA will continue to proactively assess the BAME employment landscape, remain an advocate for change and progress, and make recommendations where appropriate."

Richard Bevan, the LMA chief executive, when interviewed for this book, said: "It is a priority of the LMA to support and encourage BAME coaches to develop their skills and equip themselves with the knowledge and experience to build long and successful careers in the game."

24

Taking The Knee

"I am not going to get up to show pride in a country that oppresses black people and people of colour."
– Colin Kaepernick, American football quarterback

Since August 2016, some American athletes have protested against police brutality and racism by "taking the knee." "I am not going to get up to show pride in a country that oppresses black people and people of colour," the San Francisco quarter-back Colin Kaepernick said. "To me, this is bigger than football, and it would be selfish on my part to look the other way. There are bodies in the street and people getting paid leave and getting away with murder."

The gesture had a polarising effect in the US, with some critics saying it was disrespectful to American soldiers and the American flag. Many American athletes would follow his lead in the weeks and months that followed, sparking a huge reaction.

Kaepernick sat and later knelt during the anthem and repeated the action on 24 September 2017. The NFL protests became more widespread when over 200 players sat or knelt in response to President Trump's expletive-filled rant calling for owners to "fire" the protesting players. "Wouldn't you love to see one of these NFL owners, when somebody disrespects our flag, to say, 'Get that son-of-a-b**** off the field right now, out, he's fired. He's fired." The NFL approved a policy that required all athletes to stand during the national anthem in May 2018.

Kaepernick became a free agent at the end of that season and remained without a team despite being seen as one of the finest quarterbacks in the sport. He took legal action against the NFL for colluding to keep him out of the league. A confidential settlement was reached in February 2019. The player effectively gave up his career to fight for what he believes in. His gesture became a symbol of the Black Lives Matter (BLM) movement.

BLM: Black Lives Matter

The Premier League restarted with all top flight footballers making a powerful statement by taking the knee as the matches were about to start, while BLACK LIVES MATTER replaced player names on the back of shirts for the first 12 matches of the restart. The players' solidarity had a global audience and became one of sports most powerful images.

Liverpool player, Trent Alexander-Arnold vowed to help push through cultural change and use his position to show the next generation they can achieve all of their dreams. The right-back takes an interest in social affairs and was involved in the #PlayersTogether initiative during the UK Covid-19 lockdowns aiming to raise funds for NHS charities. At Goodison Park, he also wore a pair of boots with the motif BLACK LIVES MATTER. In an interview with digital magazine *The Journal*, Alexander-Arnold spoke about racism and why he believes the treatment of black people has been wrong "for centuries."

"When black lives do matter as much as everyone else's, then all lives will matter, but that's not the case now and it hasn't been the case for centuries. We have to push for change. It's been too wrong for too long. When you're able to reach so many people, especially young kids, you have to make sure that you can help them feel like anything is possible and help them grow up to have equal opportunities. They shouldn't feel different to others and be denied the same chances in life because of their skin colour. They shouldn't feel different because of where they're from or their background. For me, education is so important to all of this, because that's where a lot of issues stem from. No one is born racist and comes into this world thinking that you deserve certain privileges. You get taught that.

"All of us have to work to undo that. I hope [people] are absorbing the messages we are putting out there individually and through #PlayersTogether. I hope kids can see how much stronger we are when we care for each other and are committed to the greater good."

Trent auctioned his Black Lives Matter-branded boots and donated the proceeds to the Nelson Mandela Foundation. "Do your talking on the pitch. I've always loved that sentiment. But now we need to speak up in other ways as well," Trent said in statement. "Tonight, my boots will carry the message Black Lives Matter. It can no longer just be our feet where we express ourselves. We have to use our profile and platform."

In 2020, the death of George Floyd while in police custodyi in the USA sparked worldwide action and protests, and players, staff and officials have offered their support. The movement was criticised in some quarters and a "White Lives Matter" message was flown over the Etihad Stadium during a City–Burnley game on 22 June, 2020, evoking considerable outrage from Burnley.

And a handful of Chelsea fans reportedly held an anti-Black Lives Matter protest outside Stamford Bridge, calling on the club to stop players "taking the knee" before matches. One fan, who appeared to be leading the protest, sang, "Roman Abramovich, we won't take a knee." The same fan opened the protest with a "message" for the club's owner, claiming the Black Lives Matter movement was racist! "We're here today to send a message to Roman Abramovich," the Chelsea fan said. "Roman Abramovich, we won't take the knee. We don't want our players to take the knee. You came here from Russia, you broke away from communism. The previous government wouldn't let you build an extension to this club. The government we have in now, they're fighting for Brexit, we want Brexit and we want you to show us you're not part of the globalist oligarchy. Black Lives Matter is a racist organisation that is Marxist and is here to take our statues down and take everything down that we love in this country. We believe all lives matter. So, the message to Roman Abramovich is do not let our players or do not force our players to take the knee. We don't want our players to be forced to take the knee. Black Lives Matter is racist – all lives matter! Football has been taken over by globalism."

Rio Ferdinand joined a Black Lives Matter protest in London with his family, wife Kate and his three young children Lorenz, Tate and Tia. He posted a string of Instagram photos of the five of them among the crowd, wearing masks to protect themselves during the ongoing coronavirus pandemic. In the accompanying text, Ferdinand wrote: "Taking my family to Parliament Square today to be a part of the protest was very emotional. The importance of supporting such a cause cannot be underestimated. Educating the next generation is an absolute must. For our children to have been a part of such an important protest is something that I'm sure will have a lasting effect on them." At the end of his message he added the hashtags "#blm", "#blacklivesmatter" and "#protest".

Adding the pictures to her Instagram too, Kate Ferdinand described the protest as "a moving and overwhelming experience. Honestly, we were cautious about going [and] taking the children, but we are so glad we made the decision to go, it's something we will all remember for the rest of our lives. It felt so good to be part of the movement. Our kids are the future, for us it's so important for them to understand what is happening in the world and be part of the change, we need to continue to educate ourselves and the younger generation. Taking one knee with thousands of protesters [and] having a minute's silence is a moment that will stay with me for a very long time. We stand united."

However, Black Lives Matter UK is seen as a highlycharged political organisation by some – the campaign has called for a cut in money to law enforcement to create a "people's budget." The UK arm of the group has also said it wants to defund the police completely, abolish capitalism and has pledged support for Palestine amid Israel's controversial plans to annex the West Bank. Black Lives Matter UK is the semi-official British offshoot of its American counterpart and has been the face of the UK's protests over George Floyd's death and racial equality. Some of the many people who have donated millions to their cause are unaware of many of the group's more extreme aims. The UK branch, like the American arm of the movement, has a number of far-Left aims listed on its website; including the Marxist "commitment to dismantle capitalism."

Matt Le Tissier agreed to wear the badge because he supported the cause but pointed out the organisation did not have his backing. "I just don't agree with some of the points of that movement – specifically the defunding of the police and the anti-capitalist points are things I do not agree with. They are the two main points for me. I am quite happy for them to have their point of view, but that is mine and that is where I sit. I think a lot of people in the country would agree with me. I will still wear the badge because I do, of course, believe black lives matter. It's a simple thing. I agree with the cause but there are parts of the organisation that I just cannot support."

The Premier League recognised "the importance of the message that black lives matter" but made clear that it "does not endorse any political organisation or movement, nor support any group that calls for violence or condones illegal activity." The Premier League have not provided any funding to BLM UK and chief executive Richard Masters told MPs that his organisation remains apolitical. Appearing before a select committee of the Department for Digital, Culture, Media and Sport, Masters made a distinction between moral and political causes, although this position was criticised by Sunderland MP Julie Elliott, who accused him of "opening a can of worms."

Patrice Evra, Jamie Redknapp and Gary Neville had all ditched their Black Lives Matter badges during Sky's coverage of Manchester United's win over Brighton. The decision came just hours after Le Tissier, another of the channel's pundits, made it clear he was asked by bosses to wear the Black Lives Matter badge, but stressed he "could not support" the cause's anti-police and anti-capitalist aims. Former Wolves midfielder Karl Henry had also slammed the organisation on Twitter. Crystal Palace become the first Premier League club to publicly distance themselves from the Black Lives Matter UK movement. Palace insisted they *do* back the "ethos" of the cause, and issued a statement drawing a definitive line between football's adoption of the anti-discrimination message and the wider demands of the movement. In a statement, Palace said: "As people will have seen from our first home game, we have placed banners over our seated areas at Selhurst Park that read: BLACK LIVES MATTER. We stand proudly alongside members of the BAME community, our players and employees, and behind the ideals and ethos of "black lives matter." However, we would like to make clear that we do not endorse any pressure group or body that carries the same term in its name, and we strongly believe that organisations should not use this important force for change and positivity to push their own political agendas. We want to be part of a world that is fair, inclusive and open to all. As an organisation, we recognise that we need to do more, and we will do more to contribute towards this goal."

Emile Heskey was the only pundit who remained wearing his Black Lives Matter badge for Premier League coverage after the BBC banned pundits and guests from wearing them. Gary Lineker, Alan Shearer and Micah Richards decided not to display any message. Sky allowed pundits to make their own decisions, but only Heskey opted to display the message. Fellow pundit Graeme Souness was also without the badge. *Soccer Saturday* host Jeff Stelling along with experts Clinton Morrison, Paul Merson and Le Tissier chose to support anti-racism charity Kick It Out instead. However, BT Sport's guests. Rio Ferdinand, Robbie Savage and Steve Sidwell joined Jake Humphrey for the programme and supported the BLM movement by wearing a badge.

The major question was how and when the Black Lives Matter momentum would manifest itself into effecting real change.

Ex-England forward Eniola Aluko knew that targets were needed to increase BAME inclusion at the top level of UK Sport. Recent data shows that of all national sporting governing body board members, 3% are black. Aluko, Aston Villa Women's sporting director, suggested a target of 30% BAME representation to the Digital, Culture, Media and Sport Committee. "There has to be something intentional about change. When you rely on self-regulation, people tend to fall back into a comfort zone and what they've always done. I think we need a target, 30% is a good one. Whether owners or directors like it or not, this is what the game needs to do. There's a lot of recycling of the same people in the game and if you do something like a target or a quota, you will start to see recruitment behaviour change."

Former Birmingham City, Chelsea and Juventus player Aluko retired from playing in January, before being named Villa Women's first sporting director. She is England's joint-10th most capped international, scoring 33 goals in 102 senior appearances. "I think there has certainly been a lot of progress from when I started playing football 20-plus years ago. There was absolutely no one I could look to in the game that looked like me, either as a woman or a black woman," she told the DCMS committee. "Fast-forward 20 years we are still seeing a glass ceiling to a certain extent."

Wolves manager Nuno Espírito Santo is the only manager in the Premier League from a BAME background and there are only four in the entire English professional game.

Paul Cleal, an adviser to several relevant organisations including the Premier League, said: "All those sports should be trying harder. Targets are useful and have helped with representation of women on FTSE 100 boards. We need to have at least two (ethnic minority board members) to reflect the breadth of diversity. People have waited until almost forced, we have seen the same with the reporting of gender pay gaps. The best organisations take a voluntary approach and go out and do the right thing."

Cleal was asked about the introduction of the Rooney Rule. The EFL was urged to go further by the Professional Footballers' Association and apply that approach to all managerial and coaching vacancies. Cleal said the EFL's approach had had "patchy success" so far.

Aluko, 32, was found to have been subject to racial discrimination by, the then England women's manager, Mark Sampson following an independent investigation in 2017. The FA eventually apologised to Aluko, who had said the body was "dismissive" when she first claimed Sampson made racist remarks towards her in 2014. Speaking to the DCMS committee, she said she hoped the approach would be different today. "I genuinely would like to believe that if a similar thing happened to another black player in the team today, it would be dealt with much differently. First of all, that it wouldn't happen, but I think it would be dealt with much differently and much more independently and without conflict."

Thierry Henry
Montreal Impact manager and World Cup winner Thierry Henry was delighted in 2020, when other ethnicities committed to standing up against racism. In an interview with Taylor Twellman on ESPN's *Banter* ahead of the MLS is Back tournament (the Major League Soccer event held to mark the return to action after the suspension due to Covid-19), he said, "We all have stories that we can tell, but for the first time other ethnicities are involved. I always said, back in the day, when stuff like that was happening, that I got insulted on the field for the colour of

my skin... I would have liked other ethnicities in my team to walk out before I walk out then that would be pretty powerful. Because at the end of the game, I don't want the journalist to ask the question to the black guy. Ask the question to everybody and see if they feel our pain. That will have an impact." In 2005, the ex-Arsenal striker launched the Stand Up Speak Up campaign along with other players, and has been a supporter of Show Racism the Red Card.

Earlier in 2020, more than 170 black MLS players had formed Black Players for Change. Their objectives are: a voice in all racial matters as it relates to MLS; increased Black representation in the MLS Players Association and the highest levels of MLS; and to have an impact in Black communities. Players from across Major League Soccer joined a pre-match anti-racism demonstration as the game returned in the US for the first time since March with a match behind closed doors at Disney World, Florida.

Several MLS players took to the pitch before kick-off and raised their fist for eight minutes and forty-six seconds, the same amount of time that white police officer Derek Chauvin had his knee pressed on the neck of Floyd, a black American man, who died as a result.

"It was emotional for the ones who were there," said Nani. "We all want to change the world. We want a better world – no differences, no discrimination. Everyone in the world should stop for a couple of minutes and think about our children and teach them how to be a better person and create a better world."

Ex-Manchester United winger Nani scored a 97th minute winner for Orlando over David Beckham-owned Inter Miami.

1:48 AM · Jul 9, 2020

As Orlando and Inter Miami players took a knee around the centre circle, players from the other teams stood around them and one by one raised their fists. Each wore face masks emblazoned with BLACK LIVES MATTER, while some wore T-shirts with slogans including "Silence is violence" and "Black and proud".

Toronto FC's Justin Morrow, also executive director of the Black Players for Change organisation, said MLS players wanted to add their voices to the movement. "This is a chance for us to take our place with them, stand up against racial inequality, fight that battle and make sure our voices in Major League Soccer are heard," he said at half-time. "What you saw tonight was a special moment that was driven by the players, and Major League Soccer collaborated with us to make that happen."

Henry took the knee to show support for the movement when his side, Montreal Impact took on New England Revolution the next day. They lost the game 1–0. Wearing a T-shirt with BLACK LIVES MATTER emblazoned on the front, the Frenchman knelt inside the technical area at kick-off and only returned to his feet after the opening eight minutes and forty-six seconds of the match.

"I guess you guys know why," Henry said after the match. "It was just to pay tribute and show support to the cause. That was basically it. [It's] pretty simple."

In the Premier League, Manchester City manager Pep Guardiola said that white people should be "embarrassed and ashamed" for their treatment of black people after watching players from his team and Arsenal recognise the Black Lives Matter movement by taking a knee prior to a game at the Etihad. Guardiola spoke strongly about his belief that much more must be done to ensure equality and inclusion. "White people should apologise for the way we treated black people in the last 400 years. I feel ashamed for what we have done for black people around the world, not just America – the problem is everywhere. We should send a thousand million messages for the black people. I'm embarrassed and ashamed of what the white people have done for the black people. How can people think they are different? All the gestures are good and positive. Everything we can do to make it conscious. It is not acceptable. We have to do a lot of things for the black people which we have not done so far."

Raheem Sterling called for greater equality insisting that taking the knee and wearing the BLM slogan was a huge message from the Premier League and its players. "I see it as a massive step for the Premier League to allow something like that to happen, and it shows we're going in the right direction. Little by little, we're seeing change. It was natural; it was organic. We saw the teams do it in the earlier kick-off and thought it was something we had to do, as well."

Burnley captain Ben Mee was "humbled" by the response to his comments about the "White Lives Matter Burnley" banner that flew over Etihad Stadium. Mee spoke out and declared he was "ashamed and embarrassed" by the banner. City and Burnley players had taken a knee to support the Black Lives Matter movement before the Premier League game on 22 June. "I think more of us should take that stance," he told BBC Radio 5 Live. "I was really humbled by the response I've been getting. It's humbling but it was nothing I ever expected to have to say and speak up about." Burnley launched an investigation into the incident and pledged to issue lifetime bans to those responsible, saying they are "not welcome at Turf Moor."

An ex-Premier League steward was handed a lifetime ban from Southampton FC. Beryl Saunders, a retired nurse, who once worked at the club, was banished after a racist rant on Facebook. Officials said the Saints season ticket holder had left them "absolutely stunned" with her "vitriol and hateful views" and said that she had refused to apologise or undergo racial awareness training, leaving them no choice but to ban her. Saunders, who worked as a steward until 1997, shared the comment alongside a picture of far-right activist Tommy Robinson and Burnley fan Jake Hepple, who had organised the plane to fly the 'White Lives Matter' banner over the Etihad. Her comment read: "This man deserves a pat on the back [Hepple], what's he got to apologise, for ffs. Let's put up a statue, don't apologise for being white. We whites are the superior race." She vowed to never return to the club, calling it offensive that footballers knelt on the "hallowed turf" in support of the Black Lives Matter movement, claiming slavery gave people "jobs and a roof over their heads" and that the former British prime minister and Second World War leader Sir Winston Churchill said Britons were "the best race".

Premier League teams have supported the movement sanctioning "Black Lives Matter" on the back of shirts, and yet, while it has given the right impression, the worry is how much of it is window dressing, lip service. As part of an *inews* investigation into the diversity of English football's stakeholders, footballing bodies the FA, the English Football League and the Professional Footballers' Association released diversity figures. Despite the Premier League's strong public stance in support of the Black Lives Matter movement, including a lengthy statement indicating that the "Premier League stands alongside players, clubs, the FA, EFL, PFA, LMA [managers], PGMOL [match officials] and all those who have come together in recent weeks to reject racism and to show support for the message that black lives matter," the League refused, at first, to reveal the makeup of its own organisation. The Premier League initially said that it collects and monitors the information internally but does not share it externally.

Former England and Queens Park Rangers winger Trevor Sinclair tweeted regarding the Premier League's refusal, "That's a kick in the teeth after clubs have done so well with their stance on Black Lives Matter." And Kick It Out's head of development, Troy Townsend, questioned how the public would know how representative the Premier League's workforce is if statistics are kept private. He tweeted: "Are all figures present and correct and up to what levels?"

Kick It Out insisted it is "essential for" *all* organisations to share their diversity data. It became the latest organisation to publicise the diversity of their staff, in figures shared with the investigation into the diversity of English football's stakeholders.

The FA, English Football League, the Professional Footballers' Association, the League Managers' Association and now KIO have been open and transparent about the information. Organisations with low figures pledged to improve or have detailed long-term plans with targets.

More than two-thirds of KIO's staff and trustees are from BAME backgrounds. "Currently, in accordance with common practice, we categorise ethnic diversity across two broad dimensions ('white' and 'BAME')," a Kick It Out spokesman told *inews*. "We believe it is time to go beyond BAME and are considering how best to target action and report on this in the future. We will be advocating that others in football do the same. Collecting and sharing diversity data is best practice. This is essential for all organisations to set and measure progress against targets."

Of KIO's seventeen staff, five are "White British", four are "Black British", three are "Asian British", two are "Mixed Heritage" and the remaining three are "White Irish", "Black African" and "Black Caribbean". Of the eight trustees, five are "White British", two are "Black British" and one is "Asian British".

The Premier League's collated data and work in that area is independently assessed. They are signed up to Ernst & Young's National Equality Standard.

It's now known that just 9% of the FA's leadership team are classified as BAME. Just 6% of the entire EFL staff team are from BAME backgrounds, but the organisation insisted it is working hard to change that. The FA is halfway through a three-year Equality, Diversity and Inclusion Plan, with targets for improvement and by 2021 aims to have 16% of all staff and 11% of its leadership team from BAME backgrounds. The EFL has "engaged with a number of employees to discuss issues of equality in the workforce, in respect of next steps to improve representation, including new initiatives and training and development opportunities as we look to embed a wider cultural shift among the League."

Only 7% of the LMA's staff team are from BAME backgrounds. Chief executive Richard Bevan told *i* they "constantly strive to maintain and build a diverse organisation". Chris Hughton, the former Brighton and Newcastle United manager, is on the executive committee and Wayne Allison, the former Bristol City and Chesterfield striker, is the organisation's technical director. "The LMA embraces diversity, through its culture and recruitment and we constantly strive to maintain and build a diverse organisation," LMA chief executive Richard Bevan told *inews*. "We run a programme of diversity education for our team members and diversity is at the heart of our personal development programmes delivered through the LMA Institute."

24% of the PFA's staff and almost half of its trustees are from BAME backgrounds. PFA's head of equalities, Simone Pound, told *inews*: "This is an opportune time for businesses to reflect and address the importance of diversity within their organisations."

Under pressure from the newspaper, the Premier League finally disclosed that 12.22% of its UK workforce are from black, Asian or minority ethnic backgrounds and the organisation says it is "in the process" of reaching the Ernst and Young National Equality Standard, which is supported by the Equality and Human Rights Commission. A Premier League spokesman said, "The Premier League head office is based in central London. The organisation has a staff of 182 people who deliver across a range of roles including football, coach development, community, youth development, safeguarding, broadcast, commercial, communications, digital, finance, legal, marketing and policy [...] we are committed to delivering equality, diversity and inclusion across the organisation."

The lack of BAME representation within governing bodies across sports was described as a "disaster" by Chris Grant, the Sport England independent board member and one of British sport's most senior black administrators. "It's more than a disappointment, it's a disaster, and I think it's a disaster for sport and for the country," Grant told Sky Sports.

Stoke City Womens manager Alena Moulton experienced two major issues of representation in the sport – race and gender. As a black coach appointed to her first head coaching role, she applauds the debate around the fact that there are only five BAME managers across ninety-one men's clubs.

The Women's Super League has made significant advancements as the majority of teams are being managed by females. "I think the focus has been just having more females involved in football, unfortunately having diversity from an ethnicity point of view hasn't," Moulton says of the women's game. "But there's still not enough black girls in grass-roots and if we look at the England senior squad it's not representative. There's a lot of work to do, but I don't think it will be a priority just yet."

A *Telegraph Sport* report found that black players make up 10 to 15% of squads in the WSL compared to 30% in the men's top tier.

Moulton says in her decade in the game she has called out "subtle" racism, but it is not a culture that lends itself to black women speaking up, "I think what Aluko represented was massive for other black females, what she went through. At the start, people didn't really believe her, and that's often the case. Recently I've spoken to a lot of my friends in the game, about what they're no longer going to accept in the changing rooms, in comments from managers. I'm not afraid to challenge people but there's people that are, because they're afraid they'll get a reputation as an aggressive black female. Women's football is really small, and people talk. That's the culture, and until people feel safe in their job to challenge, then I don't understand if it's really going to change."

Moulton benefitted from the FA's BAME mentoring scheme in 2016. The Premier League, EFL and PFA now have announced work placement schemes for six BAME players. However, she says these sorts of programmes do not even touch the sides in addressing systemic inequality. "I was the first cohort for the FA in 2016, four years later has it changed the way clubs are employing people? No,

I'd question it. Yes, it was really good in giving me the work experience, helping me to network, and that's really, really positive for me. But when you look at five BAME coaches across ninety-one clubs, are these six people getting work experience going to change [that]? I really hope they are, and they do, but initiatives like that probably will not have a bigger impact over the bigger picture of those making the decisions."

Issues like the Black Lives Matter badges being politicised as far-left distracts from what is being achieved. "I have previously had negative experiences that have made me think I don't want to pursue football any more, but now I've come to think that if I don't do it then who will inspire other people in my region to do something in football, get the coaching qualifications?"

Down Under, the former Adelaide United star Bruce Djite, now director of football at the club, believes it will take more to instigate lasting changes. "It will fade. In our news cycle things only stay relevant for a certain amount of time," Djite told ESPN. "Seeing what the Premier League did was powerful. These guys are heroes, but it's not enough for permanent change. If you've been racist for 20 years, then seeing these guys wear Black Lives Matter on their shirts and take a knee won't make you anti-racist, but it will get you thinking. It's sad that such a devastating event or sequence of events has to happen to get everyone to sit up and take notice of what surrounds them in their own communities. It's always been there. It's not like racism doesn't exist then suddenly does. Racism is always there, lurking in the background, at the backyard BBQ among friends and relatives, in boardrooms, in places where values and political ideas align. The rallies and protests are important for awareness. They bring attention and get people thinking, but to speed up the rate at which things change, real initiative needs to be taken."

Born in the United States, Djite, who is of Ivorian and Togolese descent, moved to Australia when he was three. "I'm in a position of relative privilege and have been my whole life," he said. "We chose to come to Australia. I grew up in a very good area and was well educated from early on. I was good at football, and, as a kid when you are good at sport, that breaks down a lot of barriers. People are more than happy to accept you as one of them. That was my childhood, but it started to become more apparent to me that if you weren't good at sport, or excelling at something, then people start to pick on your colour."

Talent wasn't enough to protect him from racism, as incidents showed in the Aussie A-League, "We aren't immune to it. Jamie Young was called a 'monkey' by a fan in 2018. Paul Ifill, Ali Abbas have been racially abused," Djite said. "We are seeing society handle it better now. People are called out on it. They (racists) might think it but don't say it – the problem is they still think it. To change that, for example, in Australian sport, it's not just about saying we need to appoint an Indigenous CEO. We need everything – Indigenous coaches, Indigenous referees, board members, administrators, players. It needs to be entrenched throughout the ecosystem."

Djite believes education is the key to implement real change. "At school we didn't learn enough about Aboriginal culture. I literally heard about the Rainbow Serpent and Dreamtime but nothing on the atrocities – maybe a little on the Stolen Generation – but not enough about what defines Indigenous people."

Kyah Simon – whose mother is Anaiwan, and whose father is Biripi – is the first Indigenous Australian player to score a goal for Australia at a World Cup. She told ESPN that football had developed more opportunities to include Indigenous players. "When I was young we really only had a few different distinct pathways. Now there's so many different pathways in terms of academies, club football, state representatives and other different programs. The struggle is if players fall through the cracks. I think there is opportunity [if] the likes of myself and Lydia Williams and other girls within the Matildas (the nickname of the Australian national womens' team) playing squad, if we were able to go out to some of those remote communities and be able to inspire those girls that football is an amazing game, it is the world game. If you can present that type of opportunity and show that Lydia and myself are living proof of going through the game, then I think that really becomes attractive to a lot of Indigenous youth around Australia."

Simon wants to spread the word, "It's just a matter of finding the right ways to really tap into a lot of that raw talent that there is in Indigenous youth and show how they can get through the different stages of football and hopefully be wearing that green and gold one day. I have a cousin, Dave Widders, [who] does a lot of stuff up north, and just speaking to him on a relatable level he's doing a lot of great stuff on ground. I guess there are a lot of people like that in the Indigenous space, locals that are really connecting with community and the mob in their area. They don't necessarily get the recognition for or the platform to display that so I guess that there's going to be – and there should be – better ways we can really encompass a lot of people's interests and ways in which we can get Indigenous kids into football.

"To answer: 'What happened to all our Indigenous players, where did they go, why did they leave the game?' Do an audit. To address the issue, we need to ask those people where the gaps are and then work together to resolve those things. Find the people with context knowledge, with lived experience. Don't go to the guys with PhDs to write a good policy for us to implement, or an advisory committee with no skin in the game. Go straight to the source. It's not that hard."

Djite's closing remarks on ABC's Q&A programme in June were: "If we don't believe Black lives matter, if those three words don't sit comfortably with you … that is the problem."

Paul Pogba

Paul Pogba showed his support for the BLM movement with his new "clenched fist" haircut, which he unveiled before the Premier League game against Bournemouth in July 2020. The symbol of the Black Lives Matter movement was shaved into his head.

Before the game got under way at Old Trafford, players from both sides took the knee, and they also had Black Lives Matter badges on their shirts. While the players knelt French World Cup winner Pogba was among those to raise a fist.

A year earlier, Manchester United arranged to meet representatives of Facebook following the online racial abuse of Pogba and Marcus Rashford via Twitter after penalty misses. United were already due to meet Twitter but decided discussions with Facebook were required because of the trend of online racism aimed at players. The club recognised the problem was less pronounced on Facebook but were determined to be proactive. Ole Gunnar Solskjær said he was "lost for words" after the abuse of Rashford. Pogba vowed to fight against racism "for the next generation."

Pogba said on Twitter: "My ancestors and my parents suffered for my generation to be free today, to work, to take the bus, to play football. Racist insults are ignorance and can only make me stronger and motivate me to fight for the next generation."

Kick It Out said in a statement: "The vile racist abuse on social media continued today. This problem will not go away and needs decisive action – that's what we'll be making clear to Twitter when we meet. Without immediate and the strongest possible action, these cowardly acts will continue to grow."

Pogba asked his teammates to wear anti-racism wristbands on Boxing Day to combat the "ignorance" in football around Europe. The United players wore No to Racism and We Are One rubber bands during the warm-up before their 4–1 win over Newcastle at Old Trafford and Pogba made a point of giving his to a fan. He organised the show of unity in response to the racist abuse suffered by teammates Fred and Jesse Lingard during the recent Manchester derby at the Etihad, Chelsea's Antonio Rüdiger experience of abuse at Tottenham, as well as other incidents involving Everton's former Juventus striker Moise Kean and Kalidou Koulibaly of Napoli, rather than one in particular.

"It was my idea to do that," said Pogba. "I mean, I've been thinking about doing this, but I don't want to go through UEFA or the FIFA. I've done it myself. I think we have the chance to have this power to show things in football, on TV. People see it so I think that will make people understand some things. I think it's ignorance. Ignorance and stuff like that, and just to show people that you are all one. We are all one. We keep seeing it again and again in a lot of stadiums. It's just to show that, to give support to all the players – I mean, black or white or Chinese or whatever who you are. But there is only one race. And just to show respect to everyone. Like I said, we are all one. We all came here to enjoy football, to enjoy ourselves and to do what we love. I was thinking about doing this for a long time. I remember when I was younger [hearing] about Stand Up Speak Up, something like this. It just reminds me of that. A lot of players in a lot of leagues – not only in the Premier League, in Italy, Spain, everywhere, keep hearing this. I don't want to be the president, I don't want to be a political guy. We are just football players – we want to enjoy that. The fans need to enjoy coming and seeing some nice football and that's it. So this is to show that we're against that [racism]. I know that it will make people talk. The teammates, we did it. Fred, Andreas [Pereira], I mean everyone, we are against that. We are just for football, enjoying football. We do what we love. We give joy to the fans, to everyone, to all the spectators and that's all we want to see in the stadium."

Benjamin Mendy
Manchester City full-back and France international Benjamin Mendy grew up in an inclusive culture and hopes the powerful messages football has the capacity to send can make a big impact in wider society. Mendy said: "It's difficult because I grew up in Paris and we all go to school, to the academy with white people, mixed race people, Asian people, black people. The way I lived with them we are all the same, all a family. When I see that around the world, I think in football we have the facility to send a big message and can change a lot of things. We can find a solution, but I think we need to be all together and send a big message because what happens is not normal

and is from nothing. Every person going to work or every person going to school, we are all the same."

Ronaldo – the original Ronaldo – the Brazil striker, insists the battle against racism is everyone's fight and called on his fellow footballers to use their voice to "scream" about the issue. He discussed Black Lives Matter with FIFA president Gianni Infantino during the World Football Summit. World Cup winner Ronaldo commented: "The fight against racism is not a fight for black people – it is everybody's fight. We have to fight it every day. No one is born a racist, somehow they learn to be racist. We have to fight when they are kids. We have to fight every day and every time. Black people follow [footballers] in this fight. We have a voice, a loud voice, we have to scream to the people about that. I was very glad to participate in the [FIFA Legends] campaign against racism because I suffered in the past too. We have to continue to fight and as former football players with a big audience on social media we have to continue to fight every day."

Infantino added: "It is important to make the voice of football heard and to show tolerance. It is a simple message that everybody should understand."

But racism doesn't just come from ordinary members of the public. It can also be directed at players from those who are there to protect the public. Danny Rose says he's racially targeted by police – regularly pulled over and questioned while out driving. "Each time it's, 'Is this car stolen? Where did you get this car from? What are you doing here? Can you prove that you bought this car?' This has been happening since I was 18, since I was driving and, each time it happens, I just laugh, because I know what's coming. It's not just football. I got stopped by the police last week, which is a regular occurrence whenever

I go back to Doncaster where I'm from," he said on the *Second Captains* podcast.

Rose is also racially profiled on public transport, he says, with train staff asking to see his ticket for a first class carriage, while white passengers are left unchallenged. "Particularly when I go home to Doncaster, I don't like to drive so I get the train, but whenever I do drive, I kid you not I will get stopped at some point while I'm in Doncaster, pulled over and questioned. My friends have been there with me a lot of the time when it's happened. The last time, last week, when I'd just been at my mum's house, I had pulled up in a car park, so the engine was off. The police pulled in and they brought a riot van, three police cars and they questioned me. They said they'd had a report that a car had not been driving correctly. So, I'm like, 'okay, so why does that make it *my* car?' I got my ID out and they breathalysed me. It's just honestly one of those things to me now. What can I do? I don't understand what I can do or who I can complain to. This happened first when I was 15 and it's still happening now I'm 30. So, 15 years of this on and off the field happening and there's no change whatsoever.

"These are the things I have to put up with, being stopped all the time and being asked if I know this is first class and to show my ticket. This is everyday life for me but I feel embarrassed to even complain in a way, or bring it up, when you see the incident in America where a man – a black man – lost his life at the hands of people who were supposed to 'protect and serve'."

Rose said that English football's anti-racism work has been too little and infrequent in the past. "Before the incident with George Floyd in America, one day in a year we wear Kick It Out T-shirts. Doing that one day a year is not really going to get the message home. It is just a crying shame that a man had to lose his life in the way he did for this movement having to happen. So, for me that's one of the biggest things I've ever seen in the world, let alone football. All I can say is that things have happened in the past, nowhere near to the extent of what happened in America and a month or two later it's just business as normal. So, I hope this is something that now will catch everybody's eyes, ears and their mind. All we can do now is wait and see and hope that nothing like that happens again."

Rose also faced racist abuse on the pitch back in his time as a youth player at his first club, Leeds United. He recalled racist abuse alongside his future international teammate Fabian Delph, while they were teenagers. Rose was sold to Tottenham in 2007 and never made a senior appearance for Leeds, while Delph become a key player during the club's time in League One before his transfer to Aston Villa in 2009.

He was "lost for words" when Montenegro were ordered to play a single game behind closed doors and given a €20,000 fine after himself and other black England players were racially abused by supporters in a Euro 2020 qualifier last March. "Whenever I do say things or complain about things, you hear people say, 'You're on this money so get on with it.' I just give up with hoping things will change because that's some people's mentality towards racism. It happens on a football pitch. That first happened to me and my good friend Fabian [...] we were only fourteen at the time. He'd been called a 'black [expletive]' on the pitch. I'm not saying I'm used to it, because it still hurts. But how I then go on about my day after that is, it's happened, I move on, and who do we play next?"

Los Angeles Lakers star LeBron James called for players to keep pushing for racial justice as the NBA season resumed in Orlando in the summer of 2020 and the wake of massive protests in American over Floyd's death.

The Lakers, Los Angeles Clippers, Utah Jazz and New Orleans Pelicans – the four teams in action – all knelt during the pre-match anthem. "In the past when we've seen progress, we've let our foot of the gas a little bit. We can't do that," said James. "We want to keep our foot on the gas." Before the anthems, TV coverage of the matches broadcast an introductory segment - narrated by rapper Meek Mill – that promoted social justice initiatives and the campaign for societal change sparked by the viral video of the death of George Floyd in Minneapolis in May. Instead of displaying their names on the back of their jerseys, several players wore a slogan from a list approved by the league organisers, including BLACK LIVES MATTER, SAY THEIR NAMES and I CAN'T BREATHE.

James, who kept his own name on his jersey, as, he says, none of the slogans "seriously resonated" with his personal goals, said that basketball has the power to make a change globally.

"The game of basketball has always been bigger than just the ball and the rim and ten guys on the floor," he told TNT. "It's an opportunity to use this platform to be able to spread a lot of positivity, a lot of love, throughout the whole world."

New Orleans Pelicans' meeting with Utah Jazz was the first NBA match in more than four months after the league had been suspended. The 22 teams with a chance of making the post-season play-offs assembled in a bio-secure "bubble" to play out the remainder of the season at the elite-level basketball facilities at Walt Disney World,

Orlando. All matches took place without fans and the opening-night anthems, performed by jazz star Jon Batiste and Compton Kidz Club, were performed virtually and displayed via video link.

25

The Media

"I've called the office crying because I've felt so uncomfortable as a black man in press boxes."

– a journalist for *The Athletic*

The media have often been criticised for the way they tackle racism. Even TV commentators have come under the microscope.

Much emphasis is placed on how the media whip up racism through their sometimes distorted coverage. Sports journalists Ryan Conway, who covers Derby County, Carl Anka (Southampton), Roshane Thomas (West Ham) and Dan Barnes (office editor) all work for *The Athletic* and all are black. They got together for a very powerful podcast, which, reports the Sports Journalist Association (SJA) "asks searching questions of the sports journalism industry in these times of Black Lives Matter." All talk about the feeling of walking into a press box and being the only black face. One says: "I've called the office crying because I've felt so uncomfortable as a black man in press boxes." The podcast shines a spotlight on what sports journalists who are "different" have to face on a daily basis "simply because of the colour of their skin."

In June 2020, *Daily Mirror* columnist and football writer Darren Lewis called for the media to "wake up" to racial equality, highlighting a letter sent out to every broadcaster and newspaper by the Black Collective of Media in Sport (BCOMS), which included a seven-point plan for all media outlets to encourage diversity. It was supported by stars such as Dina Asher-Smith and David Beckham.

Lewis believes the media can help in the battle for equality in sport but must look at itself too. He wrote: "With cricket joining football in finally waking up to real issues of racial inequality then we in the media must do so, too. "A hard-hitting letter sent out by the Black Collective of Media in Sport outlines the reasons why newspapers and broadcasters need to better reflect society. It calls for training to open up pathways to leadership positions, give employees the skills to address racism and to understand the lack of diversity, and education in conscious and unconscious bias following the revelation from England boss Gareth Southgate that he benefited from his skin colour as he moved into management. The BCOMS letter called for career development for staff across all areas and a commitment to producing readily available progress reports on the number of BAME people being employed and any pay gaps.

"In my 20 years at *Daily Mirror Sport*, the team's commitment to addressing football's lack of black managers, the FA's lack of black leaders and the game's racism problem has been unrelenting. Having kept the focus on sport, however, we must also keep progressing. We are seeing a sea change in our industry. Athletes across a variety of sports recognise that calling out insulting names and gestures from either fans or opponents is not enough. Black squares and warm words are failing to appease frustrated athletes, upset fans and members of the media industry with their noses pressed up against the glass. To address and deal with sport's racism and representation problem we need a media better equipped to highlight it and also one better placed to reflect the society it is serving."

Jermaine Jenas

In his opening column for the *Daily Express* on 16 October 2019, Jermaine Jenas wrote that nations should be banned from competition for racism on the terraces and called upon UEFA to act.

"Racism was rife on England duty," Jenas wrote. "I could pick half a dozen games where it stood out and we thought: what the hell is happening here? But one night in my England career stands out.

"Playing against Spain in the Bernabeu in November 2004 was a shocking experience. We lost 1–0 but the noises that came down from the terraces were terrible and condemned right up to the level of Prime Minister Tony Blair.

"Shaun Wright-Phillips, Ashley Cole and, in other games, Emile Heskey would be the ones who got targeted the most. You would hear the monkey chants really loudly. How does that feel as a person of black heritage? It is very hurtful.

"Different players experience different emotions. It depends on the individual. I was raised by a dad who played semi-professional football for Kettering Town, Shepshed, and lots of clubs, and I used to follow him around the grounds as a kid. Racism in the 80s was massive. When it happens at grassroots or semi-pro level, it is loud and feels very personal because you can hear every single word from people close on the touchline.

"I remember my dad Dennis instilling certain values over racism on the pitch. It was always a 'ram it down their throat on the pitch' mentality – be strong, rise above it, don't react. He always used John Barnes as a role model.

"Others, understandably, are hurt in a different way. I have had chats with Danny Rose about what he felt like when he went through it. It got him down. It upset him. When you are an elite athlete playing at the top, top level it only takes a 5% drop in your mentality to lose your concentration.

"Most players can deal with a raucous atmosphere, even threatening behaviour. When it starts to be about something you have no control over, the colour of your skin, something you are proud of, and people still think it is acceptable to do Nazi salutes and monkey chants… that can really bring down some players.

"As an England player, I remember there being no support at that time from the FA. No talk of walking off the pitch. It was just like – deal with it and we will talk about it afterwards.

"I am not having a go at people for that. No one thought it was acceptable, it was just the way it was 15 years ago. There was no protocol to follow. There was no step-by-step process to deal with it. Everyone knew it happened, no one really said anything, other than 'that was a disgrace' and you moved on.

"What we are seeing now is a group of England players who have a good support system. They have a process to follow. I know they are discussing in-house how to handle situations. They have strong role models. Look at Raheem Sterling, and how he has taken the fight on personally.

"I watched the game against Bulgaria and was thinking: stay on the pitch lads and ram it down their throats. All those goals went in and they remained professional.

"The players acted with so much class from captain Harry Kane back to Jordan Pickford.

"Look at Tyrone Mings, a very intelligent young lad. As offended as he was, he kept his mind. It was his debut, he kept focus and allowed the authorities to deal with it. Nations should be banned from the competition for racism on the terraces. It is up to UEFA to act.

"I know there is still an issue in England. I think it is more individual here. You can pick out the two or three offenders when it happens. As a country in the mid-80s and early 90s, we were banned from Europe because of hooliganism. That is the kind of stance I want taken."

James McClean

Republic of Ireland's James McClean criticised the football authorities, his Irish teammates and the media over their response to racist and sectarian abuse he had suffered.

"I receive and have received more abuse than any other player during my nine years in England." The Derry man has been the victim of online abuse throughout his career and received sectarian taunts from opposition fans over his refusal to wear a poppy during the annual remembrance period every autumn.

British soldiers shot dead civilian protestors in McClean's home city of Londonderry in 1972 in what became known as Bloody Sunday. In a lengthy Facebook post, McClean said the lack of support from his teammates over his decision left a "sour taste." McClean described the racist abuse directed at his fellow Republic of Ireland player, David McGoldrick after comments were posted on social media just hours after the arrest of the 12-year-old boy who had taunted Wilfired Zaha as "horrendous" and something "nobody should be subjected to." "Twelve-year-old boy gets arrested for posting racial abuse online to Zaha – again rightly so [but] has anyone ever been held accountable for mine? No. Have I ever had my abuse condemned by the media? No! In fact, quite the opposite. The slightest thing that I do that might cause offence to anyone is highlighted by them," he said. McClean asked if the discrimination he suffered was different to other racist abuse. "I have seen some of my fellow Irish teammates post a black square in support of anti-racism as well as post[s] condemning the discrimination, and again rightly so! Have I ever seen any of them ever post a public condemnation of the discrimination I get, which funnily enough is a discrimination against them also? That would be a no! Does one kind of discrimination hold a higher bearing over another act of discrimination?"

McClean went into greater detail in another post, this time blaming the media for not doing enough over his sectarian abuse and revealing he has had death threats to him personally and his three children. He received bullets in the post during his time at Sunderland from 2011 to 2013 and more recently messages expressing hope that his family would die of Covid-19. "I've been getting horrendous abuse, I've had police at my door taking fingerprints when I was at Sunderland because we've had bullets sent. To my family home. We've had letters, birthday cards, it's all been very well highlighted and attention has been brought to it by myself, but it all seems to fall on deaf ears," he continued. "I've made mistakes, I'm no angel, at the end of the day, and people say, 'You've brought it on yourself,' but all this abuse started well before I'd done anything. Sometimes I get annoyed and I am an emotional guy and sometimes the emotions get the better of me and I'll act out. But I'm acting out based on retaliation from all this abuse I shouldn't be getting, and the media – they jump on it and they add fuel to the fire. And before you know it my reputation is up in flames and people see me based on what they see in the media.

"The media has got a big part to play in how I'm being perceived. I'm just asking for equality, I'm just asking to be treated the same, I just want us to be treated as one. It's a bitter pill to swallow because I'm thinking we're in the same profession here, we do the same job, nobody should be allowed to do or say what they want without repercussions and up until now that's just the way it has been. I've had messages where people are saying they hope my three young children contract Covid-19 and die – I shouldn't be receiving this, I shouldn't have to put up with this. People scratch their heads and wonder why I do sometimes react the way I do, at the end of the day if I wasn't a footballer and I wasn't in the limelight … You're trying to tell me any other father in any other profession would just accept that, and that's okay? I listen to talkSPORT in the morning and on the way home from training, and yesterday when I was listening to the show and callers were very annoyed and upset at the abuse Wilfried Zaha and David McGoldrick took, and I was just thinking, 'Where has that passion and level of annoyance been over the years for my abuse?' That's where the frustration and the post that I wrote yesterday came from."

When asked for a reaction, McClean's club, Stoke City, said there was "no comment at this stage."

McClean praised the football authorities and Staffordshire police for their responses at the time of the incidents with the bullets and threats against his children. Two months later, McClean was fined two weeks wages by Stoke and agreed to delete his Instagram account after he posted a picture of himself wearing a balaclava in front of two children, with the caption "Today's school lesson – History" along with a laughing emoji.

Raheem Sterling

Raheem Sterling said that the battle for racial equality is the most important issue facing the world, claiming racism is "the only disease right now." Speaking to Emily Maitlis on BBC *Newsnight*, Sterling said: "I know this might sound a little bit cheesy, but the only disease right now is the racism that we are fighting. This is the most important thing at this moment in time because this is something that has been happening for years and years. Just like the pandemic, we want to find a solution to stop it. At the same time, this is what all these protesters are doing. They are trying to find a solution and a way to stop the injustice they are seeing, and they are fighting for their cause. As long as they are doing it peacefully and safely and not hurting anybody and not breaking into any stores, they continue to protest in this peaceful way.

"There's only so much communities and other backgrounds can take – especially black people. It's been going on for hundreds of years and people are tired and people are ready for change. This is something that needs more than just talking. We need to actually implement change and highlight the places that do need changes. But this is something that I myself will continue to do. [I will] spark these debates and get people in my industry looking at themselves and thinking what they can do to give people an equal chance in this country."

In December 2018, Sterling suffered abuse from fans during City's 2–0 defeat at Stamford Bridge. Sterling posted on Instagram the following morning questioning the media's portrayal of black players and saying it fed prejudice and aggressive behaviour. The post highlighted the different treatment of Manchester City youngsters Tosin Adarabioyo and Phil Foden – both of whom had bought new houses for their mothers – in newspaper reports. Journalist and broadcaster Musa Okwonga said, "What was so powerful about the post was that he was not doing it for himself, he was doing it on someone else's behalf. It was almost like he had weathered the storm, playing the role of big brother or uncle and saying, 'They've come for me and I've dealt with it, but they're not coming for anyone after me'."

When Sterling was presented with the Football Writers' Association Footballer of the Year award in 2019, chair Carrie Brown cited his public stance on racist abuse as being just as important as his exploits on the pitch. In the same year, Sterling condemned the abuse in Montenegro, offering support to his younger teammate Callum Hudson-Odoi who claimed he could hear fans making racist noises during the match. Again, in 2019, He called out Leandro Bonucci when the Juventus defender suggested that his teammate Moise Kean was partly to blame for the racist abuse he received from Cagliari fans. Sterling described Bonucci's comments as "laughable."

"He's not a traditional spokesman, he's a regular guy – a man of the people," Okwonga said. "He's an everyman and that's why his messages are so powerful. It held up a mirror on the media's treatment of black players in a way which had never happened before."

Host of the England team's YouTube channel Craig Mitch added: "For me, Raheem is a massive inspiration. He's taken so many metaphorical bullets. Metaphorically speaking, he's a martyr because he's saying, 'You're not doing this to this player or any others.' And on social media, he's got a bigger platform than the newspapers or the media outlets to say, 'This isn't right and I'm not standing for it.' You're seeing things unfold and thinking, 'Who is going to be the brave one to stand up and say something?' Lo and behold it was Raheem. He's decided enough is enough and since that post he's just carried on standing up."

John Barnes challenged Sterling to use his growing influence to further conversations in wider society. "He's started the debate about the influence the media has on perceptions of black players but rather than talking about millionaire footballers who get racially abused, I'd like him to – because he's got that voice and people are listening to him – to talk about the black community in general," Barnes told a 5 Live panel. "I think now footballers should – rather than talking about how terrible it is in Croatia or Montenegro – talk about the wider issues that really affect the black community in the UK who are disenfranchised, disempowered, whose kids are giving up hope because they are not given an education or social opportunities. Racism has been around for ages so we have to look at different ways of tackling the problem, and the way of tackling the problem is to stop talking about getting more black coaches or black people in positions of power, and to start changing the perceptions we have of the average black man in the street, not black superstar footballers, or Barack Obama, or Beyoncé."

"In six years, we'll be talking about him making his 100th England cap," said Rory Smith, chief football writer at the *New York Times*. "And in eight years, we'll be talking about him as a leader of a generation. For players like Callum Hudson-Odoi, he's a standard bearer. He will go down as one of the most important England players of the early 21st century."

"I would liken Sterling to Muhammad Ali," said Mitch, on England's YouTube channel "[When Ali was first fighting] he wasn't looked at as a legend, he was looked at as an unruly individual from the Nation of Islam. No one gave him props for standing up for what he believed in, and Sterling is going through the same stuff now. He's changing people's minds, he's being brave, and we can see how it's working out for him. We need characters like that because it takes them to another level outside sport and cements your legacy within humanity. And if he keeps going, he'll go down as a legend. He symbolises the dream that you can be from a different country, grow up in the UK and rise to the highest level of football and perform consistently at the pinnacle of the game. He's a living example of someone who's still playing who is trying to make history by winning a domestic treble with City and trying to win trophies with England. Any creed or colour can look at him as an inspiration. And that's the highest act a human can perform: inspire. He's one of the top role models we have right now – not only in sport but in popular culture."

26

And Finally...

Question: How many black players were there in the England World Cup squad in Russia?
Answer: Nobody was counting. It didn't matter.

Here, to round things off, as Kick It Out continue its vital work, Clive Tyldesley writes about his association with the organisation.

I think there is a major misconception about Kick It Out. It is not an anti-racism body. Or it isn't *just* an anti-racism body. What I love most about the essential motives and aims of Kick It Out is that they are, above all, pro-fairness. Fairness in football is always a matter of opinion and degree, but the reason that the world's game embraces uniform laws and regulations is to try to produce a playing field that is level for all.

Once upon a time, it was a talking point but not anymore. The England team is the country's greatest meritocracy. The only requirement for selection is that you are good enough. There is evidence to suggest that when Paul Ince became the first black player to wear the England captain's armband

25 years ago, skin colour was still an issue with some senior FA officials. It is important to remember the progress of the past when addressing the problems of the present. Kick It Out has driven much of that progress over those 25+ years.

The organisation may have been borne out of a campaign for racial equality, but it is now every bit as committed to supporting victims of discrimination on the grounds of gender, disability, religion and sexual orientation. It makes no distinctions between the sources of prejudice because there are none. People disadvantaged on the grounds of their age, their accent or their economic and educational backgrounds are not headline news in the way that other minority groups may be but Kick It Out is still on their side.

Unfairness is institutionalised, so it needs counter-institutions to set about dismantling it. When I first volunteered my support and involvement to Troy Townsend a decade or so ago, I made him probably the most unusual sales pitch he's ever heard. I told him that what Kick It Out needed was some white, middle-aged, middle-class, overweight, overpaid, male spokesmen on board! *Why?!* Because we know the enemy.

A lot of influential, institutionalised people that fit the above description are as racist as they are sexist and a hundred other "-ists" besides, but they don't know it. They are not terrible people. They actually want to be "better" people, but they live in bubbles that create little access to influences that might organically refine and correct their outdated attitudes and approach. Kick It Out is in the business of popping bubbles. I, for one, reel against any public mention of the "black community" or the "gay community" because I see them only as further bubbles promoting distance and self-interest. Something has got to rise above all of that in order to create true diversity. Kick It Out is trying.

Promoting greater understanding and tolerance may need a kick start from the law makers from time to time and Kick It Out has both the credibility and the energy to start campaigns for increased opportunity and representation for minority groups. It is positioned to knock on the door of Westminster and Wembley when the pace of change slows. Lord Ouseley has a particularly loud knock. His organisation spends a lot of time reacting to instances of abuse or injustice, but he knows that Kick It Out is at its best when it is proactively leading initiatives and crusades to give everybody a fair chance.

The greater breadth of Kick It Out's work is illustrated by its "Raise Your Game" series of events. They do not target one issue or group but rather look to prepare everyone to seize any opportunities when they do arise. Adaptations of the Rooney Rule can only work if there are strong BAME candidates in place, qualified and ready to excel in interview situations. If "Raise Your Game" can seat a budding Asian coach across a table from a football administrator that regularly conducts such interviews, he or she inevitably becomes a stronger candidate. Organic, natural progress is far more valuable and lasting than change enforced by legislation.

The greatest allies to Kick It Out are our children. They see no skin colours, they are at ease with any sexual preferences, they embrace all cultures. The next generation are ready to stride through the barriers that the Kick It Out pioneers of the last 25+ years have broken down. When Cyrille Regis died, he was universally recognised as one of those pioneers. He endured the taunts and jibes of baying imbeciles with an unbelievable dignity that eventually persuaded the majority that his only difference from the other strikers in English football was that Cyrille was better than most of them.

Pioneers rarely volunteer. When Jacqui Oatley was cast as *Match of the Day*'s first female commentator, she didn't know that she was breaking ground that Vicki Sparks and Robyn Cowen would be able to tread with a little more acceptance and confidence one day. When Justin Fashanu revealed that he was gay, he was in need of more support and endorsement than, frankly, football was ready to give him. I don't know but maybe he would be with us today if Kick It Out had been 25 years old when he took his life back in 1998. In over two decades since then, it is a body that has gathered status and credibility enough to be able to defend and champion the cause of anyone that feels isolated in football.

Because Kick It Out is public and 21st-century, it has its critics. They go with the territory. The complainants that decry its financial dependence on the FA, the PFA and the EFL never climbed the four flights of stairs to its old run-down office above a pizza place in Clerkenwell. They don't know how little of their riches the football powers bestow on Kick It Out. They don't "get" what this 24/7 organisation of the low-paid and their interns is doing to fight fights that a multimillion-pound industry like English football should have long since won. Like many things in football, you would only miss it if it wasn't there. It's been there for over 25 years and it will be needed for many, many more to come.

Just be grateful for Kick It Out.

Afterword: Time to Purge Racism

It is remarkable that anyone should still need to write about racism in football. It surely should have become a chapter in the history of the game which readers today saw with a mixture of repugnance and surprise. Yet it is still high on the agenda. And it needs to be.

When I became the first independent Chairman of The Football Association in 2008 it was said I had the good fortune to take the role in a golden age – the hooliganism and overt racism that had stained the game for generations was said to have all but vanished. There were many black players at the top of the English game and a significant number had earned the right to play for their country. It was evident that, in spite of their ability and leadership qualities, it was rare for one to become captain and the reasons given were the stuff of mythology. They were said to hate playing through the English winters; they would not guide other players although they were amenable to being guided; they hadn't experienced captaincy in their club teams – generally for the same reasons.

It was obvious nonsense. You didn't have to spend much time with Rio Ferdinand or meet Paul Ince to recognise the presence of a leader or the respect they enjoyed. But the "wisdom" of the time was that the problems of racism with minor aberrations had gone away. I accept that in 2008 it was better than it had been ten years earlier but it is hard to ignore the outbreaks of racism or to miss the atmosphere of a hornets' nest which might at any time be poked with a stick.

It was my good fortune to know Lord Herman Ousley throughout the period I was chairman. His dynamism in Kick It Out and the people he brought in to make it a remarkable team of activists were an asset to football and wider society. He was always a source of great wisdom on the deep-set problems facing people of colour in football and had time to advise on the not infrequent occasions when the form of racism was anti-Semitic. Just as I was frequently told it was a great sign that a Jewish chairman had been appointed, to be followed by another in the exceptional David Bernstein, I was equally frequently reminded that the appointment was at best a curiosity.

It was a curiosity in England where at a meeting of the Premier League Board an occasional member would ask me if I had "chosen" to be Jewish to get the extra holidays (the Jewish New Year and the fast of repentance) and whether it wasn't a bit of an inconvenience for others when they disrupted the scheduled meetings. But I can't and won't say these irritations compared with the grim experience of black players and the massive lack of opportunity for black coaches and managers.

Nor did they compare with experiences on the road. The England team playing away in the World Cup qualifiers in Eastern Europe were always subject to abuse – abuse which has obviously become worse. When I raised it with the Chairman of a former Yugoslavian nation, he laughed and told me it was just part of the game and asked if I had particular reasons myself to be sensitive.

So, it's a longstanding and ugly reality which needs to be dealt with now and perhaps the stimulus of Black Lives Matter will give the fight more intensity. Raheem Sterling and others have rightly propelled the issue to the front of our attention. Over 20 years ago I read a remarkable account of the same sorts of experience by Richie Moran who described himself in a serious academic work as "a black ex-professional footballer who actually quit playing the game because of the direct, indirect, overt and covert institutionalised racism that exists within the sport" (*Soccer and Society, Vol 1*, p 190). Moran, a gifted Birmingham City centre-forward, said he was almost always astonished when he focused on the source of screamed abuse. It would be a white, middle-aged, male, home supporter, face contorted with hate, and often with an affectionate arm around his child who would be stridently imitating his dad.

Of course, it all goes back far further into the past. The first black outfield player in professional football was Walter Tull who, in 1909, played for Spurs. He served in the Middlesex Regiment as an officer and was killed in action in March 2018. Having made the first team, he was dropped to the reserves after sustained abuse at its worst at Bristol City. The event was described by a Football Star reporter under the headline 'Football and the Colour Prejudice'. He was also said to be the first black infantry officer in the regular British Army and had been commended for the Military Cross which the Ministry of Defence has refused to award posthumously. However brave, or however skilled on the pitch, some barriers appear insurmountable.

I recount these points to show how long these prejudices have been in football – indeed they date back to the first black professional – and to show how easily racist hatred can pass between generations in the atmosphere of a football ground and how hard it actually is to take on the problem because it becomes inter-generational.

At the start of last season 150 racist incidents related to football were reported to the police. They had risen by 50% over the previous season and were double the number three seasons ago. The reaction from football itself became more clear-cut and sustained. In England, The FA and Kick It Out recognised the problem as growing societally and in football and demanded better behaviour from everyone – not least the politicians who routinely use divisive language to the extent it has become normal. Gary Neville, to his credit, named leading politicians including the prime minister, Boris Johnson, for making casual racism more acceptable. They certainly had some far better ministerial examples to follow including Home Office Minister, Baroness Susan Williams, who has been consistently spoken about the problem as a white people problem inflicted on black people.

Consistency in effort has also been clear from the weekly meetings of Kick It Out, the UK Football Policing Unit and The FA which aimed, from early 2018, to create a proactive agency to support police activity and educational programmes. Some clubs have shown serious intent. Manchester City imposed a lifetime ban on supporter Ian Baldry for racist abuse of Raheem Sterling. It is instructive that Sterling was playing on his home ground and Baldry was a City fan. The abuse was straightforwardly because Sterling is black.

In Europe players who hear abusive chants or shouts can now report them to the referee, their captain or the manager. The game is halted, and a warning read to the crowd. If the abuse persists, that could be the end of the match. It is also true that FIFA then often imposes a derisory fine on the offending club or national football federation, a sum which looks absurd given the financial strength of so clubs and football organisations.

Each of these steps is welcome, but they hardly seem to me to do much more than scratch the surface of the issues. Statements about racism and behaviour are great but they are made all the time and saying things is nothing like so potent as doing things. 'Our society will not tolerate ....' needs to be followed by what our society will *do* in the event the activity continues. Small scale fines cannot be the remedy as everyone knows the wealth at the top levels of domestic and international football. Even the poorer footballing nations have TV income from internationals which demonstrates they have far deeper pockets than at any time in their history. And where players allege the discrimination has come from a fellow professional and the case is proved, a ban for no longer than a straight red card is felt as a nuisance rather than a permanent blemish.

It will not be popular, but it is surely true that the time has come where the powerful sentiment behind taking the knee translates into steps that hurt racists or those who turn a blind eye. I am not advocating a lack of proper process, but it is imperative that processes themselves are transparent and as rapid as they can reasonably be. This needs to start at the very top.

The late President of the South American Football Federation, the Argentinian Julio Grondona, served as his country's football president from September 1979 till his death in 2014. He was a long-term vice president of FIFA and very close to its leadership. He was a man in the true traditions of FIFA. After his death in 2014 he was alleged to have approved 47 corrupt payments to football officials and sports executives during 2007. By then, he was not around to answer the charges or be extradited to the USA. But Grondona had form in other respects. In 2003 when discussing in public who could referee major matches, he said "I do not believe a Jew can ever be a referee at this level. It's hard work and, you know, Jews don't like hard work."

In a heated discussion with him on the fringes of a meeting of the International Association Football Committee – we were in disagreement because I wanted the introduction of goal line technology and he didn't – I told him how offensive I found his anti-Semitic comments. He told me it was a pity Hitler hadn't finished the job. In short, the problem reached the very top and it had never harmed Grondona's career.

In competition at club and international level, the punishments must persuade the large number of supporters who cannot stand racists that they have every interest in identifying them and getting them kicked out. A set of sanctions could be designed with that outcome. Serious points deductions, no home games for the rest of the season but all games played on opponents' grounds, all home games for a season behind closed doors or fines equal to the club's weekly wage bill. No doubt there could be mitigations for supporters who point out the culprits at the time of the offence and clubs who always ban culprits for life. Immediate life bans for proven abusers was the minimum penalty I wanted at Wembley Stadium. For player on player abuse – a ban for at least a season and commensurate pay deductions.

And in matches, whilst an initial warning would give stewards, other supporters, and the home administrators a chance to act immediately, I can see no reason to press on with a game after any repeat behaviour. The match should be forfeited to the side on the receiving end. It cannot be up to players to say they want to go ahead. That removes the imperative to make sure they and their successors never face the same viciousness again. Of course, players want to be brave to let their skills do the talking, but this has become about everyone else's behalf.

There is nothing in this which would remove the need for a proper and convincing examination of evidence. But I feel certain the international federations, the leagues, the clubs, the players and the supporters will choose not to allow the intolerable to be repeated. The first few harsh examples may well be the last few.

Might it penalise those who had no part in the abuse? It might, but these more innocent parties are subject to sanctions now. It is a matter of degree and objective. I feel confident they will be precisely the people who conclude there is no merit in or justification for silence. The broadcasters who want and need football as the key content for their business models will be equally clear. They will tell everyone they are paying for the football and not for the ranting of those who simply want to abuse the stars of the show. Time for everyone to pull together and use the restart after this pandemic-induced interlude to launch a very specific new new. One purged of racism.

David Triesman
The Rt Hon Lord Triesman of Tottenham
First Independent Chairman of The FA (2008-2010)

Postscript

There can be no more significant postscript to this book and why the "white, male, and stale" notion still persists, than the events within the Football Association, separated by a few days in the autumn of 2020.

On 10 November – two weeks after the FA announced a new code for diversity that had been described to me as a "game changer" from the more enlightened within the organisation – Chairman Greg Clarke, spouted such unacceptable language in front of an All Party Parliamentary Commission that he was forced to resign his post in disgrace.

Clarke had been called to give evidence to the Department for Culture, Media and Sport select committee about the Premier League's potential bailout of English Football League clubs and the structural reforms proposed as part of "Project Big Picture."

Clarke was talking about racist abuse of players by trolls on social media when he said, "People can see if you're black and if they don't like black people because they are filthy racists, they can abuse you anonymously online." He had earlier spoken of the need to attract people into the sport from a range of communities: "If you go to the IT department of the FA, there's a lot more South Asians than there are Afro-Caribbeans. They have different career interests." He attracted further criticism when referring to gay players making a "life choice" and recalling how a coach had told him that young female goalkeepers did not like having the ball hit hard at them. Most damningly of all he referred to black players as "coloured footballers."

He was forced, at first, to apologise and then, soon afterwards, resign. Hours after Clarke resigned, with the FA facing a barrage of condemnation, Kick It Out said his remarks should be "consigned to the dustbin of history."

As Clarke departed, former FA Chairman Greg Dyke reacted to the news telling *The Times*, "My advice to anyone offered the job is: don't take it. The governance structure of the FA is archaic, and unless they bring in an independent regulator separate from the clubs and the grassroots, it will not be effective."

An FA spokesperson said afterwards that Clarke acknowledged his language was inappropriate. "Greg Clarke is deeply apologetic for the language he used to reference members of the ethnic minority community during the select committee hearing today." But the apology was insufficient, and Clarke had to go. "As a person who loves football and has given decades of service to our game, it is right that I put the interests of football first," added Clarke in the statement confirming his departure. "2020 has been a challenging year and I have been actively considering standing down for some time to make way for a new chair now our CEO transition is complete and excellent executive leadership under Mark Bullingham is established."

The condemnation of Clarke's language was instant and damning. Sanjay Bhandari, executive chair at Kick

It Out, said Clarke's comments were outdated. "I was particularly concerned by the use of lazy racist stereotypes about South Asians and their supposed career preferences. It reflects similar lazy stereotypes I have heard have been spouted at club academy level," he said. "Being gay is not a 'life choice' as he claimed too. The casual sexism of saying 'girls' do not like balls hit at them hard, is staggering from anyone, let alone the leader of our national game. It is completely unacceptable."

A statement from Show Racism the Red Card said Clarke's comments "only serve to demonstrate the power of language and the damage of stereotyping groups of people."

Nigel Huddleston, sports minister, said, "Greg Clarke's comments have caused deep offence and were completely unacceptable. I acknowledge his decades of service to football and his apology, but he was right to stand down as chairman of the FA. We must ensure that opportunities are open to everyone in the sports sector – from athletes to board members – and all forms of discrimination must be tackled head on."

David Bernstein, former FA chairman, told BBC Sport: "I am just surprised that the chair of any organisation who's got a feel of what's going on in the year 2020 could use those types of words, that sort of language. It's just inappropriate."

Darren Bent, former England striker, said, "Slip of the tongue was it? Awful just awful." Anton Ferdinand, former West Ham, Sunderland and QPR defender, asserted, "Clearly education is needed at all levels."

Julian Knight, DCMS select committee chairman, stated, "It's right that Greg Clarke apologised before the committee, however, this isn't the first time that the FA has come to grief over these issues. It makes us question their commitment to diversity."

Alex Davies-Jones, committee member, was keen to stress "The language used by Greg Clarke in our meeting this morning was absolutely abhorrent. It speaks volumes about the urgent progress that needs to be made in terms of leadership on equalities issues in sport. I can't believe we're still here in 2020."

It wasn't the first time Clarke had put his foot in it. Three years ago – in front of the same parliamentary committee – he was criticised for referring to institutional racism as "fluff." He apologised after being chastised by MPs and was reminded that language matters. He didn't seem to learn. Maybe this latest episode highlights the endemic institutional racism at the FA that his predecessor Greg Dyke talks about in this book.

"We can confirm that Greg Clarke has stepped down from his role as our chairman," said an FA statement issued at the time. "Peter McCormick will step into the role as interim FA chairman with immediate effect and the FA board will begin the process of identifying and appointing a new chair in due course." Any chance he would be from the BAME community? Following his resignation, Clarke said: "My unacceptable words in front of Parliament were a disservice to our game and to those who watch, play, referee and administer it. This has crystallised my resolve to move on. I am deeply saddened that I have offended those diverse communities in football that I and others worked so hard to include."

Gareth Southgate said there was "no alternative" but for Clarke to resign. "We can't just keep standing in front of the cameras talking about change." The England manager added: "We are seeing a lot of change in society and football needs to be at the front of that. What's a shame for him [Clarke] is he has done a lot of work behind the scenes to support the diversity code and make inroads into relationships around Europe. But what he said wasn't acceptable and there was no alternative but for him to go." Southgate praised Paul Elliot, the chairman of the FA's inclusion advisory board and a reported contender for the role. "The reforms Paul has helped to put in place deserve a lot of commendation. What I admire about someone like Paul is he has committed himself to football administration. There are a lot of hours to that."

Match of the Day presenter and former England striker Gary Lineker told ITV's *Good Morning Britain* the organisation was full of "lots of old white men" and said he believes real change can only be implemented if the FA, the English Football League and Premier League work together. Former England winger John Barnes said the issue of racism needed to be tackled by society, not just football. "A lot of people are now looking at this problem as if it's unique to football," he told BBC Radio Wales. "But if you look at the higher echelons of any institution, a lot of white men over 50 have the same ideas. This is the way society is and this is what we have to tackle, society as a whole."

Former FA chairman David Bernstein said Clarke's comments highlighted the FA's need for structural change. Bernstein was among a group who launched a manifesto for change in October 2020 called "Saving Our Beautiful Game", demanding changes at the FA, as well as an independent regulator of English football. "The FA has been resistant to serious change over the years and frankly if you have an organisation that is not modern, that has not been updated, then this sort of thing is much more likely to happen," he told 5 Live. "I hope there are progressive people across the board who feel strongly about this. I think the FA has to think very carefully about the sort of person who is brought forward to lead the organisation next time."

Former England and Manchester City centre-half Joleon Lescott described Clarke's comments as "very disturbing" and told BBC Radio 5 Live that "One hundred percent of black players want to see change, but that's not going to happen." He believed Clarke's comments hinted at structural problems within the FA and said any successor may be unable to instigate real change. "I don't think a 63-year-old man in 2020 is using that phrase for the first time, and that's the problem. So, we now expect the next person in line will have heard this and have been a part of this. Now he's going to step up and we expect that person to take us forward. How do you expect change if the people that are in charge have the same mindset, or similar mindset?"

Casey Stoney, Manchester United Women's head coach, railed at Clarke's crass comment that the lack of goalkeepers in women's football was due to girls not liking the ball being kicked at them. Stoney was hopeful Clarke's successor would strive for real change at the organisation in order to develop a progressive culture of inclusivity and diversity in football. "It just shows how much work we've still got to do," the former England defender said. "They are completely unacceptable. I think it was the right thing to stand down. It's extremely disappointing when the person at the top of that chain is making those comments and making them so flippantly and easily. It's extremely disappointing. Hopefully, you have to see this as an opportunity for positive change now. I think this is a really good opportunity for that."

Former Manchester City defender Nedum Onuoha told 5 Live, "It's outrageous to be honest – it sounds like something from 20, 30 years ago. That language has been inappropriate for decades now, so it shows in some ways that perhaps he's lived in an echo chamber where things like this are acceptable to say." Onuoha thought the new diversity code was a "step in the right direction" but there was a need for further change: "It's not the answer to everything. Behaviours will have to change as well and ways of discussing these things, as we have seen today." Former Manchester United and England striker Andy Cole remained optimistic things were moving in the right direction and said people should wait to see whether the new code made a positive impact. "We need to make progress now," he told BBC Breakfast. "I'm hoping, seeing what we are going through now, that within six months there will be progress, and I want to see where we are at."

Former Huddersfield and Gillingham striker Iffy Onuora, who is an equalities officer at the Professional Footballers' Association, said it shows more education is still needed about the effect of certain words and phrases and why they are offensive. "It's just so outdated. There's certain terms we don't use any more about disabled people or gay people – we've moved on," he told BBC Radio 5 Live. "It's as much the message it sounds. Don't forget people in the FA are looking up to the chairman to provide leadership, to provide that voice and to drive on some of the initiatives they are doing, as is everybody in the game."

With Clarke gone there were nine on the FA board, including acting chairman Peter McCormick. Of those, four board members were women and one was from a black and minority ethnic (BAME) background in line with reforms agreed by the FA in 2017, which pledged to increase BAME representation on the board to at least 10%, have 10% representation from the LGBT+ community and 40% female representation. It also pledged to add 11 new members to improve the diversity of the 122-strong FA Council, which was overwhelmingly made up of white men over 60.

Dame Heather Rabbatts, who spent five years as the only woman and BAME member on the FA board before resigning in 2017, said Clarke's comments "revealed the fault line" in the sport. "The leadership and management of football, one of the most diverse games on the planet, is still controlled, fundamentally, by white men," she told BBC Radio 4's *Today* programme.

Mark Bullingham, the FA's chief executive, said the recruitment process would be an open system. "Our process will be open and conform to the Diversity Code, ensuring that we are able to select the best candidate from a diverse talent pool," Bullingham said.

***

The FA delivered the Football Leadership Diversity Code, an 11-page document, to clubs, convinced it would be a "seismic shift" with a minimum of 15% of senior leadership or team operations roles – including the boardroom, and jobs such as director of football – should be performed by people from a BAME background. In addition, 25% of coaching appointments should be BAME, while that figure is 10% for "new senior coaching" roles with the first team. Alternatively, clubs can set their own targets based on the demographic of local areas if they meet the FA's criteria allowing for negotiation. The FA will carry out checks with clubs and post results of progress, confident their reforms will finally make a significant difference.

At present, only five of the 92 Premier League and English Football League managers or head coaches are BAME.

Paul Elliott, head of the FA's inclusion advisory board, insisted the new code will "hold football to account."

Elliott was instrumental in drawing up the code. Elliot said that its ethos is "ensuring boardrooms and leadership positions across our national sport better reflect the society we live in and the people who play the game." The code was developed over a five-month consultation period, with Elliott speaking to several leading players including Harry Kane, Tyrone Mings and Lucy Bronze.

Nineteen of the twenty Premier League clubs agreed to the voluntary code. Southampton were the only exception, stressing they were "wholly supportive" of the code's objectives but were waiting to see how it fits in with the Premier League's own Advanced Equality Standard before revising their recruitment processes, which they say are the culmination of a "five-year equality and diversity journey."

More than 40 clubs signed up in total, including sides from the EFL, Women's Super League and Women's Championship.

Manchester United instantly endorsed the FA's plans. Richard Arnold, Group Managing Director, said: "I want to restate our promise as a club to champion diversity and to promote equality for all. Manchester United has been and will always be a club open for all. We are very proud of all the efforts that we have made across the club over many years to campaign for equality in football and society and to diversify our workforce. Our most recent initiative, All Red All Equal commenced in 2016 and through that, we have challenged hate crime and discrimination, raised awareness of mental health issues and promoted the empowerment of women amongst many other initiatives.

"However, there is always more for us to learn and to do in this area. We welcome the work of the FA to support the good work that has already been done and to challenge us to raise the bar even higher. We had no hesitation in signing up to the Football Leadership Diversity Code.

We now look forward to implementing a plan that will be adopted and embraced throughout every department of the club.

"While this is a topic that is rightly moving to the forefront of conversations in boardrooms across every industry, we are proud that we have been leading, and executing, in this area within our organisation over many years. We have seen the benefits of having a diverse, talented senior leadership team at the club. By having our people coming from a variety of backgrounds, we will be able to continue to innovate, adapt, raise standards and uphold our reputation in the industry.

"The message is clear. Manchester United is a club that is open to all. This national effort will enable the game to make a huge leap forward, reinforcing football's popularity for the next generation of fans, coaches, players, staff and volunteers.

"We want to create greater diversity in leadership positions. We are trying to modernise football, so it stops relying on its 'little black book' and group of networks and gives equal opportunities to those who are qualified. This isn't about tokenism; this is about equal opportunities. To be the same as everyone else.

"What really inspired me to create the code was a comment from Raheem Sterling, when he said he looks up to the directors and senior leadership and doesn't see people like him. Also, Jermain Defoe. He's had such a wonderful career and has thoughts about being a coach but wonders whether it is worth getting qualified as he doesn't think he will get a job. We've lost three generations of players who have been denied opportunities, we can't lose a fourth."

★★★

While the FA heralded their initiative as "game changing," Raheem Sterling was leading fresh calls for social media companies to take decisive action after a groundbreaking study revealed the alarming scale of online racism and abuse aimed at footballers.

The PFA Charity's study was backed by Kick It Out and carried out by data science company Signify, which analysed 825,515 tweets directed at 44 selected players during the six weeks of Project Restart. They identified 11,000 posts deemed offensive or controversial, and over 3,000 that were explicitly abusive messages. Of all the discriminatory abuse 56% was racist; 43% of Premier League players experienced targeted and explicitly racist abuse on Twitter; and 50% of the online abuse was received by three players, Sterling, Zaha and Akinfenwa (all of whom had spoken up on Black Lives Matter). These posts have not been deleted and the accounts have not been banned. The sickening posts significantly increased *after* the trio called out racism, highlighting the repercussions players face when they attempt to take a stand. A total of 29 of the racist abuse came in the form of emojis, and the length of time that some remained visible, due to their context not being automatically detected by Twitter, highlighted "a weak point in Twitter's efforts to deal with racism." The issue was labelled a "blindspot" for the platform.

Sterling said: "I don't know how many times I need to say this, but football and the social media platforms need to step up, show real leadership and take proper action in tackling online abuse. The technology is there to make a difference, but I'm increasingly questioning if there is the will."

Akinfenwa said: "Players don't want warm words of comfort from football's authorities and social media giants.

The time for talking has passed, we now need action by those who can make a difference."

The study found "the worst, most threatening messages are sent via private, direct channels."

The 44 players targetted for abuse came from all 20 Premier League clubs, some represented more than once, four different EFL clubs, and five playing abroad including Jadon Sancho, Romelu Lukaku and Chris Smalling. The accounts of ex-players including Alex Scott, Ian Wright and Sol Campbell were also reviewed.

Along with racist abuse, six players were sent homophobic posts, five received ableist abuse two messages were sexist, two were generally xenophobic and one was anti-Semitic. One player alone received a third of the homophobic abuse. Based on the study's findings, it is estimated that 40% of players "are suffering discriminatory abuse from fans on a routine basis."

Zaha highlighted the scale of the problem when he posted a string of messages he had been sent directly on social media ahead of Crystal Palace's trip to Aston Villa in July 2020. This led to the arrest of the 12-year-old boy.

Rhian Brewster was appalled that it took the BLM movement to galvanise action. Three years before, he had spoken out about his experiences and his frustration about the authorities' lack of action. Brewster said: "If this didn't happen in America with George Floyd, would it be like that now? Would we have BLM? Something serious had to happen for people to say 'Wait, let's protest and start talking and stand up for everybody.' That is excellent but it took someone to die for this to happen."

Brewster is one of several young footballers using their platforms to raise awareness. "When someone was racist to me, Liverpool gave me their full backing from the manager and players all the way to the owners. That helps a lot.

Back in the day, the black players didn't have the backing that we do today. Raheem and Marcus speaking out helps as well. You see them talking about it and think 'why can't I talk about it as well?' We all have different platforms, some bigger than others, why not use them and show people we can all come together."

Tottenham winger Ryan Sessegnon was "not even surprised any more" after receiving regular racist abuse on social media. The England Under-21 international was on loan at German side Hoffenheim when he posted an image of the racist messages on his Instagram account. Sessegnon, 20, described the abuse as "unbelievable" and "disgusting." The account that sent the racist messages was removed from Instagram. Bundesliga side Hoffenheim posted on social media: "Our player Ryan Sessegnon was racially insulted in the worst way online. Hoffenheim stands for tolerance, integration, and respect. We reject all forms of racism, discrimination and exclusion and say no to racism."

When Nigeria suffered a national emergency with violent demonstrations in protest against brutality from a now-disbanded section of the police called the Special Anti-Robbery Squad, British-based footballers of Nigerian heritage, including Odion Ighalo, Wilfred Ndidi and Tammy Abraham used their platforms to speak out, but also to call for aid for people affected. Manchester United striker Ighalo said: "I'm not the kind of guy who talks about politics – but I can't keep quiet any more about what is going on back home in Nigeria. I would say the government are a shame to the world – for killing your own citizens, sending the military to the streets to kill protesters because they are protesting for their rights... I am ashamed of this government. I'm calling on the UK government, calling all those leaders in the world to please see what is going on in Nigeria and help us – help the poor citizens."

When the internationals resumed in 2020, it was a time for the England manager Gareth Southgate to reflect on the moment one year earlier that he nearly led his England team off the pitch in During a 6-0 victory against Bulgaria the team were subjected to monkey chants and Nazi salutes from the home crowd. He recalled: "It's not a night you ever want to be involved with and it's not a type of night I ever want to experience again. My thoughts throughout were how do we look after our players, how do we protect our players, both going into the game and during the night? To experience the pressure of it, as a head coach because of the spotlight we knew existed, and the fact the decisions we were going to take were going to resonate around Europe, if not the world, was a unique experience to be in.

"We tried to do the best job we could, everyone will have a view on what that should or should not have been. We highlighted an issue that is unacceptable, and we were the first team at international level to bring a game to a halt for those reasons. It's not something that I'm particularly proud of; it's not an evening where pride is the right word for how we dealt with it.

"I felt we sent a strong message, and we sent a positive message. I think as a squad and a group of staff as well, we continue to do that. We care for each other, we're united and we don't see discrimination of any sort as acceptable. We'll continue to try to have a voice because we hope to make a difference."

Chris Powell was a new member of the England team's coaching staff in October 2019. He recalls the events surrounding that night in Bulgaria: "Gareth, in his very astute way, spoke to me a week before we got into the camp. We spoke for about half an hour on the phone and he just said, 'If you were a player what would you want from me as your manager?' I thought it's such a great question because we knew we had intelligence that the team may suffer racism in Bulgaria, and he wanted to be well prepared. Gareth wanted to make sure that the team were prepared for what was coming. I just said support. "Support from you, support from the chairman, support from everyone, staff included."

"I know some people felt maybe we should have walked off, but we were the first international team in the world to stop a game to complain about racism. We did step one when it was first heard at Tyrone Mings and we were prepared to go to step two which was right at the end of the half. We were prepared to do step three. I know some people agreed and some didn't. I felt the way we behaved, the way we handled it, the way we discussed it with the referee, the fourth official and the way our chairman and everyone who is part of the FA organisation felt, we handled it brilliantly as a group.

"Our behaviour was very calm. We all knew what we were doing, it wasn't someone doing something off message; we all knew how to behave. I felt that showed the rest of the world that this was a football team, a nation that was united in what they believed in. I was very, very proud – not only of the players and staff, but actually our supporters on the evening. They can get a bad press at times, but I felt their support of everyone that evening and how they were singing and how they were proud of not only our display but our behaviour, they mirrored our behaviour. It was a huge moment. I was very proud to be a black Englishman that night. I can't say anything more than that. People won't always agree in what we did, and I get that, but I felt it was the right way for us to go."

In the England squad for the 2018 World Cup in Russia, 11 of the 23 players were from a BAME background, and the FA wanted to reflect that and introduced the Elite Coach Placement scheme which aimed to address the issue of under-representation of BAME coaches in the game. Chris Powell was appointed to Southgate's backroom team in September 2019.

Powell said: "It's a great honour for me to be part of the England men's set up. I know how big a role, not only for me personally, but in the wider scale of things, what it would mean to be seen working among the elite players in the country. I think how that works, I have to build relationships and trust with those players.

"I would be lying if I said to you I haven't spoken to the black players quite casually because I think it's important that they feel comfortable, especially if you are a new player to the group. You have got to get used to your surroundings and how it is to be an England player and how to carry yourself. If there are certain issues that people haven't dealt with before and I'm not only talking about culturally, but it could also be just something that is quite simple.

I'm there to encourage and inspire, but also to make sure they feel part of the group and what Gareth is trying to build as a culture for the whole group."

Southgate commented, "There are two things. One is the coaching scheme that has brought diversity to the teams and also visibility for other coaches that might aspire to be [head] coaches in the future. I also have to point out that in our junior teams, we've got seven teams and three of our head coaches are from black or minority ethnic backgrounds. We've taken positive steps, but those people got those roles because they were the best people for the job. Combined with that, we have also committed to giving opportunities on the coach placement scheme as well. I feel that more and more young coaches are coming through from those communities. There are some outstanding coaches coming through who will be role models in the future. With any scheme like this, you need role models to inspire people going forward. People need to see it is possible before they are prepared to commit to further education and learning in order to be a coach."

Southgate reflected how BLM had brought the agenda to the fore: "I think that everyone would react differently because the story moves forward. At the time [in Bulgaria one year ago] we felt we took an approach that was appropriate because it was unique really. Nobody had ever gone as far as we had. We also recognise that we wouldn't stand and accept it happening to us again.

"You can sit here and talk without the responsibility of living through something. I think the whole world over the last few months has moved forward. Educationally, I think everyone has moved forward. I think the events of the last few months have caused the majority of the world's population to stop and think and recognise that there are things that we've all got wrong in the past and there are things that we all need to learn more about. That can only be a positive because education in the end is a critical part of improving the situation."

Wales manager, and Manchester United legend, Ryan Giggs is "immensely proud" to be Welsh and mixed race; the 46-year-old's father, ex-rugby league player Danny Wilson, is black and his mother, Lynne Giggs, is white.

Cardiff-born Giggs suffered being made to feel "different" in his youth and had the "shock of facing racism" for the first time when his family moved to Manchester. "I didn't experience anything in Cardiff," Giggs told ITV Wales. "I was seven, so I can't remember a lot before that. It wasn't until I moved to Manchester. Where I lived my dad was very well known, because he was such a good player. He was probably the best player in the team in that town. As you can guess, to look at me, you wouldn't think my dad was black. But obviously everyone knowing that was my dad, and my dad quite clearly being black, that's really when I sort of experienced the first time. Which was a bit weird because I'd never experienced that before."

A long-time supporter of Give Racism the Red Card, it was an easy decision to take the knee along with his Welsh players at international games, to show the nation "didn't put up with discrimination or racism."

"There was no hesitation with myself and with my staff and with the team," he said.

***

Yan Dhanda is thriving in a Swansea City team chasing promotion to the Premier League. But the 21-year-old was told he would not make the professional game because of his British Asian background.

"When I was young I got a lot of racism, being Asian, probably because I was better than other kids," Dhanda said. "I got a lot of kids saying, 'You should be doing this job or should be doing that.' or 'You're not going to make it – you're Asian.' There were obviously a lot worse words than that, but I am not going to say them."

Dhanda, a former England Under-17 international from the West Midlands, is one of only 10 British Asians among around 4,000 professional footballers in the United Kingdom. The support of his mother Zoe, who is English, and father Jaz, who was born in England to Indian parents, was key in helping him deal with abuse he faced as a child.

"I think because I had so much self-belief and I knew I was better than everyone, I never let it affect me," Dhanda said. "But I can see it affecting other kids who don't have the backing of their parents, or don't have the self-belief I had or the relationship with their dad that I had. My dad would always say 'You are better than them – don't let it get to you and we'll see where they are and where you are in the future.'"

Dhanda spent five years in Liverpool's academy before moving to Swansea in search of first team football in 2018. Dhanda's background is never far from the conversation. "On social media I get a lot of messages with people asking for advice. They want to become footballers – how do they do it. Or they are proud of me and what I have done. Because I hear it so often, I am so aware of the lack of Asians in football. There's no point sugar-coating it and saying it's fine because it's not. I am quite passionate about it, that things need to change, and Asian kids need to get more opportunities and not get overlooked."

Dhanda is happy to be viewed as a role model. "I am so proud of where I am from and my family's background. I want to be the first person of Asian background to do great things. The lack of Asian players now – it can't get any worse. But the number of Asian kids I know are playing football and are really good – they are going to be coming through in the next few years. I think a lot of Asian kids, because there are not a lot of professionals, are stereotyped as not strong enough. I think with the right coaching and with someone believing in them, anyone can do anything – no matter where you are from, what race you are and what background you are. Asian kids need the same opportunity as everyone else. They need to be given a chance."

British Asians make up 7% of the UK population; 0.25% of professional footballers are British Asians. "There are twice as many people of Asian heritage as people of black heritage in the UK yet there are 100 times more black pro players than Asian pro players. That's a massive statistical anomaly," said Kick It Out executive chair Sanjay

Bhandari. "It is clear that football has a long-standing problem getting British Asian players into the game and it is getting worse. Football needs to address this."

Maziar Kouhyar was called a "terrorist" by a teammate during his time at Walsall. Kouhyar came to Britain aged one because of conflict in his native Afghanistan, where he had played for the national team. He made 33 Walsall appearances before being released in 2019 and says while there were "a lot of good experiences" at the club. There were also "a lot of racist things I experienced that made it a bit sour," he said. The worst was during a warm up before a training session. "One of the lads said something to me, something about being a terrorist," Kouhyar said. "The guy said it again, so we ended up having a confrontation, pushing each other. The lads split it up." Kouhyar expected to "get called into the office" to discuss what happened. When nothing was said, he stayed quiet because he "didn't want to be a troublemaker."

Kouhyar, a midfielder, now works as a car salesman. He says "racist banter" was "thrown about" during his time in the professional game. "It's sad to say but that's just the banter. If you don't play along with it, you are not going to get along with the lads. Now I work at Toyota, there's no racist banter. Why is it okay as part of football culture? It doesn't make sense to me."

Greg Clarke's public comments that forced his resignation as FA Chairman was a major blow to those trying to encourage Asian youngsters to play the national sport, with the numbers of British Asians playing at the highest level disappointingly low. Only two players currently feature in the Premier League, Neil Taylor, the Wales and Aston Villa defender, and Hamza Choudhury, the Leicester City midfielder. In 30 years of the Premier League, four British Asians made appearances, the other two were Newcastle's Michael Chopra and Zesh Rehman, who made three appearances for Fulham. Responding to Clarke's comment that South Asians and Afro-Caribbean people had "different career interests," Baljit Rihal, a football agent and founder of the UK's Asian Football Awards, said the comments strengthened stereotypes that already held back talented players. "Most Asian kids aspire to be professional footballers," said Rihal. "But when we hear these comments, that sets it back. It galvanises the stereotypes. The FA have got a lot of bridges to rebuild. Some scouts, if they are given the choice, would be more likely to pick the non-Asian player."

Sanjay Bhandari, the chair of anti-discrimination organisation Kick It Out, told BBC Radio 4: "This isn't about the one word that he used, this is about a litany of absurd stereotypes. A combination of evidence says 'You don't really get it. You don't understand the importance of equality, diversity and inclusion, particularly in your organisation and this is a strategic objection for you.' It's absolutely crucial that somebody that is at the top of the tree does get it."

ANNEXES

Kick It Out Annual Reporting Summary: 2018/19 Season
Discrimination in both professional and grassroots football rose significantly in the 2018/19 season with reports up by 32 per cent.

Statistics from Kick It Out show reports rose to 422 in 2018/19, up from 319 in the previous year. Incidents of racism continue to rise, the most common form of discrimination in professional and grassroots football, constituting 65 per cent of reports – a 43 per cent rise from 2017/18. indicating discrimination across the game is still an issue which needs ongoing and constant education and the application of appropriate sanctions.

Faith-based discrimination, which includes Islamophobia and anti-Semitism, rose higher than any other across this period, with reports increasing by 75 per cent from 36 to 63. Discrimination related to sexual orientation increased by 12 per cent from 61 to 68. Reports related to gender remained at the same level (eight), while disability discrimination reports dropped from 15 to nine.

In the overall figures, which include social media incidents, discrimination reports increased to 581, a 12 per cent rise from the season before (520).

Discrimination reports in the professional game rose by 46 per cent to 313, with an outcome received in 62 per cent of cases.

The statistics are compiled from all levels of English football, including the Premier League, English Football League (EFL), FA Women's Super League, non-league and grassroots fixtures. The 2018/19 season saw a change in the way online discrimination is recorded. The organisation received 159 discrimination reports from social media in 2018/19. Again, the most common form of reported incidents was racism (62 per cent).

Racist Incidents: 2019

January 27 – Racist chanting. Millwall's FA Cup win over Everton. The Lions pledged to ban fans for life if found guilty.

March 18 – Chelsea lodge a formal complaint with UEFA. Racist chanting aimed at Callum Hudson-Odoi during a Europa League game at Dynamo Kiev.

March 24 – Number of England's players racially abused during a Euro 2020 qualifying win in Montenegro.

April 2 – Everton striker Moise Kean, then of Juventus, abused by sections of the Cagliari support during a Serie A match. Teammate Leonardo Bonucci later said Kean should take "50–50" of the blame.

April 5 – England and Tottenham defender Danny Rose says he cannot wait for his career to be over due to racism.

April 7 – The EFL declares itself "saddened, disappointed and angered" by numerous instances of alleged racist abuse at games. Derby, Wigan and Northampton all reported abuse of their players.

April 8 – Watford striker Troy Deeney reports abuse on social media.

April 11 – A video of Chelsea fans singing a racist song at a Europa League game in Prague is condemned by the club. Three fans denied entry to the game. Arsenal launch an investigation into their owns fans after Napoli player Kalidou Koulibaly is allegedly abused during a Europa League tie.

April 12 – The Ligue 1 game between Amiens and Dijon is suspended for several minutes as Amiens defender Prince Gouano suffers abuse from the stands.

April 13 – West Ham say they are "disgusted" by a video on social media of a group of fans singing an anti-Semitic song.

April 15 – MK Dons and Tranmere condemn racist abuse of Dons forward Chuks Aneke on social media. Notts County impose 'indefinite club bans" on some supporters.

April 17 – Manchester United's Ashley Young is abused on Twitter after his side go out of the Champions League to Barcelona.

April 18 – Leading players undertake a 24-hour social-media boycott in protest at the ongoing abuse. Twitter says it was suspending three times more abusive accounts within 24 hours.

April 26 – UEFA orders Montenegro to play June's Euro 2020 qualifiers with Kosovo behind closed doors as a result of the racism from the England game in March.

August 8 – As a new season begins, Kick It Out condemns a number of incidents from the opening weekend, with Fulham defender Cyrus Christie alleging his sister was hit and racially abused. QPR's Under-18s walk off in the second half of a friendly against AD Nervion in Spain after abuse.

August 14 – Chelsea's Tammy Abraham is targeted online after missing a penalty in a Super Cup shoot-out. Manager Frank Lampard says he is "disgusted with a so-called Chelsea fan".

August 18 – Reading's Yakou Meite is abused for missing a penalty.

August 19 – Manchester United condemn racist abuse aimed at Paul Pogba after he misses a penalty. Teammate Marcus Rashford says, "If you attack him, you attack us all" but is later abused himself. Pogba says he will fight racism for the "next generation".

September 2 – Inter Milan's Romelu Lukaku is abused at Cagliari, though the club deny his accusation.

September 4 – Twitter says it has taken down 700 examples of "hateful conduct" in the last two weeks.

September 23 – A 43-year-old man is arrested on suspicion of a racially aggravated public-order offence during Hartlepool's match against Dover.

October 7 – Aston Villa condemn social media footage of fans chanting a racist song which references their own players.

October 14 – England's Euro 2020 qualifier in Bulgaria stopped twice due to racist abuse from home supporters.

October 19 – The FA Cup qualifier between Haringey and Yeovil abandoned after allegations a Haringey player was abused. The players walked off after 64 minutes.

October 20 – Hearts and Bristol City open investigations following allegations of abuse from their fans.

October 21 – Manchester United eject a fan for alleged racist abuse during a Premier League game with Liverpool.

October 29 – Bulgaria ordered to play two matches behind closed doors, one suspended for two years, and fined £65,000 for the abuse of England's players on October 14.

November 3 – Brescia's Mario Balotelli kicks the ball into the stands in protest at abuse suffered during a game with Verona.

November 16 – Sweden striker Alexander Isak, 20, was subjected to racist abuse by Romania fans during a Euro 2020 qualifier.

December 5 – Italian daily newspaper Corriere dello Sport accused of fuelling racism with its front-page headline of BLACK FRIDAY alongside pictures of Inter Milan's Lukaku and Roma's Chris Smalling.

December 7 – A 41-year-old is arrested on suspicion of 'a racially aggravated public order' offence during the Manchester derby. Play temporarily suspended in the Sky Bet League Two match between Forest Green and Scunthorpe after a Rovers fan allegedly directed racist comments towards visiting defender Jordan Clarke.

December 16 – Serie A used three paintings of monkeys to illustrate a campaign to stamp out racism.

December 21 – Millwall say they will fully co-operate with an investigation into alleged abuse during their clash with Barnsley. PFA calls for government action after the Premier League game between Tottenham and Chelsea sees three stadium announcements reporting abuse, with Chelsea's Antonio Rudiger reportedly the subject of monkey-chanting.

Football Leadership Diversity Code

The FA's Football Leadership Diversity Code was launched by Paul Elliott, chair of the governing body's inclusion advisory board which clubs can sign up to with a view to increasing diversity and equality in football boardrooms and leadership positions, particularly coaching roles.

A steering group and expert panels were tasked with devising the code.

Watford striker Troy Deeney, the club's manager Nigel Pearson, Tyrone Mings were among those selected to spearhead the initiative.

Deeney and Aston Villa and England defender Mings were vocal on racial equality in light of the Black Lives Matter movement. Tottenham executive director Donna Cullen has agreed to join the steering group with Chelsea chairman Bruce Buck and Crystal Palace supremo Steve Parish. England senior team coach Chris Powell, England Under-21 coach Michael Johnson, former Newcastle and Brighton manager Chris Hughton and former player Rachel Yankey are also involved.

The steering group are tasked with developing the voluntary Football Leadership Diversity Code with the aim of delivering it to coincide with England's UEFA Nations League fixture against Belgium at Wembley, which also marks Black History Month.

The FA is also developing four independent expert panels, which will be consulted regularly throughout the development of the code. Deeney chairs the players' panel, the coaching panel co-chaired by Hope Powell, manager at Brighton & Hove Albion WFC, and Liam Rosenior, first team coach at Derby County. The clubs' panel will be chaired by Buck, the grassroots panel will be chaired by Sue Hough, chair of the FA Women's Board.

Deeney says he hopes his "bullish approach" will help to improve diversity within football after being appointed to the FA's Steering Group. Deeney's role involves helping to develop the Football Leadership Diversity Code as part of a newly formed group. He especially wants to use his role to improve black representation in dugouts and senior roles within clubs and governing bodies. "I'm thankful enough that I'm on Premier League boards now, and FA boards to talk and affect change, but it's a long process. It's short term goals, midterm and long-term goals, is the way it will work. Hopefully, my bullish approach might get things a bit more through the door, but you know, I'm not going to sit here and say I'm not willing to put myself on the line and try and push the needle forward. We've got a lot of things we need to work on."

Deeney hoped that having black representation on panels reviewing racist incidents will result in tougher punishments for those guilty of abuse. "Legislation, simple things [need to change], if there's a disciplinary in regards to racism, to have people of colour on the board to sit in – simple things that you know, people might go, 'Well, why shouldn't that happen?'"

Meanwhile, the FA have issued an announcement that clubs could face stadium closures under their measures to punish discrimination was definitely a big step in the right direction. The rules come into effect next season, but the significance will only be seen by the way the FA implement the measures. They apply to all domestic competitions, with teams penalised for incidents such as discriminatory chanting by fans, and offences could lead to full or partial stadium closures and fines. Players and coaches can be banned for six to twelve games for almost all acts of discrimination.

If an offence is "in writing only or via any communication device", or there are other mitigating factors, the minimum ban is three matches.

The FA conducted a consultation process with focus groups and stakeholders such as Kick It Out, the Professional Footballers' Association, the League Managers' Association and various representatives from clubs and leagues. An FA statement read: "The fact that an incident of discrimination by an individual took place in private or outside of a standard football setting will now not be a barrier to the FA issuing proceedings." The

FA's director of legal and governance Polly Handford said, "We are committed to investigating, charging and sanctioning all forms of discrimination with consistency and transparency."

The announcement came a couple of weeks after FA chairman Greg Clarke was left "disappointed" claiming the professional game representatives on the FA board blocked a move to try to improve the diversity of its members. English football's governing worked behind the scenes to try and promote Paul Elliott, who is chair of The FA's inclusion advisory board, on to their full board. The FA are committed to improving diversity within the organisation and wanted a BAME individual as executive member of their board as a key target.

Clarke's attempt to add diversity to the board was blocked by representatives from the Premier League and the EFL. It comes against the backdrop of players in the Premier League and EFL taking a knee before the start of matches in support of the Black Lives Matter movement, the Premier League showed its solidarity, with players' names replaced on the back of their shirts with 'Black Lives Matter' for the first 12 matches of the restarted season, and a Black Lives Matter badge featured on all shirts for the rest of the campaign. In a letter to the FA Council Clarke said a number of options were discussed at the end of July board meeting, including making Paul Elliott – chair of the Inclusion Advisory Board – a director. He says the representatives of the EFL and Premier League "were against such a review"

Clarke added that they believed the changes introduced in 2017 "were sufficient". Although the National Game representatives were said to be "sympathetic" to a review and consultation, Clarke said they "did not want to oppose the professional game". He wrote: "Without the support of the professional game and national game, who have a majority of directors, a review of the FA board composition is not possible. I had hoped that the FA, as the game's governing body, would have been able to examine whether its own board was appropriately constituted to represent a diverse game and share its thinking with council. This process is happening across football but will not now happen with respect to the FA board. For the Council to exercise this important function it must have timely access to information and be able to challenge and question it. Changes to Council meetings to encourage questions, without notice, and schedule time for them in the agenda has been important to me in my role of Leader of Council. Transparency and accountability are important attributes for any governance system worthy of the name.

"I wrote to you earlier in the year about Paul Elliott's work to develop a voluntary code for equality in football. Sue Hough, Rupinder Bains and Mark Bullingham are working with Paul together with senior individuals, of all ethnicities, from across football. In parallel with the work Paul has been leading, I have been talking to leaders across the Professional and National Game to encourage progress in inclusion. Our game is diverse. We have doubled the number of women and girls playing football in the last four years.

"Across the whole game nearly 20 per cent of males aged sixteen and over playing football are from BAME communities. The figure for women and girls is even higher. The FA Board has made good progress on inclusion since the reforms approved by Council in 2017. Ten per cent of FA Board members are from a BAME background and 10 per cent come from the LGBT+ community. 40 per cent of the FA Board is female.

"At last week's FA Board meeting we debated the need to evaluate further reform to improve inclusion and effectiveness on the FA Board for consultation with Council. We discussed a number of options including: making the Chair of the Inclusion Advisory Board a Director and giving the Professional and National Games an extra Board seat each that could provide the flexibility to allow appointment of diverse candidates should they be the best qualified person for the role. Both our Independent Directors offered to stand down to create opportunities for a more diverse Board, but the Board was united in declining their offer."

He added: "As FA chairman, this disappoints me. As Leader of Council, I felt honour bound to inform you of the situation. It seems to me better to be open on the issue now rather than surprise Council when Paul Elliott publishes the recommendations of his working group in October."

Other options discussed included giving the professional and national Games an extra board seat each "that could provide the flexibility to allow appointment of diverse candidates should they be the best qualified person for the role."

BBC Sport spoke to one board member who described Clarke's statement as "bizarre" and "divisive" and said he had been urged not to issue it by members of the board this morning when he made them aware of his plans.

There are three representatives of the professional game on the FA board – former Premier League chairman Peter McCormick, who is chair of its legal advisory group, English Football League chairman Rick Parry and lawyer Rupinder Bains, who jointly represents the Premier League and the EFL.

The reforms in 2017, which they deemed sufficient, led to BAME representation on the board reaching 10%, 10% representation from the LGBT+ community and 40% representation by women.

Several high-profile players, including Manchester City winger Raheem Sterling, have called for greater diversity in the hierarchy of sports organisations following the Black Lives Matter campaign.

Kick It Out chair Sanjay Bhandari said, "Black Lives Matter has rightfully caused organisations across all industries to consider how they attack systemic inequalities and better reflect society. That process must start at the top with the senior leadership team. It is only right that the FA should seek to seize the moment, to reflect on the composition of its leadership team and whether it represents the players, fans and participants in the game. I applaud Greg Clarke's effort to do so. It is disappointing that this effort has been rejected. Before commenting further, we would need to understand better the professional game's reasons for rejecting a review."

Clarke toned down his displeasure and later said in a statement that he had "not intended to be divisive" in the letter and that he "intended to highlight an issue that we all care deeply about across both the FA Board and the FA Council".

A Premier League and EFL joint statement said Clarke's letter "did not reflect the true nature of the discussions held at the FA Board meeting last week" and they said they welcomed his clarification. The statement added: "It was agreed at last week's FA Board meeting to undertake an evaluation of diversity and inclusion within the FA in a consultative but efficient manner."

Kick it Out welcomed Clarke's attempts to diversify the FA board but says real change can only come from setting targets. KIO chairman Sanjay Bhandari says change needs to "start at the top". "I welcome the fact that the FA are doing that review or wanting to do that review," he told BBC Sport. "Every organisation should be thinking about its leadership and its board, and the FA and other football organisations should be no different." He added, "The giant leap forward is making people accountable for targets and creating targets for coaches and senior leadership – that's how you drive inclusion."

Bhandari, who became Kick It Out's chairman in November, supported Elliott's potential inclusion on the board and said football had shown a "willingness to change" since the Black Lives Matter movement had become more prominent. But he said football organisations should be more co-ordinated in their initiatives. The English Football League has a version of the Rooney rule, which makes a provision that BAME candidates be interviewed for coaching positions, and the Premier League, FA and Professional Footballers' Association have set up a coach bursary scheme – but positions are only with EFL clubs.

"Part of the typical response of many organisations, and not just in football, to any major external event is to come up with one initiative and put all the hopes in that," Bhandari said. "What I'm really after is more whole system thinking and lots of initiatives, but that are connected. That's the bit that's missing at the minute. I'm not sure we have enough of the targets, and I don't think the initiatives are connected in any meaningful way."

He added, "I can understand why some of the schemes might start coming through the EFL because that's a traditional pathway for some things like coaching. But that's all they are – a helpful start. Having interview quotas or bursary schemes that apply to a relatively limited number of people is not really going to move the dial. It does feel to me like there is a willingness to change. What we need is to turn that into meaningful action.

ABOUT THE AUTHOR

Harry Harris is a double-winner of the British Sports Journalist of the Year award, with special affinity to the KIO cause, and winner of the Race in the Media award, the only football writer to receive it. He was presented with the British Variety Club of Great Britain Silver Heart for "Contribution to Sports Journalism". Double-winner also of the Sports Story of the Year award, he's the only journalist ever to win the accolade twice, he boasts a total of 24 industry awards.

Harris has regularly appeared as a football analyst on TV news and radio sports programmes, including *Richard & Judy*, *Newsnight*, BBC News and ITV *News at Ten*, Sky, Setanta, BBC Radio 5 Live, BBC Radio 4 and TalkSPORT. Interviewed on *Football Focus*, he formed the original *Hold The Back Page* and Jimmy Hill *Sunday Supplement* on Sky.

He is arguably the most prolific writer of best-selling football books of his generation with over 80 books to his name, including the highly acclaimed best-seller in the UK and United States *Pele – His Life and Times*. Other books include: *Gullit: The Chelsea Diary*, *All The Way Jose*, *Chelsea Century*, *Chelski* and *Wayne Rooney – The Story of Footballs Wonder Kid*. He has worked on the autobiographies of

Ruud Gullit, Paul Merson, Glenn Hoddle, Gary Mabbutt, Steve McMahon, Terry Neill and Bill Nicholson's *Glory, Glory – My Life With Spurs*; and biographies of Roman Abramovich, Jurgen Klinsmann, Sir Alex Ferguson, Jose Mourinho, Terry Venables, Franco Zola, Luca Vialli; as well as George Best's last book, the best-selling *Hard Tackles and Dirty Baths*.

Harris has directed four documentaries, on, respectively, Ossie Ardiles, Kenny Sansom, Kerry Dixon and Ron "Chopper" Harris. He is co-owner/director H&H Sports Media Ltd and Football30.